The Rain Tree

The Rain Tree

A Memoir

MIRABEL OSLER

BLOOMSBURY

LONDON · BERLIN · NEW YORK · SYDNEY

First published in Great Britain 2011

Copyright © Mirabel Osler 2011
Rain tree illustration by Frances Carlile

The account of Sureen's adoption was first published by Granta.
Reproduced by permission

Mirabel Osler has asserted her right to be identified as the author of this Work

Bloomsbury Publishing Plc
36 Soho Square
London W1D 3QY

www.bloomsbury.com

Bloomsbury Publishing, London, New York and Berlin
A CIP catalogue record for this book is available from the British Library

ISBN 978 1 4088 1548 9

10 9 8 7 6 5 4 3 2 1

Typeset by Hewer Text UK Ltd, Edinburgh
Printed in Great Britain by Clays Ltd, St Ives plc

MIX
Paper from
responsible sources
FSC
www.fsc.org   FSC® C018072

To the new friends – indispensable and generous, and they'll know who they are – who have surprised and delighted me in old age.

The '*arbre à pluie*' gets its name from the sound of
rain falling through the folded leaves at nightfall . . .

CONTENTS

Preamble

I have just been to seek out a shroud. There's a young woman who makes environmentally friendly felt shrouds decorated with leaves. Sounds lovely. Sounds suitable for me. For the way I think. I've never believed in an afterlife. Never had the comfort from faith in a divine being concerned with each one of us – God won't let me. Instead, not believing in immortality, I find solace in contemplating space: that tempting void without significance. Considered against infinity, how can we be anything but disintegrating dross floating through time?

Anyway if I'm wrong, how is there no answer to the classic question: Why is a lightning conductor necessary on a church?

Edmond de Goncourt when discussing immortality with Alphonse Daudet said, 'We are mere ephemeral gatherings of matter.' That is how I feel. I'm a nothing – agnostic if a label is needed – and because I want to save my children from coping or feeling guilty if they don't send me off with a fanfare, or in theatrical splendour, I decided to get the practicalities sorted. A felt shroud or cardboard coffin would suffice.

To evaporate like dew at sunrise would be my aim, but life isn't like that, nor seemingly is death.

This isn't an autobiography but a paean to friendship. Janus-faced, looking both ways – love and death, ends and beginnings – the unavoidable human apophthegm of those who mattered in my life before I was a sentient being. I write of the *upside* to old age in spite of loss of faculties and physical prowess, or of the necessity of making lists, of repeating a word aloud so that I haven't forgotten by the time I reach the top stair.

As a non-believer with nothing to hang on to, I write of the compensations, the unexpected liberations and friendships I have not anticipated as I've grown older, in a series of seven episodes – the fifth being the reason for the book's title – or parts of my life as I jump about like a grasshopper on speed between loss, writing, gardens, friendship, food and grief; Europe, Asia and finally, today, facing the edge.

The taproot is mine, and although I begin with a few pages on gardens, it's the accumulated letters, diaries and photographs that are the catalyst in an attempt to leave my children some sort of background to where they've come from. The chapters, not in chronological order, are disparate chunks of recollections prompted by a letter, painting or photograph of the people and the overlapping lives of those who have been germane to me and my family in England, Thailand and Greece.

My past is the shadow I can't avoid. Now in old age, through corridors of memory these people still reverberate.

1

'That Pretty Blue Thing'

The act of shared gardening, not the garden, was what mattered when my husband Michael and I returned to our house in England after years of living abroad. We had no intention of 'making' a garden. Certainly not anything that imposed sophisticated geometry on the landscape. Rather, as though we were painting colours and shapes on a vast canvas, we were drawn into an activity where neither of us had been before.

Our intuitive feelings had grown from nowhere cerebral, nowhere ambitious. They came from standing about ruminating on our stream, the undulating land, fruit trees long past their use, sheep grazing in meadows beyond our boundaries. Design hadn't come into it, nor had horticultural wisdom, and that holy cow of gardening – lawns – was non-existent. All that was needed was a light touch where sporadic blotches of floral enhancement seduced both nose and eye, where old roses followed the contours, bulbs appeared among unmown grass, and primulas, irises and ferns grew beside water.

Unintentional, arbitrary, were our spontaneous responses as we succumbed to what was surrounding us. How could a tug at our primeval senses not tempt us to scatter a few plants about the place? At least that's how we began. With no plan or know-how. Stone, water, bulbs, trees and roses were to be our ingredients with the built-in proviso that we could leave it all for little bouts of travel.

Idiots! Slowly, surreptitiously, we were coerced. We had no idea we were moving into a world of blackmail where on a summer's day, slumbering among bees and an infusion of scents from the shrub roses, a coil of bindweed throttling a hollyhock threatens all thought of inertia. I call it floral blackmail. And that's why, when I used to visit and write about gardens, I knew instantly if they were the work of proper or improper gardeners. Proper gardeners don't sit. They can't. They have a couple of benches – one on the patio, another beside the 'water feature' – from where, in less than a minute, they catch sight of some neglected chore and involuntarily spring up to make amends. Once up they keep going. The improper type, however, have seats scattered about the place like a beckoning finger offering hospitality and unrestricted idleness.

I started writing about our garden through no volition of my own; it just happened. I found that the process of grubbing about in verdant corners provoked thoughts that had nothing to do with me. Unprompted, they rose to the surface from some deep source of stillness: lightweight or puzzling. Ever since I'd first picked up a spade I'd felt an undertow to gardening, like the statue in the rock waiting to be hewn by the carver. The enigma lay quiescent, yet impossible to ignore.

On scraps of paper kept with a pencil in my pocket, I wrote them down. Abstract or trivial – the layers of geology that had gone to make a tree; how pointless it is the way gardeners devote hours to something that's entirely perishable; how like a rosary of stones was the arrangement of pebbles I'd put around the thick stems of *Lewisia*s to protect their necks from winter wet. And as time passes – unlike food past its sell-by date or lines on a face – a garden goes out in triumphant florescence.

Think too how few gardeners exult: we meet, commiserate and complain. Only in June did I encounter people who spoke with rapturous buoyancy about the beauty of their gardens. The rest of the year we spend apologising. Cooks hold their tongues, never admitting that the sauce shouldn't be like this or the soup is really from Neal's Yard, but gardeners only say, 'You should have seen it last week.' Other things intrigued me as I moved among the roses: the tyranny of birds. Nesting close to the house just where I wanted to work, their black eyes would watch me. Intimidated, they annexed my territory, forcing me into a Groucho Marx crouch in an effort to keep below their eye level.

Lurching was what Michael and I did. Inconstant, erratic or just pure foolhardy: wild and unstructured, the place evolved. Through mutual cohesion our commitment burgeoned – but we hadn't intended to be taken over this way.

Whatever the pundits advised, however fashions changed – from white gardens, to grasses and gravel, to exotic rarities or Japanese gardens – roses never lost their bloom. 'A rose-red city – half as old as Time', as Walter de la Mare described Petra, was just one of the childhood rosy recollections we shared:

> . . . Oh, no man knows
> Through what wild centuries
> Roves back the rose.

For us, Michael and me, they became of primary importance after we'd visited a rose nursery in full spate. All their flowing, tumbling effect, their huge loomy mounds and the porcelain perfection of single-petalled blooms took precedence over herbaceous borders or lawns.

Gardens are as unpredictable as human relationships. There are no right ways to make one, only alternatives, and nobody knows what you haven't done – a comforting thought when faced with disillusion over plans made while lying in the bath or before going to sleep, when I haul in garden thoughts like net-fulls of kelp. We soon learnt that death is a part of gardening as inherent as slugs or our fickle climate, and though disappointment may be a built-in ingredient, surprises proliferate. The first time I saw the waxy petals on our *Clematis armandii* I realised I had an asinine smile on my face. Another time I was misled by a thread of brown bootlace on what I took to be dead clematis until in the spring I found a pinhead of green at its base. Blessed pinhead, auguring life. And how comforting it was not just to contemplate the plants that bloomed against the elements with such bravado but to look at some of the dismal black sticks of winter. I could put out my hand and know with certainty I was touching the colours and scents of next summer.

Starting a garden is the beginning of making a series of mistakes. Books don't warn you; they tell you how and when, but never hint at the capriciousness – the quintessence of gardening. Another thing: until we began gardening I hadn't realised we were taking on potency behind those gentle words – the annual resurgence meant whatever happened one year would never happen again – timing, performance, weather, disease or sheer overwhelming luxuriance proved the garden's transience. How different from the written word.

And until summer ended, I hadn't appreciated the bliss of hip sockets. After months of stooping or shuffling behind a

heavy wheelbarrow, standing upright and walking with swinging limbs along autumn lanes I discovered my body with all
its moving parts had been returned to me. How exquisitely
contrived was my thigh to my hip.

But strange things happened. Unexpected percipience lurked
about gardens. I would be weeding, hearing the intricate song
of a blackbird, groping at the root of things in some over-
grown corner, when feral abstractions came into my head
with such arousal that I looked round to see where they were
coming from. I was being manipulated. Pulling up a weed
before realising it was a flower, I'd push it back with apologies
and heartfelt supplications for its survival: 'Live, please live.'
But when I heaved on a recalcitrant dock, whose root was so
deep it broke in half, quite contrarily my pleas became curses:
'Die, you wretch, die!'

The emotional pendulum was exhausting.

Less dramatic were the shared moments at dusk when
Michael and I pottered together among our shrub roses, grown
into floral mounds big enough to live in. Lingering, surrounded
by scents, textures and colours, we knew – each flower being
ephemeral – that those moments were not to be squandered.
Subtly we'd been appropriated. We were no longer in control.
We'd become possessed by the fecundity of the place. And we
marvelled. Astonished at what we'd started, we looked at each
other wondering, 'What have we done?' There is no doubt
that for raw gardeners, inexperienced, naive, the amazement
of the first summer's production can take your breath away. It
certainly did for Michael and me.

Slowly, surreptitiously, our days and nights were spent
discussing what next bit of land to annex, what decorative
climber to plant beneath a tree, or where to make another

sitting place among the bosky shrubbery and cool galleries of greenery.

One was a platform with two seats made high up between a pair of trees beside the brook. Reaching it by a flight of wooden steps, we viewed our roses with the eyes of a bird. From a rope on a pulley in overhead branches, we hauled up a wooden tray made specially to hold the bottle of wine we'd left cooling since morning in the stream below.

On summer evenings we surveyed our floral landscape with the same passion I imagine a diamond dealer does his jewels in Hatton Garden. I know it's easy for eyes to become unseeing – as though with cataracts – until we no longer look with primary and pristine clarity, yet it would be hard to find one gardener who wasn't still occasionally confounded by a rose.

As the dusk deepened, and feeling agreeably mellow, we were never certain whether it was a breeze or drink making our platform sway imperceptibly among the foliage.

The green light of summer was transformed, and the season of cobwebs turned our listless days into some of the loveliest of the year. Waking to a barely perceptible shift in the garden, we found that autumn had arrived – for some it brings contentment, for others only despondency.

Weeks later, we'd pull back the curtains to a cataleptic world of frozen grasses and leaves brittle and sculptural. Rime outlining spires of plants left standing, the seed heads of *Eryngium*, spiky as porcupine quills, turned to artefacts. Then there would be a morning when the room was full of light reflected from a snowfall during the night; we'd hear the flapping of a tortoiseshell butterfly against the window pane, and with rising excitement we knew that winter had arrived. Proper winter: not the grey days, dismal and short, but the winter of childhood. Michael would get out his skis, and I'd saddle my horse, put a washing line round my waist and pull him up beyond the Nordy Bank, higher still, to the top of the Brown Clee Hill from where he could ski all the way home and I could return via lanes full of snow, cantering through a silent landscape. This was before snowploughs: the village would be cut off for days and we lit our oil lamps by mid-afternoon.

It may surprise proper gardeners, but we loved the garden in winter for the restful tones under a leaden sky, the grades of ashen gloom, the sallow shadows on the bark of trees. Pissarro or Sisley captured the luminous tonality of misty distances, and as for Bruegel, Michael and I never forgot standing in the centre of a gallery in the Kunsthistorisches Museum in Vienna surrounded by his paintings of the Flemish landscape in the petrified grip of winter.

Out of curiosity I tried sitting blindfolded to experience an invisible garden, an attribute that isn't always in the forefront of garden literature although touch, smell and sound are as fundamental as the most recherché planting and supersede any verbal descriptions. Even the photographs and letters I've been wading through aren't as potent as smells and sounds to resurrect the past. Homesick for the gardens of England, a friend in Thailand struggled to grow sweet peas among orchids and frangipani, hoping to be carried back to his childhood. Primroses do that for me. Their damp, fresh smell instantly epitomises an English spring.

Personal and idiosyncratic, we each respond to remembered scents more potent than anything tangible. The smell of toast, of Boots the Chemist, wallflowers in the sun, bonfires – and in the Far East how we longed for the smell of ground coffee! The list goes on.

But how sad that now everything is always! What I mean is that the rhythm of the seasons is no longer defined by the arrival of the first rhubarb or strawberries in the shops. And how many times visitors commented on our old shrub roses that only flowered once. Fine with us – who wants snowdrops in July or peonies in December any more than year-round raspberries?

After a few years working in the garden, Michael and I discovered another thing.

Perversely, the more beautiful it became, the more we left it. Not for the reason of a fleeting escape, but for the bliss of coming home. If you don't go away, you forego an unforeseen pleasure: the return – when we would walk among our shrubs remarking on every altered detail. There was sense in our capriciousness. We couldn't have done that at the beginning when the place was raw, but once it became swarming with roses and the trees had grown mature enough to make their own shadows, we became aware of this other dimension to our garden. Returning home to what we'd been loath to leave intensified the effect. It was a simple device for renewing our eyes, for sharing the floriferous creation surrounding us.

Besides, there was a spin-off. We controlled time.

At home, days trickled by unobserved; years dissolved; familiarity scooped up hours with relentless inevitability. A month would have passed since Christmas while my mind was still with the children opening stockings. But escaping even briefly, we tweaked life to move at our tempo; we lived elsewhere, experienced other places, people, things that gave us the sense of once more filling our skins with living rather than the mundane process of existing.

Experiencing elsewhere meant – without the use of marijuana – that time became prolonged. *Elsewhere* was a hallucinatory means of manipulating perpetuity: 'Was it only yesterday we were breakfasting in the kitchen? It seems like years.'

So why did Michael and I both surrender at the same time, work so well together, spend evenings making lists, hours visiting arboretums, chasing 'open days' listed in the *Yellow Book* and perusing coffee-table books of immense weight and glossy pictures?

The answer lies in our differences. When it came down to it, our gathered inspirations fragmented so that, although nothing was planned as to which of us should do what, we each took on the bits that physically pleased us. Michael, being good at mechanics, took over tinkering with the grass-cutting mower when it went wrong as all lawn mowers regularly do. (I've never understood why they have this inbuilt defect when the Singer sewing machine I inherited from my mother has never failed.) He created 'architectural grass-mowing': paths where the blades were adjusted to allow different levels to make patterns among the orchard trees. Michael held the place together. He used his machine and scythe to give it cohesion like a piece of textured material. Uncut in places, this allowed for wild flowers to seed under the ancient fruit trees, which did little of productive value except blossom each May, when we'd sit on a bench drinking wine under their branches, listening to the hum of bees overhead.

I wanted no flower beds: my idea was to try growing shrub roses in the way we'd seen wild roses abroad. Being planted in the unkempt turf allowed them freedom to festoon and sprawl, filling the place with colour, scent and abandonment.

But no book gives you the one essential fact, no rose catalogue explains (among the information on height, season, colour and so on) that what matters is their characteristics. Had we known their habit, their deportment, I wouldn't have made so many mistakes, would have known how the roses with a compliant disposition were a godsend to ignorant gardeners. It was their behaviour – the swooners, the thrusters, the supple or the inflexible all planted in the wrong place until we despaired as we tried to cope with a thorny *rugosa* or the languishing elegance of a *gallica*. If I'd known beforehand how old shrub roses – with their twiggy, lax or heavy-headed blooms mottled or silky, some on wine-dark stems – have fundamental characteristics, we might not have planted so many in inappropriate sites.

But what an unforeseen learning curve as we discovered progressively that mistakes in the garden are not disastrous or as irrevocable as they can be in relationships or finance. Plants can be repositioned – even in an experimental, reckless manner – and yet survive. (I used to think this about places where we'd lived: a feeling I could be dibbled in various parts of the world and thrive as long as my family were there.) Roses, we found, were equally transferable. Even huge ramblers are agreeable to this treatment of being cut back and repositioned without harming their lusty vigour the following spring.

Bulbs galore also went to our heads. Besides the vast narcissus family there is the whole spectrum of tulips, where once again we ignored proper procedure and instead let our imaginations go wild with visions of tulips growing with abundance among the rough turf. Some worked: the little species tulips for instance. But the photograph in *A Gentle Plea for Chaos* belies reality, I'm afraid; those peerless lily-flowered tulips you see in the picture did not fulfil my expectations. We'd assumed that, like daffodils, they would appear year after year. And in spite of consulting the RHS Gardens at Wisley, who advised us to plant each bulb twelve inches deep – which we did – their origins in Persia got the better of them. Without baking summers they slowly dwindled over the years. Other bulbs, though, were a triumph. There was something touching about finding fritillaries with their fragile stems thrusting through the tussocks every year. Others too were survivors, such as the pools of blue *Anemone blanda*, dependable and long-lasting.

Another thing Michael and I discovered was how gardeners are always on the way but never arriving. We couldn't wipe our hands and say, 'Well that's finished!' because it never was. Death, being an inbuilt element to gardening, meant every year was different, but the returning seasons gave us another chance. Gardens are beneficent. So after trying to grow something three times (such as rosemary, *romneya* or magnolia) before accepting defeat, there were the other times when we'd be bamboozled by discovering life in our bay tree struck down one severe winter.

Gardening isn't uphill all the way, but there were few days when I could confidently coast downhill with my hands in the air. 'What shall I do next?' asked the sixteen-year-old Lady Jane Grey of the custodians surrounding her as, blindfolded, she groped towards the block. This was a question I had not infrequently asked myself.

One area Michael and I shared was planting trees: fruit or decorative. We visited Westonbirt Arboretum to make lists and to overcome our ignorance of what full-grown trees looked like. This was a place that would force any gardener to raise their eyes above the flower bed. Although we knew this was a long-term arboreal investment, we had no idea of what an enjoyable venture we were starting. Planting trees, I reckon, is one of the most satisfying horticultural occupations, knocking messing among the rockery, or with bedding plants in the border, off the calendar.

Before we started, we needed wheelbarrows. Those objects that can rend gardening compatibility apart. Marriages may founder as each person tries to be the first to find the empty one. As tree planting needed a collection of equipment transported about our land, we increased our two wheelbarrows to four. The excavated earth needed one, the disinterred stones needed another; there were stakes, compost, a fork, a spade, an axe, a hammer as well as several watering cans to be carried across the hummocky ground before we started on the pleasurable four-handed business of planting a tree.

The optimism of such an occupation is indisputable: the belief that this small tree will, in the years ahead, seasonally change the outline of the horizon was something to celebrate as we walked home with aching backs. But we couldn't stop there: the following year we planted a small spinney of serious trees.

Our evolving garden led Michael into another unexpected dimension: photography. He used to record our progress by taking photographs which I then stuck in my 'Idiot Book' alongside notes of everything we'd planted, where and when. 'Idiot' because I could never remember the Latin name ('Oh, you mean that pretty blue thing over there?' was my usual response to an erudite garden visitor), nor could we always remember where we had put anything, especially as we were always moving plants about, transplanting roses, shrubs and trees that we'd placed too close together or in the wrong climatic position.

Michael became fascinated by the limitations of the camera's eye. It gave him power to record only the beautiful, leaving anything ugly, diseased or in need of pruning out of the frame. With his tripod spread-legged at some strategic spot when at dawn or twilight the light was particularly enhancing, he would peer through the lens with tireless dedication. He'd always been a patient man, so much so that he was well known by his family and friends for saying, 'I never knew it was so late!' when he arrived breathless for a meal with others who were far from forbearing about his mistiming.

In the garden his perseverance to immortalise a particular moment of light dissolving the colour of petals was inspired. Twelve pages of his photographs appeared in *The World of Interiors* with a double-page, slightly out-of-focus view of our pond at dusk, impressionistic and transitory. This catapulted him into more work, and had he lived longer he would have been on the threshold of discovering how, at whatever age, a whole new occupation can open up.

Besides having patience, Michael had the insight to understand my need for periodic solitude. This is not a charming affliction: it's tiresome and selfish, and for those who aren't sufferers it appears as self-centred indulgence – a debility that never afflicted him. For me a need to walk from empty room to empty room was at times an imperative as natural as breathing. A few hours would do. All it needed was Michael and the children to go off to do the shopping, and like a dry well I found myself filling up until I anticipated their return with serenity.

Now, from this distance, I think how fortunate Michael was. To die when he was on the way is surely better than after a protracted decline? His photographs commemorate those years together working in the garden when more than half of them appeared in *A Gentle Plea for Chaos*.

His years on the stage are gone for ever, but not this legacy.

2

Grazing the Edge

Why do we always mistime our goodbyes? I mean the final ones? The ones that count. The opportunity creeps up until it's too late: the person has already lost their wits, is enclosed by pain or drugs, or in a stupor. And even when we know the disease is terminal, can we get the timing right?

Was there a morning when on wakening I felt certain this was the day to make the ultimate goodbye? I doubt it. So we slide sideways round that one, avoiding the unbearable, hoping always that there's still time, that death can be postponed for another day. When we are young we don't think about the final farewells, but later, heading for the edge, we know one of us will go first – yet the thought remains unspoken. A kind of safeguard. By ducking reality we hang on a bit longer and dodge the subject.

Since Michael died in 1989 there have been days when I've caught sight of an elderly couple struggling out of their car, stooping to pick up a walking stick, fumbling for the shopping list, and the indelicate thought has come to me: 'One of you has to go before the other. Which will it be?' And relief overwhelms me as I acknowledge I have been there. I can't go through that again.

The desolation that lies ahead eclipses any momentary envy I may have for those couples still intact, sharing their old age together as they leave the surgery arm in arm.

'One of you must go before the other.'

As I don't want to end as an expensive cadaver, a few years ago I went to our Citizens' Advice Bureau to inquire about alternative ways of being dispatched. I gave no name, nor did I know the name of the woman I consulted. Usually they deal with housing benefits and tax or neighbour problems. Nonplussed, faced by questions she'd never had before, she conferred with a colleague next door and returned with a book of rules.

'There are choices, you know,' she said, consulting the relevant pages. Green burials? At sea? On non-sanctified land? In your garden or field?

'But if you do that, you have to be aware of the water table.'

Heavens, I couldn't imagine my children resting on their spades while measuring with a ruler the depth in the field to check on the water table where Michael and I had planted two acres of broad-leafed trees. (His ashes are sprinkled there, but I can't bear to walk among them. If there really are particles of my husband in the ground, treading there would be unbearable, but if the casket contained the cleanings of that day's cremations, I wouldn't need this formula, a specific place to mourn. I talk to him as I walk about my house. I grieve for him as I lay the table; playing Happy Families with our grandchildren; visiting the vineyards of the Napa Valley in California.)

My conversation with the Citizens' Advice woman became more and more surreal until we were talking of surplus body bags; how soon rigor mortis sets in; and if I bought the cardboard coffin in advance to keep in my cellar – depending on how long I lived – might the corners go soggy? And when

I learned it wasn't necessary for the family to be present at a cremation, my mind was made up. A shroud made of felt reduced to ashes was the least declamatory.

Attending the inevitable proliferation of funerals as I grow older – where 'Jerusalem' appears to be a prerequisite, and where people who never attended church need the comforting formulas of ceremony – I want nothing solemn or ritualistic when I die. At too many funerals the sterility of some of the eulogies, which have little to do with the deceased, leaves me thinking thank God I'm not a Christian. (Surely the perfect oxymoron?)

People who work in the Citizens' Advice office are volunteers, and I'd put this one through it. Leaving, I thanked her profoundly.

'At least you'll have plenty to dine out on.'

However, should my family want to make something of a celebration, please let it be among beloved friends. Transform the expense of a classier coffin into a meal in France – a festivity beside a remote river in the Cantal, Ardèche or Lozère. Or if not France then Greece at a table on the terrace of a taverna in the Pindus Mountains where once we were offered 'fresh eggs, fresh liver, fresh bread. Tomato salad, sheep's cheese and wine . . . whatever you want . . . whatever you want' – so said the owner as she offered us each a glass of *gliko*.

We ordered wine, salad, cheese and liver.

Suspended in sunlight on that far-off day, in air clear as a note of music, we heard a nightingale singing in the ravine far below and goat bells threading through a wilderness of juniper and arbutus on the opposite hillside. The moment was idyllic until, across our view, a goat was led past. Horrified, we leapt up.

'No, no. Not that fresh.'
We settled for an omelette.

With our children David, Tamsin and Sureen in mind, and not wishing to leave them a house full of years of accumulated sediment, I need to jettison stuff and attempt to justify the rest, including a chest full of letters.

Who writes letters today? Not my grandchildren; they text. They're forever at it, while their parents prefer to email. Neither method is anything but expendable, whereas what I have here, spread across the table in large envelopes – sorted into their relevant years – is a personal, descriptive or trivial collation that might intrigue my great-great-grandchildren as quaint.

Beginning in 1959, when Michael and I first went to live abroad, the letters end in the eighties. We neither of us kept diaries. In the last ten years or so batches of letters have been returned to me from friends and relatives clearing accumulated correspondence after the death of their own parents, who had, for all those years, kept our letters.

Michael and I had to be thankful for a corrupt postman who steamed the stamps off all the letters we'd written to friends and family during the five weeks we were in Kathmandu early in 1961. It was a time before the road had been finished from India to Nepal in preparation for Queen Elizabeth's visit later that year. All the erotic carvings under the eaves of temples were being spruced up with gold and scarlet paint to catch the eyes of the monarch and her consort.

Aborted, our letters from Kathmandu never arrived. We learnt our lesson. From then on we kept copies of our copious correspondence as we travelled about in that part of the world – Nepal, Java, Bali, Laos and Malaysia – while we were based in Thailand.

The letter-writing habit remained after we'd moved to Greece, hence the piles now lying on my table.

But what shall I tell my children? What bits of past detritus, in the lives of those dead before they were born, is of any importance? How to bring bygone generations into the foreground? How, even, to breath life into moribund wodges of other people's lives?

I need to distil the past, leaving them a hereditary celebration, not a lament.

Temperamentally I'm an optimist. There's a right time for things to happen, and I've found that too often going against the grain, pushing at frontiers, hasn't been successful. Remaining receptive means that some of the best things have happened when I've been facing in another direction. Being alone, not answerable to anyone, opens up vistas of freedom unavailable previously when hedged around with family commitments. These are opportunities not to be dissipated. Six months after Michael's death in 1989, my first book was published.

There is no Plimsoll line that cautions us from risking a plunge into the deep end. There is no cut-off age for starting a new venture. There are those ossified at forty yet others in their seventies who respond to the song of the Lorelei. I was in my sixties when *A Gentle Plea for Chaos: Reflections from an English Garden* was published. I wasn't looking for authorship. It arose from the chance meeting of someone I hadn't yet met with an English publisher at a party in New York.

Liz Calder from Bloomsbury was the publisher who on her return from America invited me to lunch at the Groucho Club to discuss a book. Eve Auchincloss, a senior editor at the New York magazine *Connoisseur* for whom I'd written some articles, was the fairy godmother who set up the introduction from across the Atlantic.

A Gentle Plea for Chaos had germinated with the same alchemy that produces summer scents from a winter twig.

I was in my bath when Michael and I first met. I was five.

Older than me by fifteen years, he had come not to see me but to see my mother Phyllis, to whom he'd lost his heart as an adolescent and aspiring actor when he found in her an indomitable ally against his father Julian's opposition to a career on the stage. Fortuitously Julian had also fallen for my mother, making him agreeably malleable. He was her first cousin. Occasionally he came from Birmingham to London to take her out to dinner, to a nightclub for a little light-hearted flirtation and hedonism. Dressed in a slinky evening gown with a bare back, accompanied by Julian in black tie and silk scarf, my mother relived a few hours of the glamour that had been missing since her youth.

When Michael remembered meeting me again, I was in my early teens. I have no memory of that occasion, had no intimation that this man – who was visiting my mother and my sister Cordelia (named after my grandmother), for whom he'd briefly fallen – was to become pivotal in my life.

E. M. Forster in a broadcast during the war had said, 'I belong to the fag-end of Victorian liberalism, and can look back to an age whose challenges were moderate in their tone, and the cloud on whose horizon was no bigger than a man's hand . . . It practised benevolence . . . had little colour-prejudice, believed that individuals are and should be different, and entertained a sincere faith in the progress of society . . .'

Amen to that. Although Forster had been born in another century and died in 1970, I too had grown up in benevolent

security. For those of my age during the war there was no time
to tread water between childhood and adulthood. Assimilation,
transition, becoming, were in a way kaleidoscoped. One
moment I was living in the sheltering haven of boarding school
– with its mandatory boundaries and where every minute of
my life was known by those in authority – the next I was
responsible not just for myself but for innumerable strangers.
Yet I never remember being frightened even though we were,
at that time, living in Cheyne Walk almost opposite Battersea
Power Station. It may sound posh considering houses in that
area now cost millions, but during the war the owners had fled
the bombing for the country and were only too glad to rent
or sell their houses – uncherished, shabby, vacant – to anyone
who made an offer. My mother was one who did so.

The co-ed boarding school where I went was in Hampshire,
where my cousins were and where subsequently our son
David also went. It was there, after joining the exclusive group
allowed the freedom of the hand-printing press, that David
was inspired to become a printer. How much better it was at
that time that there was not the pressure on everyone leaving
school to go to university. Instead David became an office boy,
a general dogsbody, first at a north London newspaper, later
at a small Kentish Town printers as the 'order clerk', dealing
with paper, ink, finishing services – spiral binding – and printing blocks. Everything, in fact, that amounted to a hands-on
form of apprenticeship. Every Saturday he went to morning
classes at the London College of Printing at the Elephant and
Castle.

Not being academic myself, I came away enriched by everything other than erudition. The school offered so much: music,
drama, dancing, debating and choral speaking, as well as

hands-on creativity – painting, weaving, dressmaking, wood-work and modelling.

The library was a haven of privacy and warmth where I spent hours in the poetry bay reading tragic epics such as Masefield's 'Reynard the Fox', Christina Rossetti's 'Goblin Market' or 'High Tide on the Coast of Lincolnshire'. Jean Ingelow's plaintive refrain, 'Come uppe, Whitefoot, come uppe, Lightfoot' plagued me for days afterwards with ' "Cusha! Cusha! Cusha!" calling' echoing in my head rather than equations. I may not have left school with scholarship, but the artistic stimulation I received compensated for my lack of brains.

The effect of the war on us schoolchildren – although coming at us obliquely – meant that every air-raid warning at Portsmouth penetrated our dreams as the school siren would go off at the same time. Leaping out of bed, groping for shoes, coats, blankets and gas masks, we traipsed in the dark across the grounds to the trenches. The sudden wakening, the chilly stumbling together and sitting on wooden benches surrounded by the smell of damp earth until the All Clear sounded left us drowsy throughout the day.

Yet freedom from fear was absolute. I was young, I was inviolate, even through the bombing in London. It's true that when the pilotless flying bombs came over and the engines suddenly cut out I did hold my breath, knowing that was the moment they fell to earth. But fear, the real thing, grows with age. It only seriously took root with the birth of my first child, and now as a grandmother fear is perpetuated for my children's children.

Joseph Conrad, who died a year before I was born, perfectly expressed how I felt: 'I remember my youth and the feeling that will never come back any more – the feeling that I could last for ever, outlast the sea, the earth and all men . . .'

Oh Conrad, the crassness of youth.

That once-in-a-lifetime buoyancy: a complacency that comes from experiencing little. My assumption of immortality kept me, after I'd left school, imperturbable whether I was hearing the wail of sirens stationed in the Royal Hospital grounds surrounded by shrubs of heavy-scented lilacs or fire-watching on a roof during an air raid. Bombs, the Blitz, explosives when – wearing a tin helmet, carrying my gas mask slung across me – two of us, recruited to stand on a tall building on Chelsea Embankment, were on the lookout for stray incendiary bombs intended for Battersea Power Station. When we saw the incandescent pyrotechnics over the City, it wasn't fear we felt but the enormity of devastation.

During the war, sheep were put to graze in Hyde Park. The sight of farm animals grazing among paths familiar to me throughout my childhood had the effect of a limitless pastoral scene, though the area is not as large as New York's Central Park. How different Hyde Park was from the secrecy of London squares. Railed round, with padlocked gates, they mystified Cordelia and me as we viewed them from the top of a Routemaster bus. Who had the keys? Who had the authority to let themselves in to these secluded spots with hiding places among the grimy bushes? And that little shed – there always was one – what went on inside? Did elite groups of chums with exclusive passes party there all night surrounded by houses where the inmates slept in ignorance? We imagined on some nights how one loner would secretly let himself in to sit on a bench and write poetry among the shrubs under plane trees with blobby fruit. Whereas the public parks were places we wandered freely through among their regiments of tulips. Sadly we never held the key to one of the squares in Bloomsbury, Belgravia or Notting Hill Gate.

*   *   *

The notorious fogs – the pea-soupers – made the capital even more perilous to traverse in total blackout. Walking across London having missed the last bus home after a party, dance or play held no apprehension, no angst, in spite of fog, blackout and the noisy racket of ack-ack guns stationed in the Royal Hospital grounds, which now, more serenely, contain the Chelsea Flower Show. (In the early days of the Show had there been a lack of sophistication when gardeners arrived with armfuls of flowers devoid of artifice, polystyrene props, cerebral acrobatics or ten-inch blooms in psychedelic colours? It's hard to make the upturned face of a pansy look dissipated, yet at recent shows it appears as if the love of flowers had been left behind in the potting shed.)

Shafts of searchlights catching glimpses of anchored barrage balloons – silver whales floating overhead – added a theatrical unreality that reinforced my sense of immortality. Fear of strangers was something alien to people of my generation. Coming up from Sloane Square Underground (where to avoid the bombs sleeping bodies lined the platforms), the fog lapped and fondled grey spectres: dense, suffocating, annihilating. I was sanguine. Finding my way home may have been hazardous, but it was the sound of footsteps that gave me confidence. I evolved a technique, a means of navigating through fog by finding the pavement edge and dragging my foot along the kerb, counting the corners and road crossings while trying to visualise the turnings in my head. Buses down the King's Road had blacked-out windows and headlights, the rare cars gave out narrow shafts of light, and once off the main road obscurity was complete.

My foot-dragging method wasn't always infallible. If I lost count of the roads I'd crossed – and it was too easy to stray into a diagonal rather than a right-angle once I left the kerb – I sometimes ended up turning down Walpole Street or Smith Street instead of Royal Avenue. Touching tree trunks – those beautiful planes with mottled bark that do so much to enhance London squares – or house railings – those around area steps which hadn't been removed as valuable metal for the war effort – meant I'd reached home safely.

'Where are we?' 'Did I mistake Lower Sloane Street for the King's Road?' 'Where are you going?' Footsteps coming towards me, or following behind, meant salvation.

Blessed, lovely, life-giving pedestrians. How welcome they were. Their presence in the midst of foggy blackout meant comfort. We would talk as we passed one another, throwing aside reassuring bulletins and directional confidences. The thought that nearing footfalls were anything but beneficent never occurred to me. Adrift in a subfusc world, every passer-by, knowing where he or she was going, could be shared as though we were playing a giant game of Chinese Whispers, passing messages from Sloane Square to World's End.

And then there were the mornings.

Wind, sky, clouds bulking the horizon where once terraced houses had enclosed a street. Sunlight from unexpected quarters, structures missing, gaps not there yesterday. Of course, here was destruction in my once familiar territory where the guts of houses lay spewed about the place. Sagging floors, charred beams, a dangling bed-head, a grate in an upstairs wall with no roof, a skewed bath clinging on by one claw were exposed to the public. Flowery wallpaper in disembowelled bedrooms; toys; a contorted bicycle; normality violated; a chest emptied of drawers, its contents trashed among rubble where a cat tiptoed through debris, was other people's history. Touching, defenceless, their intimacy revealed in full-frontal exposure. At the corner a postman scrambled over tumbled bricks to clear a space before he could open the door of a pillar box. Across the road the milkman negotiated his way through wreckage to deliver bottles to a single remaining upright house.

In spite of the bombing, the shortages, the blackout, the sirens and the lack of shopping for clothes as everything was on coupons, girls of my age had a wild time, being in demand for parties and dances to cheer up those on leave. London was full of servicemen of all nationalities: our Allies preparing for the 'Second Front'.

I don't remember ever hearing of my contemporaries being attacked or mugged as we travelled across the city in the blackout. And when the war ended we all migrated, like birds at the end of winter, to Piccadilly Circus for the celebrations that went on till dawn.

For us who were young it was a jubilant and forward-looking time, but for others, the older women, there was a certain loss when the war ended. They had discovered freedom; for the duration they had replaced household drudgery with work in factories. War work was a release. They'd never enjoyed life as much, and for years afterwards they looked back to the hours spent at their machines listening to 'Workers' Playtime' with nostalgia for lost comradeship and laughter.

When Michael and I married – after our spasmodic encounters – at the register office in the King's Road where on the next floor you could get your corns done, I was a prototypical hippie: long hair, black stockings and clothes suitable for Prue Sarn, a Mary Webb heroine.

As we were second cousins, Michael loved to think our grandmothers had been sisters. In one of the letters among the bundle I've been going through, he wrote, 'Have we something to say to each other because we are both off-shoots from the same line in space? And why do we meet now after all these intervening years while I have lived so many years away from you: a forgotten relative with wires across your teeth? Perhaps our life-paths were destined to touch when I first saw you in the bath?

'The same strand runs through both of us, though your grandmother, much younger than mine, was less earnest. She was warmer, more "twinkly". And she never exiled Mary [his sister] and me to the nursery when we went to tea with her, but allowed us to join her in the drawing-room where we played spillikins made of delicate pieces of ivory or Pope Joan with a painted board, shells and mother-of-pearl fishes. It's not surprising that her daughter, your mother, turned out to be a maverick among all that strait-laced lot!'

Living in Shropshire after we married, where we had a small farm with neither electricity nor mains water and where each spring a stallion bedecked with ribbons walked the lanes servicing the mares, we often made the journey between the country and London, a slow and un-trafficky journey through the Cotswolds before the age of motorways. In his open-top Sunbeam motor that had to be started on a handle, with wide running boards and a bovine-sounding horn, Michael kept me enthralled with tales of his school days. Having been brought up in a co-educational, free-thinking milieu where the emphasis was on opening doors in a child's mind and offering a whole world of possibilities, I found his accounts baffling and deliciously appalling.

From his anecdotes, diaries and letters I've distilled what sounds like a barbaric life at his public school. A set-up about which, years later, when we were living in the Far East, a couple of young American friends working in the embassy would ask him to elaborate. Mesmerised by Michael's account of nannies and maids, prep and public school, they'd learnt about this sort of England from old black-and-white movies. They couldn't hear enough. He fitted exactly their idea of a WASP – a White Anglo-Saxon Protestant.

'Tell us more,' they urged. 'What did the butler wear?'

From his father, on the eve of his departure to public school, Michael received mystifying advice.

'I was summoned into his study. Among editions of Scott, Carlyle, Macaulay and prizes – Livy and Tacitus with the school crest tooled in gold – and the Etruscan marble clock presented to my father on retirement from the family firm, he warned me: "I . . . er . . . hope you'll never let another boy . . . er . . . take hold of your . . . er . . . you know . . ." '

'I thought my father had gone clean off his head. Why should another boy want to? Later I found out. My house-master at Shrewsbury used to have a group of us boys to tea where a good deal of er . . . you know . . . went on.

'At school I lived in terror. The desks, linoleum, the smell of disinfectant, chalk, the fustiness of the masters' gowns, the high, wire-netted windows closed by ropes clanged with a jarring clatter that made us jump every time. The gym was my incubus. I should have felt confident being adept on the horse, springboard, ropes and parallel bars . . . instead it was persecution. Below the wall-bars were the mats, the licensed battleground where old scores were settled, vengeance or recompense claimed, punishment and torture supervised. "You cheeky little squit," some senior boy shouted at me. "I'll bust you! To the mats!" And to the mats, the dust-filled pile – coarse, scrubby, breathing in long-dried nose-blood, sweat, salty tears, splinters of spectacles and pocket-fug – I would be frog-marched while the master turned his back. And then, pinned down by a bottom on my chest; an alien crotch too near my nostrils; blue bony knees against my ears; an ink-stained thumb pressing on my jugular, I accused my father. He'd been head boy at the school. Why hadn't he warned me of this ritual awaiting every new boy?'

Nor did the masters intervene.

'They were sadists in their caps and gowns, their nicotine-soaked pipes ... *Magister* ... *magistrum* ... dead people teaching a dead language. But it was the emphasis on masculinity that undid me. When in my first week I mentioned my sister – two years older and capable of climbing the highest trees and un-squeamish about killing a rabbit – I was ridiculed mercilessly. It was not done to have a sister. I was expected to take bullying "on the chin", my father told me. My sister was much nearer to his heart with her tomboy habits.'

I would visit Michael's home in Birmingham – a respectable district where the large houses were protected from the road by a high wall and a drive flanked by leaden-leafed shrubs. In the drawing room, permanently dark from the gloomy trees in the garden and the heavy brownish curtains on the windows, the fragrance of roses trapped in bowls of potpourri was as comforting as the smell of a warm cat.

'I could isolate every scent as I entered the house,' Michael wrote. 'The liniment, knife polish, plant fibre in pots of hyacinths with roots like unkempt hair my mother grew in glass jars, their sweetness overlaid by traces of escaping gas from light brackets along the hall. In the drawing room – where charity ladies who smelt of Cologne and never took off their hats came for committee meetings – I avoided being introduced by hiding under the grand piano shielded by a Cashmere shawl that hung to the ground. Afterwards, if my father weren't around, I'd have a quick slide down the banisters or escape to the basement for the warm haven of the kitchen.

'Each afternoon Milly, white capped, with starched ribbons floating behind her, emptied the diminutive pillar-box on the hall table handing the letters for posting to William the chauffeur in charge of the 1911 Daimler with its vase of flowers, glass partition, and speaking tube. On a silver salver Milly carried the letters to the drawing room where my father demanded quiet and my mother – who had never recovered from the gross obscenity of sex on her wedding night – painted water colours. And on Sundays we had lunch with uncles, aunts and cousins at my grandmother's house – a committed suffragette whose portrait hangs in the Birmingham Art Gallery – upright and kindly but never indulgent, she was an autocrat. Humour had little currency at these gatherings . . . quite unlike her sister, your grandmother. If anyone started to gossip she'd admonish, "Hush dear, we talk of things, not people."

'But Mary and I were growing up to be little snobs – not from our parents, whom we saw briefly – but from our daily walks with nanny we became connoisseurs of class. Beyond the streets of net curtains, aspidistras, and signs saying Dressmaker lived "the poor", a district we never penetrated. A straight drive gave the impression of substance, where the garden would be at the back of the house. A front garden was lowly, without privacy. And houses on a tram route had no status at all. How smug we were.'

He might have been describing life in another century – it sounded stultifying.

Class distinction was an aspect of Edgbaston life my bolshie mother Phyllis had repudiated instinctively. If that's how she grew up, no wonder she rebelled and gave my sister and me a freewheeling childhood.

Education for middle-class sons was prescriptive: prep school, public school, university. Money opened the doors of academia with no need to jump scholastic hurdles. Cambridge, for Michael, would naturally be followed by joining the family business, into which generations of conforming uncles and cousins had been absorbed, and this was why his father insisted on his son reading engineering, not English – Michael's preferred subject. He wrote of it with bitterness: 'At Cambridge you were either an aesthete or a philistine. Beer-swilling sporties talking motor cars and nightly hunting shop girls, I avoided and when I could the lecture theatre, the ghastly labs, the hiss of mercury lights, the smell of leaky gas rings and the drawing office where silently forty heads, bent over cartridge paper, draw intersection curves of cone and cylinder. I wasted years over Ohm's Law, the Binomial Theorem, Elementary Electricity and Magnetism instead of *The Rubaiyat of Omar Khayyam* or Arthurian literature. Stagnant, I became a brainless automaton who never read a book ... well nothing that counts as literature. And I got a third.'

The firm of F. & C. Osler, which Michael was expected to join, had created the crystal fountain for the centre of the Great Exhibition of 1851 in Hyde Park, known as the Crystal Palace. The thirty-foot fountain was spectacular. To enable Queen Victoria's voice to be heard above the sound of splashing, the mechanism – concealed behind glass shells and flowers – had to be silenced. In 1936 the palace was removed to another site where the ingenuity of a year and a half's labour went up in flames. Nothing remained of the masterpiece but fragments. (The original drawings are in the Birmingham Art

Gallery.) Some Osler glass was exquisite, some bizarre. Among decanters, goblets and posy holders, candelabras, chandeliers and wall lights with 'fish-tail' gas burners were crystal chairs with baluster arms and velvet seats, a crystal long-case clock for the King of Nepal and a monumental crystal cabinet of inspired vulgarity.

The business – started by Follet and Clarkson Osler early in the nineteenth century – finally closed in the 1970s. A minor resurrection took place in 1991 when Mallett, in Bond Street, London, held an exhibition entitled *Osler's Crystal for Royalty and Rajahs*. Visiting with my family, I coveted, among all the tinkling splendour, a small, round glass table with the underside intricately cut into geometric shapes. By using copper, not the usual cobalt, this gem of a table was the blue of a sapphire, the iridescence of a kingfisher in flight. Unable to afford it, I wonder who did.

When Michael refused to go into the family firm, his father was apoplectic: 'What, foregoing "the Works" for the theatre, an actor chap – messing about in front of footlights?'

The acrimony remained like an infestation between them: 'When I read "Following in Father's footsteps" by John Betjeman I knew it had been written for me. Betjeman, by choosing to write rather than go into the Birmingham family business, displeased his father in just the same way as mine. Neither parent forgave their sons.'

Yet Julian did have a felicitous side – not with people but with roses.

Away from 'the Works' – at their country house in Grafton, Worcestershire – Julian created a small garden. Lilies, lavender and hollyhocks; evening primroses, sweet williams and campanulas. A summerhouse festooned with honeysuckle, pergolas sagging with roses – where pansies clustered at their roots – was the epitome of a 'cottage garden'. There were vegetables and soft fruit; damson, plum, pear and walnut trees. Beyond was the apple and cherry orchard. Further still, the song of skylarks could be heard high above Bredon Hill.

Julian – a relic of a repressed, unemotional upbringing who signed letters to his son even when Michael was in India during the war, 'Yours, Julian Osler' – resembled so many bottled-up men of his generation. When Michael first told me this, I was incredulous: I'd assumed all families were tactile, embracing and affectionately articulate.

Julian's romantic alter ego found fulfilment in the face of a *centifolia* rose, the cabbage or the moss, not in his wife. It wasn't orderly beds of raised bare earth, planted with floribundas and hybrid teas, which loosened his libido, but the damasks, the bourbons, the *albas* and *gallicas* and the species roses. Flowers of such exquisite delicacy that by June the garden was overwhelmed by an abundance of dishevelled blooms.

Over the flushed face of 'Madame Pierre Oger' Michael's father bent as adoringly and tenderly as any lover.

Was it Julian's garden, one of the prettiest small gardens I'd ever seen, that inspired my love of roses? Oh yes, I do genuflect to the man and his roses. His dual personality may not have been endearing when his devotion to flora never extended to the other distaff members in his life – his wife and daughter – but his sensitive dedication to his shrubs was steadfast. The cosseter of 'Queen of Denmark' or 'Great Maiden's Blush' in his other bed (the flower border) was in contrast to the overbearing paterfamilias who never forgave his son for turning his back on the glass trade to become an actor, or even his daughter when she trained to become a doctor – a profession he thought unsuitable for a woman.

Although in Birmingham Michael's family lived with servants, electricity and hot water, Julian remained unconcerned for his wife coping without electricity or mains water in their country house: 'We suffered unbelievable austerities at Grafton, a perverse morality, unconcerned with the trivia of comfort in accordance with my father's Unitarian principles. But Mary and I loved the place, not least because our father became agreeable. For us there were no shortcomings.'

Even though in the country they did have the charmingly named Mrs Mantle for inside help and Mr Coates for outside chores, 'We were expected to help our mother wash up with water from a kettle boiled on the kitchen range, and go to bed by candlelight. The kitchen was vast and cold, with a stone-flagged floor and two coppers in the corner for boiling the clothes. We bathed in a tin bath on the floor. But lack of comfort was compensated by wonderful produce. Hare, pheasant, duckling and partridge, asparagus, fruit tarts and cream and butter. Our home-made cider was the most potent, the peas the sweetest, and my mother's summer pudding the best ever. Yet few visitors came to stay after one night.

'When your mother, with her love of the country in short bursts, came for a brief visit, Mary and I thought she was enchantment. She brought laughter, midnight feasts, gaiety and charades into our lives. My lasting memory is the time she came to say goodnight to us wearing a silky dress, green glass necklace and quoted Harold Monro's poem: "Nymph, nymph, what are your beads? Green glass, Goblin, why do you stare at them?" and her green eyes were as luminous as her beads.

'I understood then that there were other worlds about which I knew nothing. Sadly, your mother never stayed long, she hated the frugality. She'd protest gently to my mother but raged at my father: "The place is impossible!" My parents did their best to calm her, thinking it was "Cousin Phyllis" not the house that was impossible.'

My mother much preferred the lifestyle of her King's Counsel Communist friend D. N. Pritt. At the magnificent Priory on the river in Berkshire, my mother purred like a cat from warmth and luxury, and to hell with ethics.

As a child I used to stay with the Pritts. With their children, we punted on the river among the swans, and gardeners tended floral borders full of butterflies. How paradoxical: the KC wore linen Cossack shirts hand-embroidered at the neck and cuffs; we ate off hand-painted pottery plates, each depicting a different peasant working with a scythe, flail, pitchfork and sickle while all the time waited on by servants, nannies, maids, butlers and chauffeurs. Quite contrarily, his wife Molly was a Catholic. Crucifixes, a Communion table and, on the landing, a four-foot marble figure of a monk with an open Bible in his hands were hers. Every time I went up- or downstairs after nightfall I crept by anticipating the touch of his cold hand on my shoulder calling me to pray for God knows what. And once, when Molly sent me upstairs for the thermometer, I laid it on his Bible. It rolled off and broke.

At the outset of the war Michael had joined up. Among the hundreds of letters he wrote from India is one to his mother: 'There are in this country a number of throw-outs from all the nations of the earth. They are contemptuously dismissed as *Chi-chi* . . . people who are as white as you and I, are classed among them simply because they are "country born". Rejected by both races the whole thing is utterly odious – all the social barriers and the tittle-tattle of the white "pukka sahibs" are tragic.' In another letter he'd written, 'Perhaps I feel cheered today because I have seen some hills! It was at a terrific stratocirrus altitude after the sub-sea level paddy fields. We passed at lunchtime through country that could perhaps have compared with parts of upper Burma or the barren stony wastes north of Kunming.'

Six irretrievable years were lifted from Michael's life. When he returned from India – driving three thousand miles through Burma from Rangoon to Chengtu in China – the world had changed, and as with the rest of his contemporaries there was no going back to where he had once been. His career on the stage came to an end.

After the war, leaving this island was our lodestar. To encounter foreign worlds in contrast to years of drab living, of ration books and contriving ... the seduction of travellers' stories describing the pre-war countries of Europe obsessed Michael and me in different ways. For Michael, who had been compelled to travel for six years during the war, the prospect now of peaceful encounters abroad was a means to eradicate bad memories. For me it was different. Mentally I'd kept a packed bag under my bed for years, always hoping for a friend to say, 'The old Silk Road is open. Come with me beyond the Karakoram.'

That never happened, but we did make short forays when limitations of money and petrol kept us within touching distance of the Channel, when Dunkirk was the gateway to the world and if we'd turned left at Lille and kept driving in an easterly direction, we could have reached Vladivostok.

Nearer home we visited Lascaux – a unique experience as it was at a time when the complex of prehistoric caves in south-western France was still open to the public. Within those high galleries 'sympathetic magic' was in the air as we stood among the contorted and twisted bodies of beasts painted in soft mineral colours sixteen thousand years ago.

How fortunate we were. Just as I feel each time I visit Venice that we are able to return again and again while the city remains afloat.

Our first serious and major journey was in 1953 when, with two friends, we drove in a Dormobile to the remote hills of Anatolia, to the ancient Hittite capital Hattusas and the weird cylindrical monasteries of Cappadocia. Fifty pounds of currency per person was the allowance in the early fifties. For three months we slept under canvas in France, Italy and down the Yugoslav coast road – then under construction – on our way to Greece and Turkey. We returned to Shropshire via the Black Sea.

Campsites were non-existent. While our two friends slept in the vehicle, we pitched our boy scouts' tent (inappropriately called 'Pal-O'-Mine'), which Michael had acquired while at school, anywhere: among falling snow in a pine forest, in great bulks of limestone wilderness where it was impossible to knock in our tent pegs, or in an olive grove in Arcadia. Tourists were rare – meeting a foreigner coming the other way, we would mutually stop to exchange information on essentials: availability of petrol and road conditions. Only once, when we trespassed onto military ground in Turkey (where we were arrested in the middle of the night, much to the delight of the soldiers whose hands wandered through my side of the car window uninvited), was there a sense of intimidation.

Wherever we went – once it was established that we weren't Germans – 'Churchill! Football! Good!' was our universal mantra. The three words worked like magic on both hearts and doors. Embraces, meals, guidance, whether from an archaeological professor in Ankara who fed us cherries and took us to a nightclub, or from a village headman who invited us to stay overnight in a communal guest house where, before going to bed on a raised dais covered with spectacular rugs, we were accompanied into the orchard by a crowd to watch us pee.

Michael described, in *Journey to Hattusas* (1957), the winding valley and the streams, the blue-green crops and cream-coloured iris decorating meadows where in the surrounding hills we pitched our tent: 'It was evening when we arrived, and the ancient Hittite citadel was quite deserted. All around us lay the ruins of its civilization, its temple, dwellings, fortifications. Fragments of pottery lay everywhere . . . the handle of what once had been a pitcher thirty centuries ago.' We were the only people there except for ghosts of the campaigns 'against Syria or the Egyptians, the merchants from Mycenae travelling to Sivas and the East and traders from Amisus making south through the Cilician Gates to Tarsus'.

The next morning we woke to the voices of children floating up from the village of Boğasköy and to the sound of bells as flocks of goats and sheep wound, in an endless procession, across the valley below. As it had been, Michael wrote, 'through the summer mornings, century before century, back to the years when King Suppiluliumas had heard them as a boy'.

Through all the years during which Michael and I travelled subsequently, driving hundreds of miles up and down Europe, we both sought a combination of travelling for the sights and galleries and for self-indulgent hedonism. However focused we were on the next fresco, Michael could never resist getting out of the car – long before lunchtime – to read a menu posted outside a hotel or restaurant in France. And we discovered that driving with others never worked successfully if they only travelled for 'culture', for packing in every single campanile, clerestory or squint till we drooped with fatigue at the end of the day.

There was no one I enjoyed motoring with more than Michael.

After our daughter Tamsin was born, we used to travel in our car with David – and my sister Cordelia and her family in theirs – through Europe for spring or summer holidays. Travel is addictive. A longing to get into the car, cross the water and keep going is not easily deflected. Returning to our pastoral life among the Shropshire hills, where curlews called from across our fields and where dog-and-stick farming was traditional, we decided we could no longer resist.

In 1959 we went to live in Asia. But first I must go back in time to the years before I was born.

3

'That Loathsome Centipede, Remorse'

Looking at a photograph of my mother, aged seventeen, when her face was oval, her eyes wide, knowing nothing of unrequited love and wearing an ankle-length skirt, a high-necked blouse, her thick hair tied back in a black bow, I pore over the image, urging her to stay that way. Don't get older. You are young; not yet a mother, you're free of limpets. I stare, concentrating, waiting for her picture to go ripply to the sound of formless music as in movie scenes.

Bereavement cannot be practised in advance and remorse is residue that cannot be dispelled. The self-accusation of words unspoken – of selfishness, of exasperation, insensitivity or obtuse responses – is not easily placated. Guilt festers. I was thirty when my mother died. I ought to have known better, yet I never regarded her as a person. For too long I'd been guarding my frontiers against her histrionics.

I never stopped to think how lonely she was in her last

years after Stella Bowen, her beloved confidante since the First World War, had died.

Phyllis and Stella – the two people who had been instrumental in my childhood.

My mother had escaped to London from the conventional mores of her upbringing in Birmingham to become a student at a school for voice training and drama, at that time housed in the Albert Hall. For someone like Phyllis, educated at Roedean – a conventional girls' boarding school on the Sussex coast – and brought up among prejudice and proscribed attitudes, this flight to London was considered a dodgy business during the 1914–18 war. But my grandmother was astute enough to push aside the boundaries of hallowed behaviour. She backed her daughter, and by accepting that she had produced a child who was far from submissive, she overruled my grandfather's misgivings. My mother was placed in an establishment for young ladies in Kensington. Here she could shed the constraints of a Unitarian upbringing where the first question on introducing a friend to her parents was: 'But, darling, who are his people?'

The move to the hostel was auspicious: she met Stella Bowen – one of the boarders – with whom she felt an immediate empathy. Stella, with large brown eyes, dark hair cut in an Eton crop and a serene personality, had broken away from even more formidable fetters. Born in Australia, she had grown up within the suffocating restraints of Adelaide, 'a queer little backwater of intellectual timidity'. When her mother had died, Stella had persuaded her trustees to allow her to go to Europe to study art for a year, but she never used the return half of the ticket. What began as youthful curiosity – a hunger for European art, a passion to escape – took her into the arms of the novelist and editor Ford Madox Ford, grandson of the painter Ford Madox Brown.

My mother, with her extrovert personality and natural presence on the stage, was one of director Elsie Fogarty's star pupils at the speech and drama classes. Small and stout, wearing a long skirt, boots and a three-cornered hat, Miss Fogarty would show some lumpish Puck how to bring gusto to the part. Stella, meanwhile – a pupil of the artist Walter Sickert at the Westminster School of Art – was learning to trust her eyes and to 'never touch the canvas twice in the same place'.

Over mugs of cocoa Stella and my mother felt instant amity. Their similar upbringings laid the foundation that would last in spite of the turbulence that periodically overwhelmed them as they supported, confided, advised and comforted each other with a constancy neither time nor distance could destroy.

'Stella was like the sister I never had,' my mother used to say.

When life at the high-class hostel for young ladies – with morning prayers in the drawing room and nightly curfews – began to pall (my mother, who never submitted to anything in life, chafed more than Stella), they escaped. They rented for the next three years 2 Pembroke Studios from an artist who was at the front.

Their neighbour, the poet Ezra Pound, looked on the young women as fertile ground for what he considered, in Art and Literature, to be worthy of their admiration. Ten years their senior, he had already published translations, and his poems had appeared in Ford's *English Review*. To my mother and Stella he was an exotic figure.

'Ezra took the trouble to occupy himself with our joint education,' Stella wrote. 'I expect it was fun for him to harangue two girls who took him so very seriously, and it was certainly fine for us.'

Pound introduced them to a bohemian world of poets and artists. In that proscriptive era – which reads like history to the young – it was for Phyllis and Stella an intoxicating revelation. Precipitated into a milieu of painters, poets and writers, conscientious objectors, socialists, political revolutionaries and hedonistic charmers, they experienced a coterie utterly alien to their upbringings. The literary conclaves at the Café Royal to which they were invited became the start of their education. There they met Harold Monro, who in 1913 had launched his Georgian Poets series in which he published contemporary writers. He also founded the *Poetry Review* and started the Poetry Bookshop in an alley near Southampton Row, where the American poet Robert Frost met Edward Thomas – the beginning of their long friendship. At the weekly readings at the Poetry Bookshop my mother often took part, and there she was asked by the playwright and poet John Drinkwater to join the Birmingham Repertory Company where he was manager. Had it been some other repertory, in some other town, she told me, she might have wavered. But neither praise for her acting ability nor a career on the stage could tempt her back to Birmingham – a place she regarded as provincial exile from which she had recently escaped.

Birmingham, in my mother's eyes, never received absolution. Not the city itself but the throttling prejudice, lack of spontaneity and passion in conforming constraints amongst which she had grown up. My sister Cordelia and I were to benefit from her freedom of spirit throughout our childhood.

London, in spite of the war, with so many young men at the front, was pulsating with literati. Parties, readings, luncheons, weekly dinner parties at Belloti's in Soho, literary discussions at the Café Royal where Phyllis and Stella met the artist and novelist Wyndham Lewis, the poets Robert Graves,

W. W. Gibson, Walter de la Mare, W. H. Davies and Arthur Waley, plus many others. Once, when my mother was reading a poem by T. S. Eliot at the Poetry Bookshop, the author turned up wearing a black satin chest-protector. Stella wrote, '[I]t was all very precious and exclusive and rather puritanical. But there were lovely things for us to admire – Eliot's "Prufrock", Ezra's "Lustra" – Gaudier-Brzeska's stone carvings and drawings of animals, and Wyndham Lewis's drawings.' (Pound had come to Europe in 1908 via Venice, where his first volume of poetry, *A Lume Spento*, was published, before moving later that year to London.) There was also James Joyce's *Portrait of the Artist*: 'Joyce and Lewis were Ezra's twin gods, before whom we were bidden to bend the knee most deeply.'

Pound taught the two girls to dance, performing in such a gangling, jerky gait that they quickly adapted to a more becoming style. The evening he took my mother to dine with W. B. Yeats she listened in rapt reverence as a decanter of port was passed to and fro between the two illustrious poets – one born in 1865, the other in 1885 – while they discussed the short-lived journal *Blast* (1914–15) edited by Wyndham Lewis. Recounting the event many years afterwards, my mother remembered being an overawed but delighted mute observer. Pound told her later that Yeats had said, 'Do tell me, who was that intelligent and beautiful girl you brought with you to dinner the other evening?'

By now, with the two young women established in their studio and with a growing number of friends coming to their beer-and-gramophone-music parties, admirers were flocking round Phyllis. Her gaiety and flirtatious vitality may have been alluring, but it was to Stella, with her basic sense of justice, her integrity, that they turned with their heartaches and frustrations. My mother too turned to Stella for sage advice, while Ezra became their constant catalyst and mentor. It was on the evening that he took them to a party given by Violet Hunt, novelist and social figure in literary London, that Ezra introduced them to Ford Madox Ford.

The introduction turned out to be critical. It was not Phyllis to whom the great author was attracted, but the quiet art student Stella Bowen.

Decades later, after the death of Ford, Stella and Phyllis, Ezra wrote to me apropos my mother's death, referring to those days when he'd undertaken their artistic education: 'I wonder if your generation that has known only the between wars and latter dreary one has any idea of what she called the period of most absolute *joie de vivre* – only that isn't her exact phrase which I cannot dig out of memory. The 1st war was different – and of the little group only Gaudier [-Brzeska] & T. E. Lawrence's younger brother actually got killed. And that before she & Stella got to London. & some of 'em grew old . . . Ten years ago I did a ballad refrain at Pisa incredulous that all of 'em wd. by then be old ladies. It was too sentimental to make a poem.'

A pity.

During Ford's courtship of Stella Bowen, my mother had fallen in love with the poet, Clifford Bax (brother of the composer Arnold). Clifford was older, more courtly than her other suitors; a dilettante, sensualist and connoisseur of women, he seduced her in no time. The affair was passionate and doomed. Two people with such effervescent egos had little chance of success. My mother, with the confidence of someone who expects to get her own way however many times she gets knocked back, believed her perfect lover was to be found in this man. Having rejected a career on the stage, knowing that she like Stella and Ford wanted above all a home and children, she found in her poet an implacable will not to surrender to her demands for domesticity.

They did, however, remain lifelong friends, and as a child I was taken by Clifford to watch the famous cricketer C. B. Fry play at Lords. Bored, I sat at the back of the box and ate strawberries throughout the match. When I was seventeen I visited Clifford at his elegant chambers in Albany, with tall windows overlooking Savile Row, where he asked me if I would pose nude for a painter friend of his and would I mind if he sat in on the sessions?

I wouldn't pose, and I would mind.

Clifford's was the first of my mother's many ruptured love affairs: affairs that left her mortified. 'The slow black oxen tread the world, and God the herdsman goads them on behind, and I am broken by their passing feet' was one of her oft-repeated laments from Yeats's *The Countess Cathleen*. And yet, due to the warmth of her spirit and her capacity for friendship, my sister and I came to know many of her old lovers who remained in her life long after the emotional lava had settled.

(Odd about men, so Cordelia and I thought: how often we were importuned by Phyllis's ex-lovers. Obviously there was something irresistible in working their way through the distaff members of a family, and – being the youngest – I was the last resort. I don't know how it was for Cordelia, but as far I was concerned their octopus tentacles lacked charm. Each was resistible.)

Desperate, her student life with Stella at an end, my mother turned to Harry, a young architect who was articled to the firm that designed the Houses of Parliament. Tall, with wavy hair, blue eyes, a lively wit, gregarious and vivacious, his friends ranged from a Franciscan monk who worked among deep-sea trawlermen to a fire-raiser for the militant suffragettes, and included men of letters, poets and painters, one of whom introduced him to Gaudier-Brzeska, who became a friend until the sculptor's death in 1915. The group used to meet at a vegetarian restaurant and read one another's papers in favour of 'sexual freedom for females'.

My aunt Ursula, married to Harry's younger brother Charles, described my father as 'an excellent dancer and something of a dandy who on occasions wore a gold fob and carried a tall cane [and] who loved both jazz and classical music'. Three weeks after the First World War broke out, he enlisted and got his commission, and in 1916, during the Battle of the Somme, he was temporarily invalided home with shell shock. He was demobilised in 1919.

My father was at the beginning of a successful career when he met Phyllis. Captivated by the radiant creature with whom he shared a love of theatricals, dancing and children, he offered her everything. They married, bought a Regency house in Holland Park, held parties, went to the theatre and in 1921 prepared for the birth of their first child, Cordelia.

Their happiness lasted ten months. From then on the dread disease that had felled so many of my father's family took over with progressive irreversibility. In those days tuberculosis was a killer. But my mother, inexperienced and knowing nothing of the plague prevalent in her husband's family, remained ignorant of the ominous signs: a husky throat, an intermittent cough. Instead, after the birth of Cordelia, she and my father spent night after night junketing with their friends at dinners and dances, oblivious to what was edging closer and about to overwhelm them.

When the blow did come and my father was diagnosed as critically ill, his ambition in a career that already promised success ended. Tuberculosis meant giving up everything: career, gaiety, festivities, weekending with friends. He was to be banished by doctor's orders to the country for a quiet life. Phyllis, bewildered and outraged at the injustice of what had overtaken them, could not become reconciled. When my father was sent to the King Edward VII Hospital near Midhurst for such treatment as was then possible, my mother fled with baby Cordelia to find solace with Stella, living her primitive life with Ford in Sussex. For someone who had never been ill, never had an operation or suffered any of the common ailments of childhood, my father's illness seemed an injustice.

In 1922 Harry left hospital: the family moved to a cottage in Buckinghamshire among beech woods, chalky soil and houses made of flints glossy as oyster shells. Here my mother did her best to love the ducks, chickens and goats (their milk was considered essential for my father's disease), for, unlike Stella, pastoral living was not her voluntary environment. Yet bits worked; there were compensations: 'I hear the tasselled hedges shout – run! Catch March by the heels, trip and hold down this brief and tardy spring.' And again: 'When trees are standing knee-deep in summer I pick strawberries warm in the sun, in autumn I gather mushrooms on days when no sunlight shines in the woods, only falling rain and the hiss and drip on small bushes under trees with branches raised to the clouds.'

But her spirit was withering. My mother railed against their contracted state. Her husband had lost all desire to resurrect a social life. Instead he passed hours in an octagonal rotating shed, made to catch every scrap of sunlight, where he'd write occasional architectural articles or create designs on a small scale. During a period of remission I was conceived. He'd longed for a family but now a fluctuating disease periodically shredded his life with night sweats, weight loss, the coughing up of blood. He was unable to speak above a whisper. With no promise of a cure, tuberculosis was pitiless.

To a friend, soon after I was born, Phyllis described her thoughts about me: 'Held within the hollow of my arm, little fragment of a thousand races, you are mysteriously myself – yet not I – mysteriously your father, yet not he – who are you? Lifted by the rhythm of your breath you may never tell the secret place from beyond the world and back of death whence your small heart beats to meet life's call.'

From my aunt Ursula I learnt about their marriage after my mother's death. With insight and frankness she wrote, 'Sadly, and ashamedly, my recollection of the small part in the drama played by your uncle and myself is one of smugness. We were maddeningly self-sufficient, indefatigable hill-walkers, and bigoted enthusiasts for the Labour Party. Neither of us (nor, for that matter, Harry) stopped to realise the desolation his illness had brought to Harry. It transformed him from a convivial young architect into a disappointed and frustrated man struggling to make something of a life doomed by a disease that attacked with such ruthless effect.'

Phyllis, who only thrived in the metropolitan vigour of perpetual stimulus, did her best to bring joy into their lives. She confidently assumed she could keep the fragments of their life intact. Friends visited. There were weekends when books, politics and argument could last long into the night, but few had the perspicacity to sense the impending desolation of my father's being transformed by illness from an optimistic, ambitious husband into a tragic introvert. His verve and wit changed to Spartan fatalism. Not self-pity, but an embittered, detached frigidity. My mother would say, with rueful resignation, that he preferred her to make a cake rather than write a sonnet.

Within such rural incompatibility, something had to give. It did. Margaret Postgate introduced my mother to Aylmer.

Margaret (aka Mop) was a school friend from Roedean, a brilliant scholar at school and at Girton. Her portrait in the National Portrait Gallery, painted by Stella Bowen, who by now had many portrait commissions, shows Margaret with a heart-shaped face, a curly mouth and dark hair: the kind that lives its own life. Though at Roedean her academic ability was at odds with my mother's sensual responses, they fused instantly, admiring each other for opposite reasons: 'Phyllis stood out among the rest of us at Roedean as some rare creature. She could act, recite or sing. In school plays she had the star parts but what a rebel. Phyllis never succumbed to the conventional straitjacket of a girl's school. I idolized her for that and she, I think, admired me for winning all the Latin and Greek prizes that she knew for her were out of reach.'

For the next fifty years my mother and Mop remained friends. (In 1922 Stella painted with free brush strokes a relaxed, half-figure portrait of Mop's brother Raymond Postgate against a background of newspapers.) The whole clan of Postgate and Mitchinson children had parties to which Cordelia and I were invited. Parties at which I was petrified by the games we had to play. 'Murder' among the dark passages and stairways was one, and 'Forfeits' was the terrifying outcome for the losers of other games.

It was during a visit to my parents in the country that Mop, now married to economist and Oxford professor G.D.H. Cole, and aware that my mother was in need of rescuing from mental starvation, invited her to a lunch party in London where she introduced Phyllis to her husband's friend Aylmer Vallance.

Aylmer was captivated. He'd never met anyone so spirited or so seductive. My mother – aware of being looked at and conscious of how she appeared – watched as though she was an object both to herself and to others. She saw herself from the other side of the footlights. Aylmer merely saw a vulnerable woman in an unhappy marriage. At the nadir of that marriage he entered my mother's world promising devotion that was for her a life-giving elixir. Urbane and courteous, he brought a certain civility and percipience that had been missing for too long. My mother had been deprived of approbation – her cardinal weakness. She needed perpetual reassurance from those around her. Neither her babies nor my father could offer this.

But Aylmer could.

There were six people sitting round the table, but for Aylmer there was only one – Phyllis. But she, bound by commitments at home – her babies being the one anchor in her life – did not at first respond: 'As I was in no position to respond I unconsciously retreated.'

Aylmer wrote to her.

I was one year old when that fateful lunch party took place. Now, from this distance, I feel freed from dubious morality to expose a love affair intense, romantic and old-fashioned that passed between them with a velocity that belied the archaic phrasing, the risible proprieties, the naivety of language alien to us whose children become streetwise in their teens. Aylmer and Phyllis's letters are as dated to me as the letters between Jean-Jacques Rousseau and Mme de Warens, or between Elizabeth and Robert Browning.

The 160 love letters I found after my mother's death between her and my stepfather Aylmer cover the first three months of 1927.

What did I feel as I put them into chronological order? Nothing, at first anyway. They were remote, unreal and intensely sad since all vitality had long ago evaporated, but as I read on, knowing of course the outcome that had affected my life and my sister's as well as my mother's, I began to feel the pitiful vacuity of their passionate vows, which in the end amounted to deceit.

Speech can be denied but not the written word. Warm, trenchant, the leavings of my mother's and Aylmer's protestations – ardent and fleeting, written between two flawed people – are of such poignancy. I trespass where I was never intended to go. Should I? Am I right to unravel emotions they had disclosed only to each other?

Yet if not me, who else?

Aunt Ursula, who'd known both correspondents, was unequivocal when I queried the probity of disinterring the letters: 'Such documents deserve to be rescued from oblivion. They're stuff of the human condition. They may lack the appeal of Samuel Pepys's diaries – but how sad if he'd exclaimed "These are rubbish" and tossed them down the privy!'

Today, what has replaced the physical legacy of written letters for lovers? In a chest are all the letters Michael and I wrote before we married. Were we among the last to put pledges into writing, into pages and pages of passion for one another?

Can abbreviated texting do it for the young?

Ninety years ago, the Royal Mail spanned the miles between lovers with three deliveries a day. Imagine! A letter posted that morning in London could arrive by late post the same day. Cupid, mundanely clad in a postman's uniform, was imbued with amorous light as he walked or cycled along the lanes of Buckinghamshire. For us in the third millennium, when email encompasses the world, an envelope on the doormat is no longer to be hoarded for later as a child saves till last the icing on a cake. But Aylmer and Phyllis's letters crossed continually between the country and the city. Whether written at a desk, at the kitchen table, in a conference room or even from the station, where my mother, arriving in the high-wheeled dog-cart and waiting for the London train taking her to Aylmer, penned a few passionate words.

A handwritten letter is intimate. Some sort of residue is left in hand-held paper: ink on paper, the hand that only a few hours before had folded the page, have been lost to us with our gadgetry. The tangibility of love letters has been forfeited.

After formal exchanges Phyllis and Aylmer wrote to each other, often twice a day.

'I hadn't intended to like you at first,' Aylmer wrote. 'Certainly not love! Anyway there are things in you of which I disapprove. You pose, you're a sensationalist, vain over silly things, a bit of a charlatan and capable of making life hell for a quiet man. [He should have stopped there. Besotted, he went on.] And yet my wonderful, brave, enchanting friend – you whose magic turns my grey thoughts to music – I would pay years of hell to have you with me now.'

On an afternoon in February, when pigeons like balls of wool perched immobile on window ledges, Aylmer wrote in his neat, academic hand, 'It's 3 a.m. less than a month since we first danced together, Phyllis, and I cannot sleep. I have established myself beside the gas fire (an unromantic but comforting object provided it's fed with a shilling) yet what I write will be but a shadow of the miracle you have wrought.'

That same afternoon my mother, sitting at her desk in the low-ceilinged cottage where the curtains were already drawn against the fading light, wrote words echoing his: 'My thoughts enfold your dreaming head as close-pressed I hold your hands in memory. How can we live closer than this . . . I need only put out my hand to find yours. To be with you is like coming suddenly into a clearing, light and warm, after walking among dark trees. How do you manage to be exactly the person I've always wanted – with all the qualities of mind and heart that I never thought to find fused in one man?'

They had not yet become lovers. My mother, married with two children, needed to define the boundaries: 'Although I am yours completely and if you can kiss me as gently as you did yesterday and I may lay my head on your shoulder, don't let's go too close to our physical selves lest we stir up what is the least important part of our relationship. We cannot mortgage the future before, as you said to me, "you are clasped in my arms for keeps," but the obligations of our present courses – mine in particular – demand this withholding. Instead I've written you a poem.'

Despite their frequent meetings in London their letters continued.

'If ever we do link our lives to each other,' Aylmer wrote, 'would you be content with simplicity and the slow river's unruffled surface? [Aylmer, stop now. Without having any prophetic intimations of how pivotal his thoughts were to their future, he blundered on, getting it all wrong.] There's a whole strain in me, and I think in you, which becomes sick by hyper-civilization. I've longed . . . to draw quietude from the soil's cool roots.'

From her parents' house, where we were visiting our grandparents, Phyllis wrote, 'I hadn't imagined this would happen – that you should love me like this forever offering security and cherishing until the end of time. I live through centuries in a few days whilst an outer life carries me at a different tempo, "The inner life – and the life of telegrams and anger." Since we parted I've not had one minute out of people's presence except now in bed. I've been "talking" to you all day until I'm sure others must hear me while in reality we were discussing the Chinese situation, the cinema, and Bristol glass.'

Aylmer, discovering the luxury of exposing remorse to his beloved with the confidence of finding absolution, wrote, 'Loveliest, you once said you'd made bad mistakes in pursuit of the right quest. You were talking of relationships. I'm not acknowledging any morality other than my own but what one does with one's body – or anyone else's – has been distorted shamefully by centuries of religious and perverted codes. Yet to make it clear what sort of man you are embracing I must explain.'

And launching into the confessional as naturally as a snake shedding skin, he described a brief liaison after the war, with a 'true-hearted woman': 'My mother gone, my friends dead I was lost, lonely and emotionally frozen. I took a mistress. *Des baisers qui n'engagent à rien* hurt no one. Imagine the mentality of the man who returned after five years in the East out of touch with art and cerebral thought which before the war had meant everything to me (a priggish highbrow in other words!).

'I believe that the lover of a woman embodies within himself elements from all the men who loved her in the past. But now, my sweet Phyllis, you have miraculously given me back all that was clean and unspoiled in my youth. I would give my life for you. For love is part myopia, part isolation lapping lovers in immunity. Your being is fused to mine, soul of my soul you will always be a spirit of pure beauty in my eyes. That is all the grandeur that I want.

'Forgive this portentous letter but if you are ready to trust your soul to my keeping, though I have done despicable things, I am re-incarnated as your immortal lover. You will never need to question my love whatever happens I love you more with every pulse beat – always and forever.'

['At lovers' perjuries, They say Jove laughs.' *Romeo and Juliet*.]

No premonitions of the future intruded on Aylmer's attempts for atonement. And although reading his affirmations of love so many years afterwards, my first reaction was cynicism. Later I felt only their tragedy.

Then something different: a letter for its evocation not of love, but of a young man's account of a grisly task in a part of the world I was to discover many years later. The letter resurrected a scene of sheer horror.

In the darkness of a winter afternoon Aylmer had let the gas run out ... the room was cold ... smoke rose from clusters of chimney pots ... curtains were drawn against falling snow leaving roofs and ledges whiter than the sky: 'My sweet Phyllis we meet tomorrow. Please, God, don't let me die before then for I am overcome by fear. A pure irrational panic of a kind that I have known only once before has taken over my being. Although it's almost ten years since the World War the sheer chill of an event that overwhelmed me with its horror, has clutched me again and won't let go.'

Motivated by a sense of impending fatalism Aylmer wrote, 'I had met the incoming transport below the harbour of Rangoon where the delta merges with the sea. The estuary was greyish-yellow like the flat, interminable fields that melted into the sky on either hand. Clumps of isolated jungle, the gold of distant pagodas, the islands precariously balanced on the surface of the river, all appeared to float as if land and water had leached into an immense dissolution. Sense of direction failed, the perpetually shifting mirages – trees, villages, temples, inverted crazily – stood on their heads, gliding along the margin of that ochre-tinted sea: an unsubstantial, bewildering world – the mouth of the Rangoon river.'

Aylmer switched on a small brass lamp that had come from a panelled cabin in an old steamship that plied between Brindisi and Patras . . . He recalled the magnificent Irrawaddy, Burma's sole arterial highway rising south of Tibet, without a bridge spanning its nine hundred navigable miles. Bears, snakes, tigers, leopards and wild cats lurked among the shadows; small birds, parrots and monkeys shuffled in the tree canopy. Through defiles, reefs, falls and swamps, the great river descended from rhododendron heights to the pagodas of Mandalay. The delta – fronted by rice mills, godowns and teak wharves – was where steamboats, barques, junks and tramps navigated in changing configurations piloted by small figures dressed in *lungyis* – cylindrical skirts folded in front and reaching to the ankles. Women, their black hair wound into coils high on their heads, plied their wares in flimsy crafts close to the coast, disappearing and reappearing in the diaphanous shrouds of rain that at times during the monsoon fell in solid slabs.

'I should, I suppose,' Aylmer continued, 'have experienced physical alarm that morning which now, from such a distance, I look back to with a reawakened sense of awe. There is something in the presence of cholera in a troopship crowded with prisoners of war that's calculated to produce an Aristotelian catharsis of the emotions.

'Pity and terror! I can see the captain's face now as he leant over the bridge to watch my launch come alongside. A little man, genial, tubby, but now with a face crinkled with fear he looked like a new born babe. Once the transport had retreated across that flat oily calm whence she had emerged with her freight of tragedy, I was left alone with my guests. Fifty-two of them all quite dead.

'So there were my guests, to be conducted far out to sea with me at the tiller of an old barge. Well ballasted with stoke-hold fire-bars they sat propped up round the gunwale in a ring their heads nodding sardonically over the indignity of man's estate, their shoulders joggling now and then as our bows caught the evening tide-rip. Far away, on the end of a long tow-rope, the launch fretted and fumed ahead while two Malay Lascars made ready the dinghy which would take me off from the sinking barge when, as host, I had made my adieux. I began to feel uncommonly lonely.

'It was one of those tired evenings of the East when the sky turns livid at sundown and seems to weigh heavily on the earth like a steely skull-cap horribly near one's head. I remember how I tried talking to my taciturn invités. But they would not respond. Allah forgive me, I cursed them foully for their indifference sewn up in their jute sacks. Their heads had been left uncovered as if for the air they no longer needed. Decent Anatolian peasants for the most part – pawns in a game of whose rules they heeded nothing, they had died with hideous reluctance. One man, with a little scrubby beard clinging to his wide, agony-distorted mouth, still wore a soiled fez tilted jocularly over one ear. There was one who was just a boy, no older than I was. So senseless.

'And all at once in that silence I was sickeningly afraid. It was as though from that sky, brooding eyeless over the empty horizon, there had echoed the ghost of a laugh – the meaningless chuckle of a minister of vengeance from the gods. One of the Eumenides.'

Laying his pen aside, he thought of the woman to whom he was writing with such irrational urgency: 'That's what I meant Phyllis when I spoke of a formless fear, a kind of foreboding, almost despair wondering whether in loving you I am letting myself become the sport of Zeus. Are the dark gods planning game with the two of us in which you might be hurt? Since I cannot help but love you I should be the better friend if I stopped seeing you. Then – no more letters, no more listening to your voice answering me before I've even spoken.

'No more you . . . Ah, my dear, my dear, I cannot.'

My mother, since moving to the country on account of my father's illness, had been living a twilight life. Aylmer's declarations of love, his trust in her, his eulogistic admiration – transcending sexual passion – restored her confidence. For anyone but a pragmatist this was heady stuff. And when Aylmer wrote, 'Lean as heavily as you wish while loving me with unquestioning trust never doubting, however much I may fail others or myself, I cannot fail you,' she believed him.

When in April, Aylmer, summoned by his father to visit him in Belgium, wrote 'How it hurts that the world of "telegrams and anger" should consume our attention . . . I've waited thirty-four years for you to come into my life!'

Sorting the letters that passed between them while Aylmer was abroad, I've reduced them to a kind of telegramese. From Phyllis, whose life was spiralling out of control: 'Beloved, since I wrote yesterday something has happened . . . last night Harry, with no preamble, asked me why I hadn't told him how much I cared for you – just think what a little thing – he heard me open your letter in bed. He knew that "there is only one sort of letter one keeps unopened over night." While I was out he found my box of your letters . . . he's being gentle but says I must choose. Divorce, or never see you again.'

Unable to dissemble she continued, 'My soul is yours – I'd give my life for you had I only myself to consider but I am racked with misery. Even you may not realize with what contempt I regard my position in my own eyes . . . sick with fear I might make an irrevocable decision any of us may regret. My babies . . . I must have a little time. We all must – though Harry wants the situation quickly concluded.'

Aylmer, faced with his culpability in the affair, sent a telegram, succinct and bleak: '*Rassures toi toujours la panache*' . . . to which my mother replied, 'I am yours ultimately and inevitably. I cannot live without you – I know that now.' Then Aylmer: 'I want you so much, my Phyllis, that I dare not write of my own selfish longing till I can see you and you see me. What matters is my love for you that will be my life till I die.' [Reading this, even from this distance, I want to shout aloud, No! No! Listen to yourself!] 'I am yours – brain of your brain, soul of your soul – whatever you decide to do with yourself. You begin and end my world. Let that knowledge keep you cherished till we meet on Tuesday, my darling.'

The following Sunday my mother wrote what was to be her last letter from the family home. Barely exposing her emotional turmoil she attempted to justify her decision.

In my bedroom is a photograph – posed, formal, professional – of the four of us: Phyllis, Harry, Cordelia and me. I'm in my mother's arms so it was presumably taken more than a year before this final unravelling. It's almost unbearable to consider the questions unasked as I see myself – one baby leg in its woolly leggings dangling down – with my mother holding me tight, our cheeks touching, and my four-year-old sister

Cordelia, in a velvet dress, sitting within the enclosing arm of my father. I've grown up knowing this photograph. Why on earth wasn't I prompted, imaginative enough to have asked my mother for details of the occasion? How we squander chances like this! How we pile up regret upon regret through indifference, sliding easily through the years without grabbing the moment to ask more questions! This photograph provokes just one of the many self-reproaches swarming increasingly through my declining years.

So I'm left guessing: was my mother's decision cold, calculated, knowing that my father had not long to live, that the children would be hers? Or was it that by remaining at home – living with a sick man whose months might linger into years – she risked losing Aylmer?

Probably it was neither. I can only surmise that, being a passionate and selfish person, she had already rationalised her commitment to Aylmer.

Simply there was no alternative: 'I am going to be as frank as possible before you talk to Harry. Even if he hadn't discovered we loved each other – if we had gone on snatching moments together and I'd maintained a double life – I should inevitably have "lowered the stature of my soul". I could have given my children my undivided love as ever – my feelings for you don't alter that – but I was being forced into an increasingly unreal relationship. Harry is their father – it's his money I am living on – eventually disaster must have followed. Don't mistake me – you were right when you said you were taking nothing from me that Harry wanted. True, but you were inevitably causing me to give him less and less of the things that I did owe him. Harry and I have talked too freely of our lack of love for each other to keep up any pretence. My own desires are clear – to live with you, love you, and be loved by you.

'Accepting one cannot uproot without pain, and knowing me to be yours for life, Aylmer, please have me. All the "telegrams and anger" ahead of us can be faced together. Forever I am yours.'

In my hand is a letter from my grandmother written to me on my first birthday – and before the catastrophe that would pulverise the family with its shocking outcome – in the spidery nineteenth-century handwriting that I've read so many times the letter is falling apart. My grandmother – who died on my seventeenth birthday – enfolded me with a scent of lavender bags and with unconditional love that lapped round her grandchildren with timeless serenity.

'You little sweet thing,' she wrote, 'how dear you are to me. I hope you will wear the little frock I made for you. My love has gone into every stitch so if you count the number of stitches you will find a great deal of love and more besides.'

A suffragette, my grandmother had been the first woman to ride a penny-farthing bicycle in Birmingham – a considerable feat considering that it was the young men who were adept at riding these ungainly machines. They were tricky to mount, condemned as 'unwomanly' – particularly when my grandmother took to wearing 'bloomers'. It's not surprising that such a feisty woman, against all the hidebound principles of her upbringing, recognised the 'rogue' daughter to whom she'd given birth. Acknowledging her nature, and being a woman of fortitude, my grandmother stood by Phyllis when she abandoned her family for London and for love.

Aylmer, knowing he was the villain, wrote to my grandparents from Paris, to which he and my mother had escaped from the torrent of family recriminations: 'Some day I hope you will let me get to know you. Please try not to grieve over Phyllis's welfare. She's had to pay a stiff price for the step she has taken. I love her so much it would be hypocrisy to apologize for what I have led her to do but there has never been anyone like her in the world. My one aim is to make up for all she has given up to give me the sweetest companionship that man ever had.'

I don't have my grandmother's reply to this appeal, but to her daughter she wrote a letter remarkable for its absence of reprehension considering the then current morals and her own flinty Unitarian upbringing: 'Darling, what can I say? The news of your break up from Harry was an inexpressible shock to Father and me – how could it be otherwise? God knows I tried to look at it all round and feel that judgement was not for me to give. You were caught up in one of the most difficult problems humans are faced with and my heart went out in pity for the terrible decision you were called upon to make. Indeed I realize my darling, what you must have been going through – and what the parting from your babies must have meant.'

Reading her letter from this distance, when freedom from Victorian morality and the prevalence of divorce are the norm, her forbearance is remarkable: 'If all goes well it will ease the pain crushing Father and me . . . but remember always, let no selfishness shatter it. Were I with you I would say more that is in my heart . . . I look forward to meeting Aylmer and hope, oh so earnestly, that we may become friends.

'Father sends his love. He is badly shaken but he is gradually trying to adjust and to look at the situation as rightly as he can. God bless you, my own child, my love and my understanding are with you. Always and lovingly, Mother.'

The fabric of the family frays; the consequences of my mother's flight from husband, home and children to live with Aylmer, the man who had hurtled into her life while she was looking the other way, shattered her parents. Such behaviour was for the frivolous upper classes, not for solid Midlands folk 'in trade'.

Closer to her mother than to her father, and receiving nothing but censorious letters from relatives, Phyllis replied, 'I was touched to get your dear letter today. You are wonderful! I'm longing for you to meet the dearest, gentlest, most understanding man in the world. We had such happiness in Paris in spite of the black moments that sweep over me at times. It means so much that you have been so sweet when you must mind deeply the break-up. I hate hurting you. I hope Father will see me – but I understand that he may not yet.'

The memories I have of my grandfather are sparse: he used to take me on his lap and read aloud – attempting to imitate the slave dialect of Georgia – the Uncle Remus tales of 'Brer Rabbit'. He was more tactile and humorous than Michael's father had ever been. My mother's behaviour remained as a black cloud when Michael married the daughter of that disgraced and wanton Phyllis Reid. There was general disapproval from all his relatives.

Thus condemned, Phyllis found support from her friends instead. Those who had watched the tragedy did understand. Stella Bowen was by then living in Paris with Ford Madox Ford, but others nearer home rallied round. They may not have condoned her actions, but they offered unconditional empathy and love.

We have forfeited the habit of putting words on paper in the way Phyllis and Aylmer continued doing even after they were together, yet felt written endearments had their own validity. Aylmer posted to her on the day before his birthday: 'I want you to hold like a glowing summer day in your heart forever, that this birthday is happier than any birthday could be. Loveliest, we are so close spoken words are not needed. This is merely another way of expressing the contentment in my heart. That I shall love you tomorrow more than today is unimaginable.'

As before she pre-empted his thoughts by writing her own letter: 'For Aylmer on his Birthday. Oh be my love – let us explore the country of the heart. I want, if I can to recapture the lover of yesterday by a letter that has to be posted. Though that man has gone forever I don't regret him – glorious dragonfly winging across my still waters – because in his place I have found the perfect companion.'

However, the perfect companion could not annul the guilt, desolate and recurring, that my mother endured when my father prohibited her from seeing her children. Confident of understanding rather than rebuke, she wrote to her mother, 'You cannot imagine what it is like all this time without seeing the children. I've made every effort but Harry won't let me see them until we are divorced. I know some day everything will be all right.' [Presumably my grandmother understood the implication of words that could not be spoken. My father was a dying man.] 'But in the meantime their absence is an inconsolable burden – no one knows just how bitter.'

The meeting between my father and Aylmer was chillingly dignified. Both – being neither acrimonious nor lacking civil proprieties – discussed the situation with honourable restraint. Such dialogues must have been repeated ad infinitum through generations of human frailties, with the same mixture of equivocation and sophistry.

The two men never met again.

*   *   *

In October the divorce came through yet nothing changed. Access to my sister and me remained banned. My father's illness made him immune to any moral obligations for our welfare. Embittered and self-absorbed by the scourge that was destroying his life, he lost all compassion or sense of justice until, in November, he allowed our nanny to take us to London.

'I saw the children yesterday for just two hours. That was all Harry allowed,' my mother wrote to our grandmother. 'Cordelia was old enough to understand when I told her I couldn't go home with her and that meanwhile she must be helpful with Daddy who was so ill he had to stay in the country. Mirabel when she saw me at once put her hand in mine. But oh, what heartache saying goodbye when she asked me to come back with her . . . I was devastated. But now, how anxiously I wait to hear if all was well on their return for who can see into a child's mind, who can know what enters their sub-conscious forever?'

For all I know, although I remember nothing of that occasion, subconsciously that separation may have accounted for the recurring bouts of homesickness that erupted throughout my childhood.

In a valiant effort to plead on behalf of her grandchildren, our grandmother wrote to my father, 'I am grieved to learn you are opposing reasonably frequent meetings. I do understand, even if I cannot agree with your desire not to dwell on what is past, but you must allow me – old enough to be your mother – to remind you that the children are, and will always remain, Phyllis's as well as yours.

'Where children are concerned it is impossible to treat a dissolved marriage as if it had never existed. However distasteful, you have a moral obligation to maintain a happy relationship between the children and their mother. You told me last April that your attitude towards the children was both wise and generous. I should indeed be sorry if I found I was mistaken in my judgement. I now make the strongest appeal to you . . . to act with generosity and wisdom in the belief you will consider all I have said.'

A sad man defending his frontiers and incapable any longer of taking a rational stance, my father's reply was implacable and pompous: 'I was sorry to get your letter. I fear that in answering it is inevitable I cause you pain. In the first place you must see that we approach the matter differently albeit the same; we approach it as parents, but as parents of different children. The motive activating you is loyalty to Phyllis; you want her desires to be satisfied. I, on the other hand, am thinking of my children and what is best for them. The action I am taking is based on my desire to do the best for them, not on any personal predilections.

'I do not think frequent intercourse with Phyllis can do them any good and will probably do them harm. If you are honest you will see that she is self-indulgent, extravagant, lacks balance and self-control – not qualities that influence children for the good. Phyllis has always wanted to have her cake and eat it. Unfortunately life is not so accommodating. I feel that frequent meetings would be disturbing for the children and for that reason I am opposing them.

'There is an accusation in your letter of a breach of faith on my part, but this is unjustified. What I said in April was that I would not exclude from my mind the possibility of Phyllis seeing the children. I know those were my words. They were carefully chosen, and I have kept them. Incidentally I would point out that I have no ties to keep me in England, and if necessary I should not hesitate to go and live in one of the colonies taking the children with me, of course. I am afraid this letter will make unpleasant reading and for that I am truly sorry, but it is unavoidable I fear.'

Unforeseen by anyone, even the doctors, my father's life moved to its inevitable conclusion sooner than was expected. Less than a month after writing to my grandmother, he died of tuberculosis from a sudden haemorrhage just before Christmas at the age of thirty-eight.

Phyllis wrote to her mother, 'Poor, poor Harry, he was so frightened the nurse told me. He called out "I don't want to die, don't let me." She got the doctor quickly but within an hour he was unconscious – he died without coming round. The children are not to be told yet.' [We were staying with my uncle and aunt – the one who urged me to disinter these letters.] 'What a senseless tragedy loving life as he did. And whatever else one can say, Harry cannot possibly be judged normally during his illness – in the end it warped and embittered him so much he had become a stranger to his family. The futility, the pain of his disease was an outrage.'

Years later, when my mother spoke of Harry and their marriage, which had begun with the optimism of youth and of compatibility, it was with sadness, not penitence nor pity.

On the threshold of summer the love letters between Aylmer and my mother ended. In January 1928 they were married in a register office. No announcement appeared in the paper; there was a tangle of formalities to be sorted, a house to buy and a school to find for Cordelia.

As for me, my father had no substance. I don't remember him. A photograph shows a tall man stooping to hold my toddler's hand as we walk along a garden path. But I tasted the word *Daddy*, rolled it round my tongue imagining the flavour, imagining his response if I called to him.

I used to – for the sheer pleasure of saying it – repeat the name of an insect with its frail wings flapping against the window pane in September: 'Daddy-long-legs, daddy-long-legs.' Cordelia, who did remember her father, told me to stop being silly over a fly.

A year after they were married, motoring through France in August 1929 when travel was leisurely and safe and the plumbing dodgy, but where the humblest village had a bistro serving fresh regional food, Aylmer wrote to my grandmother, 'Leaving Dunkerque at eight in the morning we ate economically a seven-penny breakfast for two at a roadside café, we lunched at a workman's restaurant in Abbeville and had "tea" in Beauvais. We ended up in great splendour at a hotel de luxe at St Germain – a reconstructed hunting box where one dines on a veranda overlooking distant Paris.' [Tantalisingly he doesn't describe what they ate. How many people when writing accounts of journeys miss out the essentials: the vicarious pleasure of having meals described with the delicacy of Proust, Escoffier, Daudet, Brillat-Savarin or M.F.K. Fisher adds a wholly other dimension to geographic information.] 'I am writing outside our small L'Hôtel des Pins, at Argelès-sur-Mer, overlooking a bay surrounded by mountains and a ten-mile beach dropping sheer into clear water. We bathe before breakfast, three times during the day, and again by moonlight. Mine host is a Catalan from Barcelona whose wife cooks for us over an open brazier as well as for a gang of Italian workmen making a road. The last two nights we had a bedroom – plus fleas. Tomorrow a four-day fiesta starts, when all rooms are pre-engaged ten deep, so we propose to sleep in the wood.' I can imagine how Aylmer would have loved that alfresco experience, and just how much my mother would have hated it.

Phyllis added a postscript: 'We have found an albergo among pine trees beside a shore lapped by the murmur of a summer sea. Last night, to the harsh strains of a mechanical organ, we danced between moonlight and indigo shadows till dawn and then ran through golden light to the sea.'

If this were a fairy tale, my mother and Aylmer would have lived happily ever after, but it wasn't like that. As a sauce made too hastily their relationship curdled. My mother, a woman with fervent responses and worldly vanities, was destined to destroy the love she sought.

She had done it with the poet, the father of her children and now with Aylmer.

Striving for more, she failed to acknowledge that Aylmer was at heart a 'dropout', uninterested in the pursuit of material success in spite of having a brilliant mind. His lack of commitment to causes, or personal ambition for pursuing a career, accounted for his charm. With the misplaced confidence my mother had in her power to manipulate life, she became myopic to what was happening until it was too late. By driving him too hard against the grain, after seven years she lost him. Aylmer, unable to keep pace with such a demanding woman, had been lured away by someone younger and seemingly refreshingly unworldly.

As my aunt put it – 'a chit of a girl in a dirndl skirt, who offered him the simple life in a Surrey cottage with dogs and peasant pottery'.

Many years later Ursula wrote to me with the wisdom of hindsight: 'Phyllis's tragedy was that despite her good looks, intelligence and vitality, she needed constant reassurance. She had to win every argument, be applauded for her every action, to be continually backed up by faithful friends ... Trapped by Harry's ill health, his behaviour in restricting access to you and Cordelia, was typical of the morality in those days and now seems insanely harsh and censorious. I can't excuse him. But goodness, it's a daunting business to recall the attitude of mind that conditioned our behaviour all those years ago.

'As for Aylmer, Phyllis blossomed under his love. He was a romantic charmer, an engaging vagabond and she, doomed, pushed her luck too far with the irrevocable consequences.'

Yesterday, as I have done for years, I had lunch with Philip and Wendy Vallance. Philip is Aylmer's son. We have been friends since his mother died when Philip was eleven. Philip is now in his sixties. His mother, Helen Gosse, granddaughter of the critic and essayist Edmund Gosse, had been the 'chit of a girl in a dirndl skirt' for whom Aylmer had fallen, the cause of his abandoning my mother for 'the simple life in a Surrey cottage with dogs and peasant pottery'.

During the summer holidays – when Aylmer was at a loss over what arrangements to make for his son – Michael and I invited Philip to come camping with David and us, down the coast of Yugoslavia. That was the beginning of my odd, lopsided relationship with my much younger half-stepbrother who subsequently spent other holidays with us in Shropshire. Some years later I got to know his older sister Margaret for whom, like Philip, I have a special affection.

At school I'd been proud to have a father who was dead. In the pre-Second World War days, before the scrolls of those killed in battle left so many fatherless, it gave me distinction, impressed my friends, made me different from the rest. But as

I grew up I longed for conformity, for suburban routine rather than returning to a flat just off the Strand overlooking the Embankment Gardens, where – Aylmer by now being editor of the liberal paper the *News Chronicle* – the place was alive with politics and jaded lobby correspondents. In a smoke-filled room full of young men going off to fight in the Spanish Civil War with burning passion and bellies full of whisky, argument went on through the night. (I was put off political polemics ever after.)

To me they were friendly enough, these poets, newspapermen, writers and idealists. Cordelia was different; being four years older, sophisticated, articulate – wearing a badge on her school blazer saying, 'War! We Say No!' – she was willing to fill the glasses of the young men, to be petted and, once, escorted by Vernon Bartlett – the diplomatic correspondent on the *News Chronicle* who reported from Spain during the Civil War – to stay with Stella Bowen and her daughter Julie in Paris.

The foreign correspondents would bring Cordelia and me strange and wondrous trinkets from their travels; their boisterous enthusiasm filled my world when really I was longing for a puppy, a toy animal on my pillow in which to keep my pyjamas, and high tea, something unknown in our house but which sounded enviably chic. Forfeiting high tea wasn't all. Instead of playing Snakes and Ladders with school friends, my sister and I accompanied Phyllis and Aylmer when we were on our way somewhere or other and, for Aylmer's sake, visited, en route, some celebrated artist, politician, diplomat or newspaper baron. Tea with Lloyd George (I remember the occasion only because he gave me a little silver pencil) or Cecil Beaton (I remember not the fabulous contents of his Wiltshire house but his large dog) was hardly an occasion to giggle with girlfriends as we pretended long slim chocolate biscuits were cigarettes.

I was dazzled by my sister's poise on these occasions. I admired her with a kind of sycophantic devotion. And when my mother chided me for only reading Rupert Bear books, chastened, I took down one of the orange Left Book Club books that lined the shelves, hoping to placate her by reading George Orwell's *The Road to Wigan Pier*. I was riveted by the account of a jerry full of pee under the table.

But could I always trust my mother?

When friends came to our house she offered them coffee after dinner. 'Black or white?' she'd ask. I was mortified. I knew perfectly well that the coffee in the pot was black.

Why did she pretend otherwise?

Reality had been a problem for me ever since, aged nine, I'd had anaesthetic for a major operation. The experience had been petrifying.

Afterwards, how did I know that I wasn't still anaesthetised? Perhaps I was still unconscious, hadn't come round from the effect of the mask soaked with ether that had been put over my face while my mother was allowed to stand beside me holding my hand. The smell had invaded my hair, my clothes, my skin. The thought that I was still in that falling, uncontrollable state engrossed me for months, never sure which world I inhabited. Another time, lying on my back in a meadow holding a grass stem with its head silhouetted against the sky, I discovered the grass was larger than the sky. Which was real?

Illusion and reality were always baffling me. If a grass head could diminish the sky, what sense was there in Aylmer's answer to my question when, aged four, I first saw a plane in flight – tiny, passing overhead? He explained that it would need more space than this garden in which to land. 'That little thing?' I was nonplussed.

Aylmer I trusted implicitly. He'd married my mother when I was two: young enough to accept him in the way small children take for granted that whatever happens is normality. I loved him: sitting on my bed he made up bedtime stories, and as Cordelia was already reading to herself they were for me alone. I treasured that brief ritual more than he probably ever knew. Having no memory of my real father, I assumed he was mine for ever, whereas my sister still had memories of a dying man with a husky voice, racked by consumption, lying in bed holding her hand.

Aylmer's absence from my life was a slow withdrawal, not an amputation but an invisible exodus of which I was unaware until it was over. It just happened. A young child soaks up affection until she learns through experience to grow a carapace. I expect my sister was much more *au fait*. As Aylmer's exodus happened about the time I had mastoid and was banished, after two operations on my ear, to recover in Switzerland, there was never a moment when I knew he was gone – he just wasn't there. Years later when he was a widower, he returned into our lives. He would come to have a meal with us in Chelsea when his relationship with Phyllis had mellowed into civilised camaraderie.

Among the letters stuffed into a drawer of my mother's desk I found a note Aylmer wrote in February 1927 (a month after they had met). It began: 'Lines to one who desired a letter should be delivered after the writer had gone to await her beyond the sun.

'My hand, with unavailing pen and ink, has striven to write what one day you shall read and know that death has found me. Yet of such tidings you will have no need, soul of my soul.

For when dawn has stirred not fraught with love of you; when your heart has spoken yet not sensed my immediate answer; when on waking you no longer are aware of my love hovering all night round your head, you then will know my dearest, that I am dead.'

And from what at first I took to be an empty envelope I found a scrap of paper on which he had written:

The Words Unsaid

> For silence past forgiving
> Blame death when I am dead.
> Forgive the lips still living
> For all they have not said.

One might be tempted to say he'd already said too much. But he went on: 'My best and only beloved, if ever – when you are old and facing death – you look back on your life and wonder how much better if you had done this, not that, your heart will answer. If you ever ceased to care for me, my love, the vital principle of my life would die.'

Sadly it took only seven years for the 'vital principle' of his life to be as fugitive as his vows.

Now, sifting through the letters, I wonder whether there were times when my mother reread Aylmer's protestations in a hopeless quest to find some lingering trace among their dead pages. And did she read again her own recollections, written after he had left her, of their first visit to Paris together in 1927? 'Under the chestnuts at the *Closerie de Lilas* in May we ate *fraises des bois*, delicate berries, laced with Kirsch, sharp on the tongue. So I remember Paris. Ah, lover lost before found

– where are you now? Should we, walking under the leafy lights of Montparnasse, recapture that impalpable, never-forgotten spring? Or should we say, as now, something was missing, something we never knew, who had found so much? Is it easier, I wonder, to remember May as it was – a sweet Illusion? Down seven years the echo of those nights rings piti-ful music. Oh how Paris was gay for us. Ardent, carefree, as we drank Pernod at stained tables to the drone of *L'Intransigeant* on the record player.

'You are gone, my love, with my life-spring's source and I must turn home to eat strawberries in an English garden.'

The pain and bitterness felt by my mother at Aylmer's rejec-tion caused her to write a sonnet beginning with the wistful lines: 'I thought that I should never turn in vain for comfort in your arms . . .'

4

The Melancholy Voice of Frogs

When I've done something particularly imbecilic I wish I lived with someone other than myself.

It's not just the careless things such as posting my shopping list with my letters or chopping something with a garlicky knife that make me long for otherwise, but, far more dire, when having spent hours writing something on my computer, I press *delete* when I meant *save*. I've just done it and know that in the same way as snow turns to slush, unless I rewrite immediately my thoughts will melt irretrievably.

The Melancholy Voice of Frogs was the title I chose for a book I wrote in 1993 about French gardens. Having written about those this side of the Channel, I wanted to find out about gardens the other side, but my publisher disagreed. The title was not PC, he said.

I had thought the title apt after gazing through the locked gate of the house where Alphonse de Lamartine, the Burgundian poet, had written, in his nostalgic memory of childhood, of 'the sweet and melancholy voices of frogs that sing on summer evenings . . .' As a title it contained the essence of too many French gardens on the brink of disappearing as their owners aged and their offspring were not interested. When Lamartine wrote, 'my eye still seeks the footprints of my mother, of my sisters . . .' he was echoing that loss I met among many owners and their gardens as I traversed from one side of France to the other.

France and Stella Bowen are linked for ever in my mind. I now write in depth about her because throughout my childhood she was the rock as steady as my mother was mercurial, and to my children, no doubt, her landscapes and portraits – which are all over the house – are so much part of their background that they never stop to wonder who these people were. Or where and when they were painted.

For me Stella is here in the foreground more than any of the others who were cardinal in my life. It is to her that I owe my way of looking, detailed observation, appreciation of food, the narrative enjoyment of vicarious living. Her paintings surround me as visual reminders of my lasting devotion.

Stella Bowen and Ford Madox Ford
'What I am now I owe to you . . .' read Ford's dedicatory letter to Stella in the 1927 edition of *The Good Soldier*. When Stella and Ford met, he was already an author of epic repute, eight years older than Ezra Pound and considerably older than the rest of Stella's and my mother's friends. His bulking stature filled their studio. Stories of meeting H. G. Wells, Henry James, Joseph Conrad, Swinburne, Rossetti and Turgenev held them enthralled.

Recalling her incredulous response to Ford, this giant of the literary world, Stella wrote in her reminiscences *Drawn from Life:* '[H]e began to tell me about himself, filling me with pride by confiding all his troubles and weaknesses. The most monumental of authors – the fountain, apparently of all wisdom, who appeared already to have lived a dozen lives now – amazingly – announced that he wished to place his person, his fortune, his future in my hands.' He revealed himself 'as a lonely and very tired person who wanted to dig potatoes and raise pigs and never write another book. Wanted to start a new home. Wanted a child'.

Ominous. Ominous. To the detached observer it all sounds slightly disingenuous. But not to Stella: 'It did not appear to me as queer that an experienced, and highly-cultivated writer should desire to bury himself forever in a country cottage with no one to talk to but a half-baked young colonial.'

Their Sussex cottage was without electricity or running water, and Stella admitted no working-class woman with any self-respect would live there, but 'I'll swear Ford never saw it like that. His geese were always swans.' He taught her that the staple ingredient to good living even when broke was gastronomy. (Elizabeth David in *Summer Cooking* describes a Mediterranean picnic provided by Ford for sixteen adults consisting of half a hundredweight of bouillabaisse, twelve cocks stewed in wine and a dish of salad 'as large as a cartwheel' with enough peaches, figs and grapes 'to bury a man in'.)

Even after their daughter Esther Julia was born in 1920, Ford continued to believe that as a robust young woman Stella had inexhaustible energy. He started to write again while she discovered that masculine egotism was boundless: Ford couldn't finish his book, he told her, if he was upset. This meant putting off meals and not telling him when they'd run out of paraffin, when the baby was unwell or when they were overdrawn and depended solely on the twenty-pound monthly allowance from Stella's trustees in Australia. At the same time Ford assumed that Stella simply lacked the will to paint. But for Stella, '[P]ursuing an art is not just a matter of finding the time – it is a matter of having a free spirit . . . Ford was a great user-up of other people's nervous energy and there was no room for me to nurse an independent ego.'

Eighty years on, her words still have a bitter veracity.

Yet Stella was able to look back to that time and write in her memoir of those years, with detached tenderness: 'Poor Ford! There was something about the sight of his large patient fingers tapping at the keys that I always found infinitely touching. He was a writer – a complete writer – and nothing but a writer. And he never even felt sure of his gift!'

In 1922 they fled Ford's vision of the 'simple life' (their cottage is currently on the market for £1.2 million) to Paris, where Ezra Pound and his wife Dorothy were living at 70 rue Notre Dame des Champs. The studio had one cold tap but immense windows from which Stella painted the picture hanging in my sitting room that I treasure for its sombre colours you still find hidden behind street façades. 'I think that any foreigner who has lived in Montparnasse leaves a little piece of his heart behind him, buried in a courtyard . . .'

During their life in Paris – liberal with friendships but short on cash – Ford reigned while Stella contrived. Using flea-market junk she turned the drabbest surroundings into somewhere decorative. Two small unframed oil paintings on rough board that she bought eighty years ago from a stall in rue du Chat Qui Pêche hang in my hall. I imagine Stella spent a few *sous* on them – my grandchildren may well consider them rubbish.

Yet in spite of their poverty, happy evenings were spent with friends at café tables where artisans, writers, painters, artists' models, seamstresses and the local *drôle de numéro* from the immediate arrondissement would stop for a drink on their way home: whores on their way to work. They drank their *fine à l'eau* at the poetically named café-restaurant Closerie des Lilas in Boulevard

Montparnasse, where once Ingres used to bring his models, before moving on to the Nègre de Toulouse. Here good food, cheap wine and discussion became a civilised event in a back room where the proprietor, M. Lavigne, always kept two tables for them and their individual napkins – coarse with red and white checks – on a rack. The *plat du jour*, written in purple ink, was inexpensive: *lapin en cocotte*, slowly cooked in dry white wine laced with a few spoonfuls of *eau-de-vie*, or maybe *gésiers confits* (preserved duck gizzards) scattered across a green salad with walnuts. And on bitter days a Cantal dish of *l'aligot* (potato, cheese and garlic puree) made with the famous Auvergne *laguiole* cheese.

They held parties: *bal musettes* where they danced to the music of an accordion until the early hours. Gertrude Stein – whose clothes were held together by safety pins – and Alice B. Toklas came, Ezra of course, his mistress Olga Rudge (the American violinist), and many others in that civilised city in the period between the wars.

In his memoir *A Moveable Feast*, Ernest Hemingway wrote of their shared insolvency: 'At the *Nègre de Toulouse* we drank the good Cahors wine from the quarter, the half or the full carafe, usually diluting it about one-third with water . . . If you are lucky enough to have lived in Paris as a young man, then wherever you go for the rest of your life, it stays with you, for Paris is a moveable feast.'

> By the time you swear you're his,
> Shivering and sighing,
> And he vows his passion is
> Infinite, undying –
> Lady, make a note of this,
> One of you is lying.
>
> Dorothy Parker

In 1925 Jean Rhys strayed into Stella and Ford's household.

The waif – destitute and unhappily married, with a manuscript in her hand – was immediately taken under the wing of Ford, who launched her into the literary world while Stella offered her a room to sleep in and advice on where to buy new clothes to replace the oddments Rhys carried in a cardboard box. Confident in both her love and her life with Ford, no portents nudged Stella's security, no inklings warned her until it was too late.

Jean Rhys's novels, peopled by bohemians and drifters, reveal a melancholy world in which women led depressing lives. *Good Morning, Midnight, After Leaving Mr Mackenzie* and, later, *The Wide Sargasso Sea* are perhaps the best known, but it was in her first novel, *Quartet,* that the fictional characters Mr and Mrs Heidler were the predatory couple who dominated the heroine Marya's life. The character of Lois Heidler, based on Stella Bowen, is a malevolent characterisation – a distortion of the woman I remember. When Marya says, 'Lois simply wants me around so that she can tear me to bits and get her friends to help her to tear me to bits' it is a calumnious portrait of Stella.

Of course I never knew Stella then, in the twenties: my memories of her begin long after the Paris years. But her fundamental integrity is constantly reiterated by those who did. Although *Drawn from Life* was written years after the Ford/Rhys affair had withered, nowhere in it does Stella mention Rhys by name, even when discretion over naming the young woman who entered the Ford household with such disruptive effect was unnecessary. Stella merely describes her as 'Ford's girl'.

'She nearly sank our ship!' was her taciturn comment.

*   *   *

In the winter of 1925, the year I was born, Stella, Ford and Julie went to Toulon. Ford – having left Rhys in a hotel in Paris – was paying her bills as well as an allowance. Not surprisingly, on their return, Rhys leached back into their lives, a move that hardly spread pleasure and contentment through the household, especially as by now it was Stella who was keeping up the payments Ford had agreed to pay Rhys. And when the messy affair finally ended, it was Stella who coped – first with Ford and then with Rhys. The former didn't want to know – he needed, he said, to get back to writing – while the latter needed pacifying.

In *Stravinsky's Lunch*, her dual biography of Stella and Grace Cossington Smith, Drusilla Modjeska put it most succinctly. Ford had broken Stella's trust: '[T]he qualities that had drawn him to her in the first place – her courage, her intelligence, her engagement with life – were precisely those that would take her away from him.' We can only gasp at masculine self-aggrandisement when Ford tells Stella how she rested like 'a precious and crystalline egg' in the palm of his hand. As a rider to this episode Stella wrote in hindsight a bitter, universal and perennial truth: 'Masculine vanity is one of the biggest motive forces in the world, and if it suffers deflation, the result is often a moral collapse.' Due to her reluctance to flaunt their dirty washing to the world, her loyalty was unwavering, however. She merely wrote that Ford, 'a much larger and more luxuriant plant than I', had gone to America to flex his emotional talents.

He had been the one great love of Stella's life. It was now perhaps that she wrote her saddest observation: 'I don't think it matters much from whom the artist gets his nourishment, or his shelter, so long as he gets it.'

*   *   *

Living now in rue Vaugirard, Stella had, after nine years, a studio of her own and spiritual space in which to take up painting on her terms. She worked on her most remarkable painting, the group portrait of the Lavignes at the Nègre de Toulouse.

Within the wooden triptych of *Au Nègre de Toulouse*, the portraits of M. and Mme Lavigne are flanked by those of their waitresses, static as beneficent angels, with safety pins holding up the bibs of their white aprons. Stella gave Phyllis the painting as testimony of their friendship and I inherited it among others my mother left me. What Stella never knew I also inherited from her was a lasting fascination for that period in France which for us, in the early twenty-first century, seems a chimera impossible to imagine.

Paris had become the literary capital of the universe, the centre for the arts where the names of poets, writers and artists rolled off the page booming with resonance. Painters such as Nina Hamnett, Pablo Picasso, Juan Gris and Pavlick Tchelitchef were there; Gertrude Stein, the Chinese translator Arthur Waley, Ernest Hemingway and Sylvia Beach with her library-bookshop Shakespeare and Company. James Joyce was described by Stella as 'the most courteous and unassuming of guests' who wrote:

> O Father O'Ford you've masterful way with you,
> Maid, wife and widow are wild to make hay with you.

But for Stella Paris life wasn't always amusing. While they were still together, finding somewhere affordable where Ford was immune from distractions – even whispering upset his muse – meant confronting irascible concierges as they led a peripatetic life. Ford may have adored his little daughter Julie, but he demanded total serenity while writing and at other times the intellectual stimulus from a motley collection of expatriates among whose reassuring admiration he could bask.

Exiling children when they became too intrusive for the male muse appears to have been mandatory at the time. Ford wasn't alone in banishing his offspring at moments of inspiration. Igor Stravinsky banned all conversation (even of his children) at mealtimes. Ezra Pound and Olga Rudge were more ruthless. Their baby Mary was fostered by farmers in the Tyrol where she learned the bitterness of loss and the local dialect, finding the infrequent visits of her 'real' parents bewildering. The 'awful king and the cruel queen', as she wrote in *Discretions*, the memoir of her father (to whom she was devoted), were more concerned with decorum than with her happiness. She expected sweets; Pound brought out nail scissors. Ford too – disappointed not to have had a son and with little to do with his two daughters from his youthful marriage to Elsie Martindale – inspired constant adoration from Julie regardless of his sporadic attention.

Others among the literati also behaved in a cavalier manner to their offspring. Wyndham Lewis and Iris Barry had two unwanted children during their brief, penniless life together. Their daughter was adopted within a year of her birth; their son, after four years with his grandmother, was dumped in an Essex orphanage where not surprisingly he wilted with unhappiness. Hemingway, who had a way of watching Lewis without appearing to, described him as having the eyes of 'an unsuccessful rapist! . . . I do not think I had ever seen a nastier-looking man. Some people show evil as a great racehorse shows breeding. Lewis did not show evil; he just looked nasty.'

Living now as a single mother, Stella depended on support from her friends. In the evenings she'd drop in on Gertrude

Stein and Alice B. Toklas in their salon, where they went in for 'a spot of cosy low-brow conversation' beneath walls covered with work by Matisse, Cézanne and the young Picasso. They discussed dealings with concierges, where to buy linen sheets or how to enjoy French provincial life. Later, Stein introduced Stella to Edith Sitwell at a luncheon party at the Nègre de Toulouse. Stella described the seemingly formidable poet – whose portrait she did in 1927 and, three years later, a painting of Sitwell's hands holding a black mask – as 'flagrantly' human: 'The English aristocrat, six feet tall, aquiline, haughty, dressed in long robes and wearing barbaric ornaments, was a strange sight in happy-go-lucky Montparnasse. But the sweet voice, the almost exaggerated courtesy and the extreme sensitiveness to other people's feeling, were so immediately winning that we all took her to our hearts at once.'

Periodically Ford returned from America to see Julie. With the coward's way of breaking off a relationship with a kiss rather than a sword, the severance was inconclusive.

Stella found his reappearances cataclysmic, hoping always for reconciliation.

In 1933 Stella and Julie returned to England. The exchange rate of her Australian allowance was dwindling; other expatriates were leaving, and without commissions for portraits she couldn't earn enough to keep them in Paris.

She had little good to say about England at first, yet out of the orbit of Ford's persona she observed, 'I was reminded of what a French old lady had once said to me concerning the vicissitudes of her life – "It was always my English friends who helped me when I got in a hole." I found comfort, kindness, uncritical friendship and loyalty – all those English virtues that I had forgotten about in my enthusiasm for France.'

Friends rallied round, Phyllis and Aylmer invited her to stay, invitations proliferated, requests for portraits bowled along: Lady Cripps, Margaret Postgate (later Mrs Cole), Raymond Postgate and his son John Postgate among many others, including my future husband Michael (just before he went on tour, having taken over the lead from Emlyn Williams in his play *The Corn is Green*), Michael's parents and his sister. As Stella was leading a nomadic life, twelve-year-old Julie – the same age as my sister – came to stay with us. They had fun taunting me, a dispensable kid of eight.

Why should I keep all these boxes of black-and-white snaps – unmounted, some milky, others curled at the edges and, worse still, without name or date to give them identity? Here they are, and here I sit – defeated. Do I hump them all back into boxes for others to deal with, or shall I do a serious culling to save my children the bother? Then I'm caught out.

Picking up a photograph of Stella sitting on a bench, I know exactly when and where it was taken.

In June 1940 Stella had escaped the London air raids to Green End, a rented cottage where she could finish the book she'd been commissioned to write, of her reminiscences of life with Ford Madox Ford. I used to stay with her there. We would wash in the kitchen before she laid a board across the bath to make it into her kitchen table. Once she painted my cupped hands holding a mouse – fragile and vulnerable – her allegorical and illustrative image of the air raids going on in London. Here at Green End she grew vegetables and cottage flowers higgledy-piggledy among fruit trees. Shamefully, as an adolescent brat hoping for immortality, I carved my initials on one of the branches.

*　　*　　*

How curious are the sources of memory that may rise from deep layers of forgetfulness to resurrect a small fragment of a lost event. Many years later, when I was visiting and writing about gardens for horticultural magazines, on the threshold of a country garden and faced by obsessive control, regimentation and conformity, where spirit of place had shrivelled to insignificance and decapitation was the gardener's credo – off with their heads to ferns, cranesbill and self-seeded poppies as nature freaked the owners out with its overwhelming fertility – Stella's garden at Green End would be inappropriately superimposed.

Cottage gardens were once ubiquitous in countryside or village – they embraced the dwelling like a garment. Nothing cerebral or contrived, no 'water feature' or polystyrene Greek urn, no decking or cumbersome barbecue lying at anchor on the 'patio'. Rather they had evolved from necessity, from an innate use of flowers among the vegetables and pots of herbs outside the kitchen door. Free from deadly diquat, dichlobenil or glyphosates, butterflies caroused among pinks and valerian appeared among cracks in drystone walls; the wigwams of runner beans and rhubarb thrusting through terracotta chimneys were interspersed with self-seeded aquilegias. Such an artless form of gardening had been Stella's method at Green End.

We'd sit together on a bench she'd put there for her old age when, she said, 'I'll be minding my grandchildren.' It was not to be. As the war progressed, Essex was designated a 'protected area'; if the Germans invaded, Green End would be commandeered as an army first aid post. Her reminiscences end with a question: 'Do we go or stay? To-morrow when I have finished this book, I must decide these things.' On the flyleaf of *Drawn from Life* she wrote, 'For Phyllis from Stella with a sister's love and many memories, London, July 30th, 1941.'

In London, just when portrait commissions were reduced to a trickle, Stella was employed by the War Memorial in Canberra as one of Australia's war artists. The assignment to paint group portraits of bomber crews with their paraphernalia surrounding them as ornamental as flowers bordering a Flemish painting was a godsend. Beneath the symbolic eagle of the RAF she painted the Halifax crew wearing their operational gear, surrounded by their hands at work on the individual jobs to which each was assigned. Another painting was *Bomber Crew*, for which her sketches of seven helmeted airmen, their names and wings in the foreground, lay on her studio table. The painting had to be completed from photographs, poignant memorials after all seven were killed on a sortie over Germany. Under the wings of the bomber their young eyes are fixed on a distance we can only imagine. 'The detail that draws my eye', wrote Drusilla Modjeska of this work, 'is the oxygen mask attached to each helmet, hanging down, almost touching their cheeks . . .' The insides of the masks were 'rather like the inside of a sea creature, vulnerable and tender'.

How I loved Stella. A woman of absolute veracity and common sense, she was the one fast colour throughout my childhood. It was she, not my mother, who with patient tenderness had undertaken to do the daily dressing on my ear when I came out of hospital following my operation for mastoid. After the first time she removed the gauze from the wound (cut through the bone behind my ear) with a quick pull, I entreated her that tomorrow she would do it slowly. From then, with painstaking patience, she gently did the dressing each morning with the imperturbability of an angel. How could I not love her? And because she was close to my mother, had experienced all her shortcomings as well as her blessings, I could always turn to Stella as the wisest, most discreet friend.

While I'm extant I can keep alive pieces of that *temps perdu*, which may have lost its lustre but which I hang on to by writing about her, since those Ford days when Ezra Pound described my mother's *joie de vivre* and Stella's emotional expenditure have long since congealed.

I lived with Stella for a time while my mother was going through a fraught relationship with a tiresome man. The tall, narrow house off the King's Road, with two rooms on every floor, had the kitchen, bathroom and telephone flights apart, and numer-ous sash windows that rattled from bombs and anti-aircraft guns as doodlebugs were coming over almost every night. I still have a note she wrote to me: 'My darling Mirabel this carries an Enormous Great Hug and many kisses from your very loving Old Trusty. It would be a great pleasure to me to have you here. I wonder whether you would care to borrow my top-floor flat during the next weeks. *Do* come. I have to start painting an old Admiral next week, but you and I could hobnob between sittings. Very much love darling, Stella.'

Without explanations – without prevarications, with no need to justify my mother's imbroglios – this simple embrace typified Stella to me.

Her 'old Admiral' was one of many assignments for portraits of Australian 'big wigs'. Sometimes I watched her at work surrounded by oddments from the Paris *marché aux puces* and the delicious fumes of oil paint and turpentine on afternoons when the high windows were half-shaded from the slanting sunlight. Being a self-centred teenager I never imagined that Stella had imperatives of her own, that she needed her space and that now, for the first time, she had a chance to live without having to compromise over concern for others. I must have been an awful bore to have around particularly as she was relishing having a place to herself since Julie, now married, was not living at home. But if I was, she never let on.

During 'hobnobbing' evenings – unless there was an air raid, when Stella insisted we should go down to the shelter in her garden as I imagine she felt a responsibility for my safety – she fascinated me with tales of Art, Love and Provence, where the buffeting of the mistral often destroyed any vestige of sanity. (Ford vividly described it in *A Mirror to France* as 'having wine forced into your limbs by a nine-million-horse-power hose. The sirocco is a parched nuisance; the föhn a miasmic breath from an open oven; the mistral is pain, exhilaration and the vastest concert of wind-instruments in the world.')

Harold Monro had offered Stella and Julie the use of his tiny, inaccessible peasant's cottage in Provence without conveniences but with views of incomparable beauty. She met other painters here. 'In Paris I had sat at hundreds of café tables with Ford, listening to talk about literature and "*le mot juste.*" In Toulon, I was able to listen, at last, to talk about painting,' said Stella.

Half a century later I remembered how different that world had been from the one my daughter Tamsin and I had travelled through, amongst the purgatory of chemical works and hydro-electric power stations (where long ago Petrarch first saw Laura) and where I'd come to write about a young woman who grew pots of flowers solely for their perfume, which she distilled to capture *Le Nez de la Drôme.*

The poet Alphonse de Lamartine may have inspired the title for my book on French gardens, but it was Stella's evocation of French markets that set me researching another book, on the legendary food of France.

Stella had described the clamour and vibrant colours of the south, its fruit and vegetables, *les violettes de Provence* (tiny green artichokes); the sea urchins, mussels and octopuses displayed next to a stall of *poils et plumes*; the hares, pheasants and partridges lying alongside pathetic heaps of thrushes with speckled breasts. Placed on marble slabs were varieties of sausages, *andouille*, hams and boiled ox muzzle for an inexpensive *museau de boeuf en salade*. Each *charcutier* would make his *rillettes* and seasonal pâtés of rabbit, game or pork. *Petit salé, jambons* and freshly made ready-cooked dishes such as pigs' trotters, pies, quiche Lorraine and, always on Fridays, *brandade de morue* – which is such a bother to make at home – plus farm butter, newly laid eggs and bunches of roses with the dew still on them.

Gourmandising in the head as she recounted long-gone meals was enticing torture. Verbal dishes can be mouth-watering and substitutive eating through the word – spoken or written – may have a certain dynamic, but it does have limitations. Toulon market was a piscine paradise for a perfect bouillabaisse. At little expense every kind of fish and tiny crabs plus saffron and a small piece of orange peel was a feast Stella made for Ford and their friends. Her description of cassoulet belonged to unattainable gluttony. Embarking on the lengthy process of creating a dish to be eaten the following day, she used *lingot* beans, pork, *saucisson*, pieces of duck or goose *confit*, belly of pork, herbs – everything – and all had to be of the best.

Sadly I have her recipes neither for walnut and garlic sauce nor for hare cooked with *verjus*, but I do remember – having saved up meat coupons – her wartime stews. Memorable, life-giving, cooked in an immense earthenware casserole needing two of us to carry it from the oven, the lid was lifted to reveal a herby aroma and gravy as glossy as velvet, dark as bitter chocolate, in which haricot beans, mushrooms, chunks of carrot and shallots like smooth pebbles lay submerged among the meat, tender as crumbly pastry. With chunks of bread we swabbed any residue left on our plates. And because Stella believed in the geniality of friendship, the symbiosis of talk and food, Gertrude Hermes, the sculptor and wood engraver, who lived a few doors away in Danvers Street (her daughter Judy was my great friend), often joined us.

The occasion was an offering to comradeship, amicable enjoyment and love. They were meals to be remembered in the golden light of conviviality.

'The Endearing Elegance of Female Friendship' (Samuel Johnson)

> And the days are not full enough
> And the nights are not full enough
> And life slips by like a field mouse
> Not shaking the grass.
>
> Ezra Pound

The woman leaning over the hospital bed spoke quietly: 'The pills are in your bedside table.' The woman lying on the bed turned her head, understanding. In the 1940s it wasn't easy to procure a phial of tablets – small, white and lethal – that guaranteed a painless escape from terminal cancer of the colon. The woman by the bedside was my mother. The one lying on the bed was Stella Bowen.

The friendship between the two women lasted until Stella died of cancer in 1947 at the age of fifty-four. Their temperaments were opposite; their lives went in different directions; but throughout periods of perturbation their devotion to each other remained indestructible with a love that outlasted more facile friendships.

'What a thing friendship is, world without end', my mother used to quote from a favourite poet, Robert Browning.

And it was a testimony to the trust they had in one another that, when Stella knew she was dying, dreading the final pain and humiliations, she asked my mother to procure something which would allow her the dignity of choosing when to go. Phyllis, who lacked neither compassion nor courage, had facilitated this request. A few days before she had written for Stella, 'You broke my heart when you spoke to me in gratitude so gently for the small things of no importance that I may do for you now. You, who for thirty years have cherished me with more than a sister's loving understanding. You were so beautiful aureoled in silver against the light – I lost my words for love of you.'

In a note to me my mother wrote, 'I know I have to embrace sorrow . . . that it's the only way, but oh darling it is heartbreaking that she should have this to cope with at the end. I feel nothing but heartache.'

And after her death my mother wrote her elegy to Stella recalling 'the winter evenings when we sat and talked by the fire amongst your pictures, for time returns and suddenly strikes the heart with longing for the quick glance, the intelligent words. Those hours together with you, who have graced my life with more than a sister's love and consolation, it is not now – but in the gathering years impoverished by your death – that I shall know the grief that passeth understanding'.

Seven years later, clearing my mother's things after her own death, I found the pills in a drawer, retrieved by my mother from Stella's hospital bedside. Stella had never used them but must have been comforted to have them within her reach.

(A salutary reminder of just how rigid Establishment morality was post-war: when Phyllis wanted to put a notice of Stella's death in *The Times*, they refused to accept her wording because it was clear that Stella had never been legally married to Ford Madox Ford.)

My mother and Ezra Pound had kept up a desultory correspondence more constant on his part than hers, as his letters became more and more indecipherable: '. . . my frien zan acquaintance – wat dey aint got is imagination & wot they have iz igurrence and how – and NO curiosity . . .' and so on scrawled across the page. A month before Stella died he wrote, 'Yes. Yes. F. [Ford] a probblum – knew more than any – see how good – is, when obeyin F's formula "n" then F. don't & cobwebs, etc. etc.'

Ezra's letters to Phyllis continued until her death. They arrived across the Atlantic from St Elizabeth Hospital, Washington, DC, where he'd been confined on the grounds of treason for his association with Italy. He harked back to Paris, to lost friends, to poetry. Often written in pencil, the missives came with the taint of someone cut off from a source of nourishment rooted in the Parisian life long since vanished: 'Fordie himself has never been properly recognized, though he was right back in 1912 when nobody else was . . .'

Living as he did, incarcerated in hospital, Pound craved news of friends from that era. Letters to my mother would end with a plaintive plea: 'I like to get news of the outer world.' In another: 'Phyllis you are invited to indulge in narrative, or reflection on remains of yr. empire . . .'

But by then her 'empire' had shrunk to a shadow of its former vigour.

Ezra died in 1972.

Stella, perhaps, had the most eloquent valediction on the time he referred to as my mother's 'period of absolute *joie de vivre*'. At the beginning of the Second World War she wrote, 'Alas! There will never again be anything like the Paris of the nineteen-twenties in our life-time . . . from England in 1940 it looks like a remote and unbelievable Heaven.'

Let's hope that's where Stella is now.

Would Stella approve my presumption in writing about her? I had never seen her angry. Impatient, certainly, at times with my mother's vanities – the trivial concerns that she made monumental, her combustible temper – these vexed Stella, but her quiet reasoning usually managed to deflect Phyllis from her tantrums. But I – now, writing this – would Stella feel I'm trespassing where I have no right to go? Making conjectures: making statements that list in one direction only? Astonished she would certainly be, but would she also be agreeable that Phyllis's youngest daughter – a skinny child so often in tears, whether finding a dead bird or anticipating my return to boarding school, I was aptly nicknamed *Misrabel* – was presuming to have insight into her life? And if I sound querulous about Ford's behaviour, I don't mean to. Not all the time: but looking back from this immense distance when mores and behaviour have changed so radically, I find it hard not to be censorious when in actuality Stella never was.

Why did my mother and Stella love each other with such constancy? Temperamentally they were hopelessly out of kilter. Was that the reason? My mother must have exasperated Stella with her impetuous reactions, yet Phyllis had a generosity unusual in someone as self-absorbed as she was. With her disregard for similarities in politics, lineage, education or taste, my mother's friends who appeared in our house were just as likely to be a lovelorn nephew who didn't know when to leave as the insecure daughters of friends who needed fashion advice or her Roedean school cronies 'up from the country'.

Like many women of her generation who had grown up with others to do their cooking, Phyllis became adept at meals based on dehydrated potatoes and four ounces of margarine, and living with food rationing of one egg a week was hardly conducive to indulgent eating. But the miraculous things my mother did with the powdered version were inventive though fairly vile. Meals depended on ingenuity. A familiar sight for Cordelia and me was Phyllis topping up the stockpot with every rescued scrap – bacon rinds, carrot peelings, leftover soup or sauce and whatever bones she'd wheedled from the butcher – for a risotto. Luckily, her priorities being at odds with those of other mothers, she would swap her weekly sweet ration of three ounces or her tea ration of two ounces for the much more crucial ingredients eggs or cheese.

'The brain has corridors,' she used to say, quoting Emily Dickinson. 'Opinions have nothing to do with friendship but everything to do with warmth, fidelity, humour, confidence and responses.' Her coterie of intimate friends outnumbered and outlasted anyone I have ever known. And in spite of our adolescent eruptions, both my sister and I knew as we were growing up that those warm responses were always available even if, at times, we walked out of the room slamming the door behind us.

Phyllis's defiant spirit embellished our youth so that Cordelia and I knew with certainty, whenever we needed it, that we could draw on her legacy.

After her death I knew I'd lost my greatest fan.

*   *   *

'We've pulled it off, darling, I'm going home,' my mother said as we left St George's Hospital at Hyde Park Corner in an ambulance. (As she was dying, I wondered if she'd only said that to comfort me.)

'Your mother has heart disease,' the doctor had told me. 'There's nothing more we can do. Take her home where she'll be more peaceful with her family around her.'

Heart disease? What – that? The organ that all her life had been molesting her, provoking her volatile temperament, causing mayhem with her lovers? Was this the thing that wouldn't stop beating?

'Yes, we've pulled it off,' I lied.

So the circle turns. I was performing intimate physical tasks that our mother had done for my sister and me when we were babies. Cordelia, with her two-month-old baby, her three other children and living out of London, felt isolated, cut off from being there with me, unable to share the tasks of trimming Phyllis's nails, combing her hair or changing her nightdress.

I dried her feet – the skin of her instep papery, toenails like washed seashells – the same feet that had walked with us over ridges of mackerel sand on summer holidays, the same feet that had clambered across Corsican rocks with Aylmer when deeply in love – 'within the rhythm of life we lay close locked in each other's arms'.

Mellow chimes of my grandmother's clock standing between books of poetry punctuated the hours. There was the Poetry Bookshop series, from 1911 to 1933, published by Harold Monro; six small calf-bound volumes of Browning printed on India paper; the mystical poems of Thomas Traherne; an old copy of Aytoun's *Lays of the Scottish Cavaliers* tooled in gold.

These are what she has bequeathed me, as well as verses from Masefield's 'The Everlasting Mercy' which she'd taught me when I was fourteen:

> The men who don't know to the root
> The joy of being swift of foot,
> Have never known divine and fresh
> The glory of the gift of flesh . . .
> Oh, if you want to know delight
> Run naked in an autumn night . . .

I used to deprecate the dash after a poet's date of birth in anthologies. It was asking for trouble. Larkin 1922– Hughes 1926– Jennings 1926– with the inferred promise of dates to follow, as though the poets were being hurried along with morbid anticipation of tidy conclusions. Why couldn't the dates be entered simply as Auden 1907, Enright 1920, MacBeth 1932, without being impatient for that other number?

Today the dashes can be completed as I open my volumes of thirty-year-old 'modern' anthologies and fill in the missing dates.

Rueful, but not satisfactory.

My mother's memory for poetry had been prodigious. She would while away journeys reciting 'The Highwayman', 'The Forsaken Merman' or Coventry Patmore's 'The Toys'. With exquisite melancholy they made me weep, submitting to tears in the back of the car returning in twilight from a journey begun many miles away. And suppose, I once asked her, the poet had been interrupted, the poem he was writing postponed, would it therefore be different because the first inspiration was lost for ever?

*   *   *

On afternoons when autumn sunlight lay low across her bedroom, when plane trees hung with bobbles of brown fruit and leaves sere and matt soughed with long-drawn breaths, I sat beside her. Whose hand was this? The same one that, when I was being anaesthetised in hospital at the age of nine, had held mine? That had tied a bow in my hair? Now, with it lying flaccid in mine, I imagined how our hands had been grafted since I'd been born.

I read to her poems she'd taught me to love, and I sang songs I'd learned from her as a child. Her voice had always been melodious whether singing lullabies, eighteenth-century French serenades, Frances Day risqué lyrics or choruses from the Players' Theatre and music-hall ditties. Time became a conundrum. She would wake from a brief sleep thinking it was another day; once she woke to tell me not to grieve. Not grieve! You might just as well ask swallows not to fly south or a sunflower not to turn towards the sun. And when she pleaded, 'I don't want to die,' just as my father had done many years before, I had no response.

I recalled her words: 'We die so often: with the first cruelty of wronged love; when our child is hurt and we have to stand by, and then with a lost friend when spring can never be the same.'

She still made pathetic gestures of outward anxieties as she groped for her glasses, fussing to hold them long after she could no longer read. Years later Michael did the same. His fretting was over a handkerchief in his pyjama pocket. These trivial signs of normality are pitiful. Do we each have a 'familiar', some trifling thing that becomes an obsession?

How lacking in dignity is human departure unless in sleep we are blessed to slide Lethe-wards into oblivion. And how immutable is a lifetime of vanities. Having always been meticulous in maintaining her looks, the habit wouldn't die even at this, my mother's most inappropriate moment. Befuddled, too many years of reflections at her dressing-table mirror kept this last reflex alive. Her ultimate vanity. Her longing for glamour: perfume, cosmetics, flowers on the dressing table topped with a peach-coloured looking glass with matching mirror and bed sheets, filled the room with scent.

And is anyone – outside novels – lucid enough to go in for deathbed confessions, unburdening long-kept secrets to estranged offspring looking for forgiveness and final benedictions? Towards the end my mother became confused as, one by one, the bonds that held her to the world were loosened. In bed lay a figure: the person was nowhere. Everything was giving up – lucidity, sense of time, recognition and bodily functions – the lot. Yet her heart, which had been both bane and inspiration, kept going day after wretched day. She who had always been a fighter lay submissive to the loosening fetters. Confused, without pain, and for the first time in her life without resistance, she imperceptibly floated away. For those who are dying, this may be the best there is. For the living it's unendurable.

Recognition was no longer reflected in her eyes.

When I kissed her she apologised for her hair, her skin and her looks. What irrelevancy – wishing I believed in an afterlife, her looks were the last thing on my mind. But not on hers. I was leaving a remnant of childhood on her pillow, angry that she was abandoning me too soon.

Two months after my thirtieth birthday.

Friends came. Some motored back from a holiday in France. Each wanted to make their private goodbyes, already too late for intelligible contact. Phyllis, their confidante and loyal companion, had left a husk on the bed. Her heart was beating – the rest had gone. And when her heart finally did succumb, the undertakers came immediately. To see my mother lying there between her peachy sheets was past bearing. I laid my hand where she had lain until I was no longer sure if I was feeling the warmth of her body or the warmth of my hand. All I wanted was to retain everlastingly that warmth of spirit which had been mine since birth.

My mother's epitaph might well have been from Edna St Vincent Millay, the economy of words being more terse than lyrical: 'I shall die, but that is all that I shall do for Death.'

For weeks after her death, letters arrived from friends – some rooted in her youth, others from the young who had always turned to her for support. All had long ago discovered her fundamental strata of generosity beneath her vanities.

Richard Church, the poet and novelist, who'd known my mother since the 1918 Poetry Bookshop days, described her as a 'most beautiful woman. Yet in spite of her vitality, her quick responses and her faultless ear for poetry she'd led a sad life owing largely to her temperament, but whatever happened she never lacked courage'.

It was due to that courage that, before she became ill, she had given me her blessing for a chancy decision I made.

The outcome resulted in ripples that affected other lives than mine.

Unable to have more children after my first child David was born, owing to trouble with my fallopian tubes (poetically named after a sixteenth-century Italian anatomist, Gabriele Falloppio), I wasn't prepared to acquiesce, to accept what I didn't want to hear. Instead, for several years I attended a north London clinic where women on the ground floor were seeking to be sterilised, on the second, pursuing fertility. What a sad collection we were, dominated by our uncontrollable biology. (This was a half-century before in vitro fertilisation.) By chance, a young medic told me of having recently read in a medical paper about a gynaecologist, Miss Moore White, who was doing exploratory work in obstetric problems. 'Why not see her?' he suggested. 'She might help.'

I took his advice and wrote to her.

'As long as you realise the chance of success is a small one come to see me on Thursday next at 2.30,' she replied.

With Michael I went to consult her.

'I'm good at embroidery,' Miss Moore White told me as she sketched out the intricate operation she was thinking of trying. 'You must bear in mind that if it doesn't work I shall need to operate again to undo it. Think about it and let me know what you both decide. I can arrange for you to come into hospital next month.'

Standing on the pavement outside her rooms in Harley Street with Michael, I was about to make a momentous decision that would affect us for the rest of our lives. We discussed the pros and cons, but what could Michael say? He knew the choice had to be mine and either way he would back me. He'd always been supportive in my quest. My sister Cordelia, already with four children, had thought I was foolhardy, but not my mother. She knew there are times when you must fight for what you want: 'Otherwise you are plagued with "what if?" for the rest of your life.'

'I'm going back inside,' I said, 'to fix a date.'

On a summer's day in July Michael drove me to London to a small hospital in Lisson Grove where Miss Moore White had gathered a group of other gynaecologists, interested in her pioneering work, who had come to watch the operation.

Our second child Tamsin was conceived seven months after my mother's death. The birth, written up in the *Journal of Obstetrics & Gynaecology*, was sadly too late for her to know her latest granddaughter.

Our third child came to us at a tangent with just as many difficulties to overcome, but alien ones. And on another continent.

5

Turning on the Curve of the World

Today, cooking a Thai curry – *kaeng masaman*, a southern Thai dish that includes coconut cream and chopped peanuts as well as the usual spices and curry paste – I think of Tongdee, our cook who came to us from the north-east at the age of seventeen and who became part of our family for the next seven years. David, Tamsin and Sureen have memories of her: their children have none. This is for them.

Michael, after his war years and in light of his inability to return to the stage, had turned instead to the healing life of Shropshire and farming. Days spent following his small herd of cows back from the pasture to be milked by the light of hurricane lamps, cold mornings rescuing a newborn lamb lying in a ditch which we'd wrap up to recover in the bottom oven, or calling his dog to round up the sheep, or turning the hay with a wooden rake were all restorative occasions that he and I shared, but it became hard financially to sustain farming on such a small scale. As our neighbours – the ones with whom we'd gone travelling to Turkey – were selling their farm, their restlessness was catching. Before going to Turkey, Michael remembered how hesitant he'd felt about that journey. 'I could feel the current tugging at me, pulling me downstream,' he'd said as he'd surrendered reluctantly.

Now, feeling the current again, he was prepared to go downstream a lot further than Anatolia. A posting overseas offered us the world. In 1959 we let our farm and, through the auspices of the British Council, went to teach English in Thailand. We chose this mountainous, forested, rice-growing kingdom with an elongated tail reaching to Malaysia because, uniquely among surrounding countries, it has none of the residue of having been colonised.

Vicarious travel has been a drug for years. Any friend who, on returning from a journey, recounts where they have been means our laying out a map to follow every detail, river, mountain or road they travelled. The more details, the more the journey comes alive. Descriptions of foreign minutiae bring distance into focus.

In the Buddhist year 2502 our map became a visual reality.

Turning on the curve of the world for two days, two sunrises, we flew low enough in a Comet to experience a journey. Refuelling often, we breakfasted at Beirut. The green malachite of the Gulf of Aqaba, the forked tongue of the Red Sea – the one I'd traced in my Phillips school atlas – made our journey impossible to sleep through. Peninsulas, ranges, karst, moraines, deltas and littorals were visible geology. An ebb tide had left miles of desert in Arabia, and beneath the sea lay trenches, abyssal zones, mid-ocean ridges. At Karachi airport dinner was served in the restaurant by waiters wearing white gloves.

Flying on eastwards, far to the left appeared the Karakoram, the Tien Shan range and the Gobi Desert, where, as a child, I'd

imagined frozen woolly mammoths with their last meals petrified in their guts. Beyond Calcutta, over the Ganges, jungles as
spongy as underwater seaweed; smudgy shadows; regimented
palm trees; nameless towns uncoiled across landmass turning
geography into actuality; rivers whose sediments – the rins-
ings of Asia – flowed into the Indian Ocean. The Bramaputra,
Salween, the powerful Irrawaddy curling into heat haze passed
in a never-ending reel where nomadic tribes, unhindered by
bureaucracy, moved freely across frontiers. The delta, the
same one that Aylmer had described in his macabre account of
escorting dead Turkish prisoners, in the letter he had written
when courting my mother over forty years before.

Life in Bangkok at the end of the fifties, before the Vietnam
War, was leisurely. An easeful charm was almost palpable at a
time before the *klong*s (canals) in the city were filled in. It was
a time when boys, swinging in acrobatic arcs from a rope tied
to a branch of a flame tree, plopped like lead into the black
treacly filth to appear choking, laughing, wiping scum from
their faces. When a dead dog floated for days nudging the keel
of one of the royal barges, and when a dish of noodles, 'wet' or
'dry', could be bought for a few coins from a street vendor on
a tricycle. Transport by *samlor*s (tricycle taxis) was a leisurely
if perilous progression behind a driver whose bare feet had
soles of rind tough enough to pedal a couple loaded down
with shopping. In the monsoon – wrapped in a sheet of plastic
– the driver like an attentive nanny fastened canvas flaps to the
hood, allowing his passenger to view the world over its rim
from the security of an outsized pram. What a loss when, in
1960, *samlor*s were banished from the city. With their disap-
pearance went an agreeable kind of hospitality when a lone
male passenger returning late at night might be asked:

'Would you like a pretty girl?'

'No, not tonight.'

'What about a pretty boy?'

'No, I just want to go home.'

As a last try: 'What about me? Would you like me?'

For our first three years Michael, Tamsin and I – the only foreigners – lived a hundred miles north of Bangkok in Lopburi, a provincial town inhabited since the sixth century where the aftermath of the Second World War had left the historical sites derelict.

We arrived with fresh-minted responses from seeing everything with pristine eyes. Just as you can never see Venice for the first time twice, so my first impressions have remained like a tattoo on my memory. As we drove north from Bangkok, humidity enclosed us in an invisible membrane. Garments clung to our limbs, Tamsin's hair was perpetually darkened, and Michael's hands slid round the steering wheel from the moisture. It was the monsoon, when young rice pierced the clouds reflected in flooded paddy fields, and kingfishers perched on the looping wires of telegraph poles diminishing into a submerged landscape. Clouds weighed Lopburi down like a migraine. Broken pavements, open drains, suppurating gutters, corrugated iron roofs, trams, concrete shops, electricity boxes with broken doors and rain-stained buildings weeping rust around the windows assaulted our senses.

In Bangkok our British Council colleagues were bewildered.

'Why on earth did you put in for an upcountry posting?'

'Anyway Lopburi is a dump. It's full of monkeys.' (True, the squalid area around the Kala Shrine near the railway station was where monkeys, among the tamarind trees, would leap onto a train and go for a ride, returning by train later in the day.)

'And you'll be bored stiff – missing out on all the metropolitan action.'

'Bridge parties, the Gymkhana Club and diplomatic receptions . . . which are always a bit of a hoot and good for free drinks.'

But later, judging by their frequent weekend visits, our colleagues came to appreciate the slow pace of our provincial life, so unlike the maelstrom of Bangkok. They enjoyed the ease of walking round the town, to the river, to the market, and the amiability of shopkeepers and – particularly for some – the 'Blue Room', a shabby brothel where we used to go for beer and dancing. The Blue Room girls, some as young as twelve, were sold by poor farmers for as little as twenty pounds. Occasionally a virgin was first sold to a rich government official or a Chinese merchant for forty pounds before being sent to work in a brothel. Our six 'girls' – more friendly than importuning – were full of surprises. Most were transvestites.

'We'd been dancing together all the evening but when we went upstairs . . . what a shock,' a friend said who, stationed in Java under the dictatorship of Sukarno when brothels were forbidden, would visit us with enthusiastic anticipation. One friend in particular, his testosterone forever pounding through his veins, used to flee to us for what he called 'the real, the authentic Thigh-land!'

When we needed bookshops, a doctor or a cinema we visited the capital. In the early sixties it was still possible to traverse the Divine City without being asphyxiated by noxious fumes. Occasionally we visited a theatre in the Chinese quarter, where actors in spectacular costumes made slow, stylised gestures to resounding music, surrounded by families eating, suckling babies, filling spittoons, kicking stray dogs. For contrast we'd visit the temples.

The temples of Bangkok, with mosaic spires, roofs of coloured tiles, gilded *garuda*s – figures from Buddhist and Hindu mythology used as symbols of the royal family – and *chedi*s – pagodas built to enclose the sacred relics of the Lord Buddha – are fabulous: glittering as shards of glass reflect the light.

Among those we returned to many times was Wat Benjamabophit, with its rich ornamentation, standing in grounds full of strange trees, and Wat Phra Chetuphon, famous for its reclining Buddha. At Wat Phra Kaew, Tamsin, awestruck by the twenty-foot demons guarding the entrance, wanted to visit again and again. And though in Bangkok we liked to visit Wat Bovonives with its magnificent Lopburi figures, we felt loyal to our shabby wats in our town with their motley clutter of gifts to the celibates: an alarm clock, a model of the royal barge, tea caddies, china knick-knacks, paper fans from Kyoto and a Christmas card of a robin. Other weekends we went to the sea, to the lonely beach of Pataya where sea warm as soup left us unrefreshed. Swimming at night, our limbs drew trails of phosphorescence like clusters of underwater fireflies.

Once, summoned to Bangkok for an embassy 'do' for visiting royalty, we were amused by the invitation with advice on correct behaviour: *When curtseying never hang on the Royal hand as you may find it difficult to come erect again.* 'What's new?' Michael muttered.

We stayed the night at the Oriental Hotel, a place redolent of old Bangkok where guests were pampered by gentle staff who moved along the passages like wraiths. (I was told recently that tourists going to Bangkok for sex complained that the revamped Oriental was the only hotel without hookers in the foyer.) At the time, the hotel was a handsome wooden building, with a lawn running down to the slow

Menam Chao Phraya flanked by timber godowns. From our bedroom, over the rhythmic gasp of a rotating ceiling fan and through half-closed shutters, came the throb of diesel engines. (Many years later in Greece, the deep pulse of fishing boats on the Ionian Sea transported me to the enervating humidity beside the soupy brown river flowing through the heart of the Thai capital.)

Joseph Conrad, during his twenty years of seafaring through the Malaysian archipelago, stayed at the Oriental Hotel. He too must have overlooked the shoals of small craft that plied up and down the river where, a century later, little had changed.

From the hotel we took a boat to the floating market where vendors on sampans, loaded with produce, touted their wares along watery alleys between small, open-fronted houses. The women squatted in the sterns of their boats on platforms worn smooth by generations of feet, shaded by paper umbrellas, as they cooked on clay stoves the food they sold to travellers passing up and down the river. Men fished, comatose in small skiffs; boys grinned and gobbed as they pulled up armfuls of lotus flowers in bud; and girls washed their hair, rising from the tea-coloured water with their black tresses, sleek as cats' tails, hanging down their backs. On balconies over the river – to the discord of a badly tuned wireless and among pots of greenery and hanging baskets of orchids – people gossiped, told fortunes or massaged geriatric limbs. Card players squatted motionless for hours; tailors tacked jackets; barbers cut hair; schoolgirls did their homework; grandfathers used abacuses; and a grandmother – pulling on a rope – rocked her grandchild to sleep in a bamboo cradle. Photographs of stern grandparents looked down from walls crowded with pictures of the king, glamour-girl calendars, and the occasional enema or hookah dangling among orchids suspended in wire frames.

Around small shrines petitioners prayed for the unattainable.

On another occasion, during the hot season when the schools were closed, Michael and I with other English teachers went to the south for a language seminar at a local college. For us it was a blessed escape. To leave behind the sweltering humidity of our small town for the coast of the Gulf of Siam with its strange, sea-tolerant casuarina trees sixty feet tall made us feel in a foreign country. Every noon we sat around a large table on the beach eating exceptionally delicious food supplied by the nearby Chinese restaurant, in blissful relaxation after the morning's teaching. Or so it was until the occasion when, at dusk, walking along the beach through shallow water – with a man who wasn't my husband (Michael was in bed with a tummy upset) – I trod on a sea snake. At first I assumed it had been a jellyfish, nasty things we often encountered and did our best to avoid when swimming. If stung, the advice was to rub the place with sand to alleviate the pain. I did just that, but as we walked further along the shore a sort of heaviness slowly crept up my leg, not pins and needles but numbness, weighty and encroaching.

'Oh help,' I said to Malcolm, a friend we often stayed with in Bangkok and who taught the young crown prince – son of King Bhumibol and Queen Sirikit – English. 'I think it wasn't a jellyfish but a sea snake.' Highly venomous, their bite causes gradual paralysis. 'We need the hospital.'

Gallantly Malcolm piggybacked me across the sand, making towards lights where a jeep was coming in our direction. But the driver, seeing a man with a woman on his back making wild gestures, kept on driving. Undaunted, Malcolm put me down:

leaping onto the jeep, hanging on the handle, he shouted at the driver that I was dying. Terrified, the well-oiled rubber planter from Malaysia did his best to brush Malcolm off by zigzagging between the casuarinas, but Malcolm clung on until the tipsy driver – defeated and with bad grace – agreed to take us to the hospital. (No doubt it made a well-embellished story for him when he returned across the border to his world of latex.)

At the hospital the doctor kept the correct anti-venom. 'There are generally several deaths a year from sea snakes if the patient doesn't arrive in time!' said he.

Blessed Malcolm. We still talk of it when he comes to visit me in Ludlow. We remember, and we drink to the drunken planter and the vee-shaped mark of snake fangs visible for days afterwards on my foot.

After visits to Bangkok we were always thankful to return to our town: to leave the glitzy frenzy of the city for the intimacy of our compound. We'd also grown accustomed to the metallic click of saucepans, the throaty Chinese voices on the surrounding balconies, and the smell of roasting garlic penetrating our guavas, pomegranates, mangoes, bougainvillea, pots of hideous crotons and a rose-apple tree in which turquoise-headed lizards lived. Distantly we heard the wavering song of a child, the hoarse call of an ice-cart man, the rattling innards of a passing tram. In the corner of the garden was the spirit house, a miniature Thai 'temple' where daily the landlord's family placed food and flowers to propitiate the *pi* – the evil spirit – with their prayers.

Our house was a masterpiece of kitsch. We loved it immediately. As the custom of walking barefoot indoors was universal, our varnished teak floors were dark and glossy like hand-polished conkers. The sparkling golden lamps and the upholstered armchairs made the place unique in Lopburi, and, as our landlord explained with pride, pointing to the louvred glass wall of the living room, we also had 'the only glass windows in town' (hardly necessary as the house had the classic deep eaves perfect for protection against sun or rain). A staircase with golden curlicue banisters led to a wide landing, three bedrooms with mosquito screens, shutters and views on to our neighbours' roofs. The bathroom had a large Ali Baba jar from which we sluiced refreshing cold water over us with a huge scoop. Ideal for life where changing clothes once a day was a necessity. And everywhere – in whatever room – was the sporadic whispering of lizards scuttling across ceilings or lying still as carvings in the shadow of a door. They were as intrinsic to our life as the nightly barking of dogs somewhere beyond the compound, their frenetic yelping cutting through the night like a chainsaw.

A lean-to at the back of the house – screened against insects and with a corrugated roof – was where the spicy cooking was done over a charcoal stove. Curious how some things were scrupulously provided, such as the table legs standing in ceramic saucers full of water to prevent ants from reaching the food, but the huge fridge, like a becalmed liner, stood next to the cook's lavatory and a narrow drainage canal crossing the floor. Except for various lapses during our three years living there, when I spent days in a Bangkok hospital with dysentery or dengue fever and – once – three weeks with hepatitis, I never regretted living 'upcountry'. On that last occasion, returning home skeletal, what joy it was to eat *dtom yam kung* (crayfish soup in a moat surrounding a chimney over charcoal that stood on the table) again after bland European food: 'the kind you can recognise', the Australian matron had assured me.

Much of our cooking was done by Tongdee (the name means 'good gold' – hardly apt for a girl who slept with some of our bachelor visitors with the same open-hearted hospitality as Penelope's maids did at Odysseus' palace on Ithaca). Slim and pliant as a willow, she collapsed to the floor like crumpled paper whenever she was overcome by laughter, her long hair falling forward in a thick, sleek mass across her face. But how she longed for curls. Mistakenly, once, she had her hair permed, which she then lamented until the dry frizz grew out.

*Ferang*s (as all foreigners were called) in the provinces weren't half as classy to work for as those living in Bangkok; consequently our cooks came and went, but not Tongdee. She stayed with us even when we moved north to Chiang Mai. Beloved by us all, she is not forgotten: I imagine her in paroxysms of bubbly laughter among her grandchildren. With her high cheekbones and wide lips, she might have been a descendant of one of the invading Khmers who had brought their art and language to Lopburi twelve centuries before.

Khmer-style Buddha heads, unadorned, square-faced, with straight brows, broad lips and serene countenances, reposed in dim chambers in King Narai's seventeenth-century palace not far from our house. (In later years the palace was restored by the Fine Arts Department, but even when we were there its faded splendour was still apparent.) Outside, squatting beside the ruined walls where once the recesses had been filled with candles, were vendors of medicines made from beetles, roots, horn, parts of snakes and coloured powders: concoctions which promised restoration of the spirit as well as of the body. Among the people seeking cures, magic amulets, soothsayers or exorcists were scavenging dogs and young children with streaky bronze hair. The first time I saw these children roasting *kluey khai* (a kind of small banana) over charcoal, I thought their hair had been dyed. I was mistaken: it was due to malnutrition. We were to see the same aberration in other parts of the country.

The male obsession with virility was allayed by powders and charms or by snakes pickled in alcohol. The female obsession for pale skin was guaranteed by traders in the white powder that young women smeared on their faces when they returned from the fields.

'Africans are over-baked, Europeans underdone, Thais are just right,' we were told.

Skin colour among Thais was an underlying prejudice that had shocked us when we first arrived. Always it was the fairer-skinned pupils who were chosen to lead at any ceremony. Tamsin suffered from this bias by having her arms touched and stroked by adults and children as though pale skin was somehow contaminating, or by sheer transference overnight they would become white as forced asparagus.

Beyond our house a barbed-wire enclosure surrounded a ruined *chedi*. For Michael the place was full of ghosts. Within these grounds, where bits of ancient carvings lay scattered among rank grass, tins, bottles and general human detritus, some of the British prisoners of war who had built the 'Death Railway' between Siam and Burma had been confined. One in three had died; attempts to escape had been punished by public execution in the camp. A friend of Michael's had been imprisoned there. He told how, in an attempt to find a modicum of shade, he and his starving fellow captives had pushed the stone images from their niches, leaving them tumbled on the ground. Now, years later, the remaining strands of wire still in situ, they reminded Michael of a sad piece of history outlasting his friend, who never recovered from the brutality. He died aged forty-one.

A few miles outside of the town at a large army camp were military trucks supplied as part of aid to Thailand from America. With the sign 'Hands Across the Sea' on their sides, these vehicles were intended to be used in a military crisis.

My mother, Phyllis Reid, as a drama student during the First World War. She shared a studio with Stella Bowen, a student at art school. Their neighbour was Ezra Pound who appropriated their cultural education by introducing them to the London literati.

The first page of a letter from Ezra Pound to my mother while she was a student, 1917.

Phyllis, Harry, Cordelia and me in 1926. My father, who had tuberculosis, was in remission when this family portrait was taken. A year later he died.

One of several self-portraits Stella painted. This one is presumed to have been painted in 1929.

Stella's triptych, painted on wood, of the proprietor of the Negre de Toulouse and his wife surrounded by their waitresses. Ford Madox Ford, the Pounds, Ernest Hemingway, Gertrude Stein et al habitually dined in a back room of the restaurant. Even after her separation from Ford, Stella used to describe the progress of the portrait in her letters to him. When we lived on Corfu, it hung against the incongruous background of the Ionian Sea. Now the picture hangs over the fireplace of my Ludlow house, a treasured reminder of that unique period between the wars in Paris.

I was seventeen when this photograph was taken. With tin hat and gas mask, two of us were assigned to stand on the roof at night watching for incendiaries intended for Battersea Power Station on the other side of the Thames.

Stella's portrait of Michael was painted before the war. Much to his father's disapproval, he chose to become an actor rather than go into the family business.

My last photograph of Cordelia, sitting serene and rested in our Lopburi garden during a visit to stay with us in Thailand in 1960. Her floral dress lies among other mementos of her visit.

Tamsin with David on one of his holidays to Lopburi, seen here against the fence through which neighbouring children would call Tamsin to play 'cooking' with them. Squatting in the path, they concocted meals from berries and flower petals using miniature clay pots.

The samlor driver who collected the children each morning to take them to nursery school.

Our house in Chiang Mai was built on stilts to withstand the annual flooding of the river. Occasionally we'd find kittens left in a box under the house. Killing them was against the Thais' Buddhist religion and we were a pushover.

The verandah, under the shade of the rain tree, was where we lunched – except in the monsoon. When the river was low, we'd watch the fishermen tossing their nets as they slowly moved through the water. They wore bell-shaped bamboo baskets on their belts in which to put their catch.

In Chiang Mai we explored the tracks leading into the forest where we'd bathe in rivers, lie under waterfalls and have picnics of curry, pieces of chicken, Thai salad and sticky rice. Each course was carried in a tier of enamel dishes called a 'pinto'. Tepid food may sound repulsive but in that humidity it was delicious.

Dousmani, our house on Corfu. Beyond the large downstairs room where swallows returned every year to make their nests and where the olives and grapes were temporarily stored is the Ionian Sea, the mainland invisible through the midsummer heat haze.

A saint's feast day procession in Gastouri village.

The back of our house and the olive tree outside the shuttered bedroom where young swallows sang throughout our siestas.

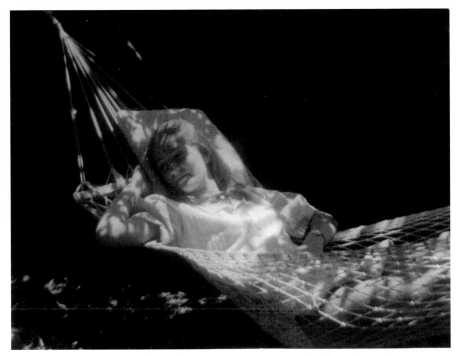

Tamsin under 'Sophie's trees' just outside our courtyard walls, where the air was heavy with the scent of oleanders.

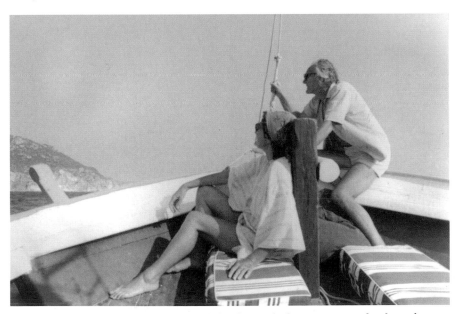

The Glenconners' caique. We'd spend the day with them, visiting islands to the north. Uninhabited and covered with cistus, we would anchor in one of the islands' bays, where we swam, picnicked and gathered red, green or translucent pebbles. Some of these now lie in a goldfish bowl of water on my window sill.

Tamsin in 1991 with Sureen who is holding Cassandra, her niece.

A shelf made from packing-case wood painted with emulsion, on which to put dug-up bits of crockery and a few pots, where a black-bird nested.

The shed at the bottom of my garden in Ludlow where a young art student painted a barn owl under the *clematis montana*.

Pragmatically and as a matter of expediency, the Thais put them to the more benign use of transporting children to and from school.

There were also horses at the camp: huge great seventeen-hand beasts supplied by the Australians. After the captain's initial surprise that a female *ferang* should ask to ride one of their horses, and after the first time when I was accompanied by a soldier to make sure I was all right, I spent many solitary hours ambling on my lumbering beast through the forest. Worn paths led across streams and through thickets to small bamboo dwellings where dogs ran round barking and the people – smoking cheroots whose smoke lingered long after I'd gone by – came to stare and ask, through incoherent mouthfuls of betel, where I was going.

These peregrinations among birds, butterflies and the occasional snake were solitary, and though pointless they lifted me into a context far from our crowded compound where we were overlooked on every side.

Led by the nose due to the pungency of the market, we walked among an infusion of spices, a fragrance of fruit and wafts of vegetation and leaking trays of fish. At certain seasons the unmistakable reek of durian – a highly prized fruit smelling of putrefaction with a trace of myrrh – overwhelmed all else. Ambrosia for some, wormwood for others, it's the longest-established fruit of the south-eastern rainforests, and *mon tong* was the most expensive variety. Within a spiky skin, black kernels are embedded in custardy pulp with such a corruptive stench that the fruit is banned from the cabins of Thai planes, as well as within the entire Singapore transport system.

(Once, at a party, when others were smoking pot, being a non-smoker and not having Alice B. Toklas's brownies to hand,

I replaced the durian stones with marijuana. Unfortunately when my metabolism kicked in next morning, the party was over. I'd over-eaten the stuff and found the effect astonishing. I remember clearly how time seemed to be extended to infinity; everything took for ever; there seemed never to be a conclusion. As I made my way to the lavatory I wondered why it was taking me so long when the bathroom was opposite our bedroom – it was a reasonable question to ask. The sensation wasn't unpleasant, only weird, but my insatiable appetite that followed couldn't be easily appeased.)

Besides the durians, which were seasonal, there was the customary produce. Mushrooms, bamboo shoots, betel and tobacco; baskets of live frogs, eels, green-lipped mussels and slim silvery fish laid in overlapping patterns; catfish and crabs scuttling underfoot to disappear beneath dripping leguminous greenery dangling from low trestles. Beetles: the huge flying sort that gathered at nightfall round street lamps until they plopped in a stupor to the ground, where children gathered them up for beetle sauce. Ground spices for *kapi* – a shrimp paste used in curries – were heaped in coral, ruby and sepia mounds as though on an artist's palette. Orchids, delicate as bone china, hung among pigs' intestines; a pot of plastic roses stood in the midst of roast ducks, fried chickens dipped in saffron and dried fish with an acrid whiff of brine. Bunches of fresh herbs sewn into parcels, lemon grass wrapped in leaves fastened by bamboo pins, bundles of roots tied with reeds lay piled up on woven trays on the ground. Every handcart, loaded with ice blocks wrapped in sacking, had to span the trays as they were pushed from riverbank to bistro.

Across the aisles came the cry '*sarapau, sarapau*' of a dumpling vendor selling stodgy white balls, stamped on the underside with red hieroglyphics, to be eaten with fish sauce. Among galleys where dishes were cooked in continuous succession alongside a gamut of delicious sweet or piquant snacks, the lad selling lottery tickets did a brisk business.

By noon the perishable food stalls had closed. Only the alleys of dry goods – bedding, baskets, garments, pestles and mortars, slabs of teak chopping boards, implements, soup bowls tied into tiers with raffia – remained open. Among caverns of swaying cloth Indian vendors offered a rainbow of fabrics: Shan, Malaysian, batik, Siamese or Laotian cotton and silk. Beyond were straw hats piled in tawny stooks, for where rice is grown, hats predominate. Not conical – as in China – but with high crowns supported by lightweight frames to allow air to circulate under wide brims.

The cultivation of rice was a source of never-ending fascination, and it was nowhere more apparent than in the vast alluvial plains of low-lying land a mere six feet above sea level north of Bangkok. Hats were as much part of the landscape as were the water buffalo. Half-submerged, with ropes through their muzzles, these clumsy beasts, covered with coarse hair and having horns that curled backwards like handles, were washed at sunset by small boys who sluiced off the mud caked on from the animals' noonday wallows.

Before returning from the market we'd sit at one of the open-air bars for a bottle of Singha beer accompanied by the Thai equivalent of Greek *meze, kai sam yang,* 'three kinds of chicken' – though there wasn't any chicken, only small red onions, tiny dried prawns, sliced lemon grass, chopped root ginger, diced lime and peanuts, eaten together in one mouthful. At a nearby table a young girl would be employed to cut a single paper napkin into four, then place the segments in tumblers.

If you live by a river you have to use it. We did: for several days we penetrated the great landmass where merchandise and produce are transported by water. For a few days we hired an empty rice barge with a raised platform under shelter at one end, where we slept. The only lavatory on board was a sort of ingenious hinged contraption with ropes through which to put your arms so, squatting and facing inwards, you could discreetly hang over the river without revealing your bottom.

On a long rope, pulled by a little launch, we travelled through landscape impossible to reach by road. To the putt-putt-putt of the diesel engine we spent leisurely days stopping at riverside habitations for food and at temples surrounded by tranquil courtyards.

My sister was our first visitor after David – at boarding school in England – had flown out during his Christmas holidays. She came in the cool season when mornings were fresh; women going to market flung towels across their shoulders, school-girls wore cardigans, and teachers tucked nylon scarves into their chaste white blouses for there was a widespread belief that when the weather was 'cold', inevitably everyone would 'catch' a cold.

Having met Cordelia at Bangkok airport, the four hours back to Lopburi, in spite of the potholed roads, was a charmed journey. Canals on either side were ornamented with white and pink lotus flowers brittle as porcelain. Flocks of ducks or the lone figure of a fisherman, his net poised for a catch, were reflected in the canals. We never made the journey without seeing a bus on its side in the water. Orange and blue, with bits of decorative chrome and canvas flaps for protection against sun or rain, the vehicle would be lying like a discarded toy. Passengers who'd been travelling on the roof among fruit, vegetables, cardboard suitcases and baskets of chickens, as well as the small pigs tied into open-work baskets and looking macabre – a bit like *jésu* sausages you see in French markets – were tumbled into the shallow *klong*, giggling and shouting, unperturbed that the top-heavy, overloaded bus had done what it always did. We drew up alongside to see if anyone was hurt. No one was. The young, the old, the babies, disentangled themselves among general hilarity. However often we came across buses in the *klong*s, a philosophical stoicism turned the event into spontaneous gaiety as the drenched driver, sodden with water and *Mekong* whisky, was wrung dry along with all the goods. We never witnessed anger or aggression.

For Cordelia Thailand was an escape from life in orbit around four children. While her husband coped at home she was able to luxuriate in the temporary freedom of a distant land where cooking, laundry and shopping were done by others. Release was instant, sending her freewheeling into fugitive self-indulgence. Forgetting her return ticket, she surrendered to idyllic evenings sitting under a coral-coloured bougainvillea and drinking ice-cold martinis to the quiet chatter of our neighbours and the clatter of large beetles flying into the lamps.

This was almost the first occasion on which my sister and I had been together for any length of time since our mother had died four years before. Although our worlds had drifted apart due to distance, we constantly wrote to each other, had visited each other and shared holidays, as well as coping with the dismal dismantling of our mother's house.

'So many times I've wanted to write yet couldn't find the words,' Cordelia had written. 'I've always been frustrated by an inability to express myself coherently – but don't think because I haven't spoken I have no deep feelings. I loved Mummy though we had little in common but she was always there loving and responsive no matter what. The gap she leaves is greater because for many years I've felt the sadness of having few mutual interests. I was a disappointment to her [she never was] but since my children were born we'd grown closer. And now they have no "granny" to give them the lovely things she gave to us when we were children.'

Sitting together outside under cascades of magenta bougainvillea, Cordelia said, 'Ever since Mummy's death I've felt guilty. I wanted so much to be with you, to share the awfulness of her protracted death.' Through the fence children stopped to peer at us before running off along the path that wound among the houses. 'I won't speak of it again,' she said, 'but I wanted you to know how, in a funny way, I was jealous of you being there during that ghastly time while Mummy was dying.'

Aware of the ease of the moment, we left the garden, secure in each other's company as siblings are who have confided in each other through an intimate childhood. We shared the same roots: however many miles separated us, there was the shorthand communication between us that never needed elucidating. With arms linked silently we entered the house.

A few days later Cordelia came with me to visit the kindergarten where Tamsin went each morning by *samlor*. Here she learned the Thai formal modes of address to her elders, and to deport herself correctly by holding in the back of her skirt as she stooped to pass her teacher. The head of a person being sacred – the *khuan*, the vital essence of the human being resides there – no child passes an adult without lowering its head. (Once, soon after we'd arrived in the country, visiting a member of the Thai royal family, we were dismayed as we sat on a couch to see that, to keep her head lower than ours, a servant shuffled all across the room on her bottom to offer us refreshment.) Amongst the many forms of correct behaviour, Tamsin learned to *wai*, the graceful way of greeting and farewell, also observed at the daily raising of the Thai flag in the playground. And with the rest of the class each afternoon, she said a Thai prayer before the children changed into pyjamas and lay on the floor for their hour-long siesta.

Nearby was the teacher training college where Michael taught in a functional concrete block on two floors. Having none of the grace and fluency of some municipal buildings with their steep roofs and rising corners like reflexive petals on a tulip, its wooden shutters creaked continuously with the sound of arthritic knuckles. Clones of this school design were found throughout upcountry towns.

'Welcome,' the headmaster, Professor Porn (sic), said at their first meeting. A lethargic alligator with a pockmarked face, he shifted from one buttock to the other with a sigh of weariness: 'Home from home. Anything you need, any problems . . . come to me.' A wide smile crumpled his pitted flesh (the result of smallpox) as he removed his dark glasses. Mildly curious, Michael asked him why some of the senior girls wore blue skirts, others black. 'Ah, yes,' said the headmaster with affable languor, closing his heavy-lidded reptilian eyes, 'they wear black when they menstruate.'

An apocryphal answer, we discovered later, but one thought by the headmaster to satisfy *ferang*s looking for sociological replies. Thais, with their immediate smiles – beguiling and charming – can at times be maddeningly amorphous. Put out your hand and nothing is solid.

Among his gentle, reverential, dark-eyed students was one, Sompet Piriyapansakul, who delighted Michael when she wrote in her essay, 'English teachers never stop talking English hour after hour as if to full the students stomaches and I am forced visit the doctors. English never fails to send me to the Land of Nods.'

At the school gates, rising seventy feet against blue sky, stood a flame tree whose flamboyant orange flowers erupted from leafless branches. The schoolgirls gathered the fallen flowers – lying on the ground like a mirror image of the tree – to pin in their hair. Giggly and shy with their English teacher, the girls' demeanour was punctilious. From kindergarten they'd learnt when handing something to the teacher to hold the elbow with the left hand; at puberty, modesty dictated that they wear blouses with short sleeves clenched tightly round their arms in order not to disclose a glimpse of underarm hair. A perennial joke among the students was the way *ferang* women thought nothing of strap-hanging in buses, disclosing intimate glimpses of their armpits. When travelling in a *samlor* both schoolgirls and teachers draped a thin scarf modestly over their knees. At the hairdresser's – a leisurely place where a girl would wash and massage heads for twenty minutes, and which I found a good place to practise speaking Thai – a piece of flowery cloth was hung over the clients' knees to prevent immodesty from splayed legs.

A tramline ran a couple of miles beyond the school before petering out among paddy fields stitched together by raised footpaths. Kapok trees, with conical spines when young, grew among thickets of greenery standing in clumps among the fields. We took Cordelia with us on the tram for a journey we liked to make for no reason other than leaving town for a landscape of humpbacked hills covered with a pelt of scrubby undergrowth. We went, too, for the sheer enjoyment of riding on a wind-up toy that bobbed along the track like a courting duck. The driver – wearing dark glasses even on gloomy days – drove his rattling contraption, rasping from lack of oil, with its frilly awning and floor covered in the husks of discarded lotus seeds, until it made a final curtsey against the bumpers before returning home.

On the day the rails were lifted to make way for the Bangkok highway we took a last tram ride with a few other Lopburi inhabitants also mourning the loss of a charming mechanical absurdity.

After three weeks Michael and I saw Cordelia off at Bangkok loaded with presents for the children, shirts for her husband and lengths of silk for herself, knowing this would be our longest parting. We weren't due any leave for more than a year. We stood together in the impersonal surroundings of the airport among returning tourists wearing Thai hats, bedecked with gold jewellery, clasping their celadon pots and carved elephants.

'I shall never have such a holiday again,' Cordelia said.

How fortunate neither of us knew how prophetic her words were. Had we known, we could never have disentangled our arms, never turned away and walked in opposite directions without premonition of the calamity ahead. The memory of her departure remains vivid – the lees of recollection cannot easily be swilled away. How I wish I had hung on to her. Held her, stopped her from returning to England, to the finality approaching her and her family.

Every time subsequently, waiting at Bangkok airport for an incoming plane, I thought of her walking through the departure gate from which there was no turning back. Caught up in the same sense of unreality which beset me in childhood, I imagined that – never having actually seen her leave the airport – suppose just suppose, by putting out my hand I might find her still there, suspended for ever in the departure lounge between reverie and destiny.

A few weeks later, when the schools were closed, Michael, Tamsin and I went to visit friends in northern Queensland. En route, while we were staying a night in a small hotel on the coast, a telegram arrived from England telling me Cordelia was dead. She had died in hospital from an abdominal operation.

We never reached our friends. Disabled by misery I knew there was only one place I wanted to be: with her family. Michael besieged the local travel agent to get us on any flight to Europe. In the early sixties there was little choice. We flew back the wrong way round the world, against the grain of time zones, across the Pacific to Los Angeles on our way eastwards to London and to Essex.

Grief is corrosive and latent. Like a virus that works by slowly consuming human vitality, it becomes a form of degeneracy, leaving an automaton in place of a person. A bane, a scourge, it never diminishes. The people who say time is a great healer are lying: they haven't yet learned the duplicity of such a platitude. All that happens is that the bereaved move across a different latitude leaving the dead petrified in time. A day, a month, a year spreads between us, Cordelia, and you will grow dim in my recollection. When forty years are gone, you, my newly born dead, will be a remembered name anchored at the age of thirty-eight with all your bright potential.

In a letter written a few days after she returned to England, Cordelia had written, 'I feel hopeless about staying here and continuing the utterly dreary domestic round. I am quite un-grown-up! I have so much love and admiration for you. Till now I'd always thought of you as my younger sister needing comfort and protection but everything has changed and now I look to you to give me these things.' Which was uncanny, for I too had been aware of our reversed roles. It should have been me who died. I felt I had more strength than she did – that I could bear being dead more easily.

Logic told me how fortunate it was that Cordelia, my mother's first-born, had died four years *after*, not *before*, Phyllis's own death. And I remembered my mother's bleak words when Stella had died: 'The dead are nowhere – don't tell me tales of reconciliation.'

I could never return to where once I was. Numbed by thoughts of Cordelia's bones buried in the cold earth of a country churchyard, her skull facing skywards with sockets full of soil, knuckles, ribs, spine – a collection of bones – and arms that had consoled me more times than I could remember, and hands that had led me across the road on the way to school. Haunted by the physical remains in the ground, I wished away her burial. It was grotesque. How much better, I thought, to have been reduced to ashes rather than left in the earth, an indestructible paradox of what once she'd been.

The year following Cordelia's death I was felled. I could no longer speak about 'last year' as a place where she had been living. Against my will I was floating away from her.

Mourning when the person is young, with years unfulfilled, cannot be the same as for those at the end of their lives. The pitch of grieving is different. Even though my mother at sixty-two was too young, compared to my sister, she had lived. So had Michael. But not Cordelia. She would never see her children – the youngest four years old – grow up.

Pain like this is insoluble, yet as long as we remember our dead they don't die. One of the small comforts left for the bereaved is to talk about them. To recall the person we have lost by sharing our memories. I hang on to this illusion as long as I can, though inevitably the number of people only I am left to remember is increasing year by year.

Writing this I think of Cordelia still at the age of thirty-eight whereas I – younger at birth by four years – am in my mid-eighties.

While outwardly the mechanics of living were carrying me along, I endured the malevolent ways of the unconscious. If this is the place where we really live, according to the psychoanalysts, if this is the intrinsic, essential part of each of us, I want none of it.

Grief returns you to the same point, continually, relentlessly. Loss. My dreams became travesties, recurring every night month after month, fooling me into thinking that both my mother and my sister had not died. How cunning of the psyche. My unconscious persecuted me, playing games as a cat does with a mouse by letting thoughts run on, letting dreams bring me deliverance that none of this was true; my sister was there, living and well, saturating them with joy. Rising through layers of sleep and tears, I remembered. Of course. Both had gone. My mother and my sister were dead. Gone for ever, and no amount of dreaming subterfuge could restore to me what I wanted most on wakening.

It wasn't self-pity but bitter, resentful reproach that made me un-resigned to the loss of the only two constants throughout my thirty-four years. Subconsciously I refused to accept the truth, which meant there was no release from nightly self-torture. Neither Michael's comforting arms nor words could penetrate a grief so physical, so painful with its involuntary force of gravity. How could my body be so deceitful, so traitorous as to play games on itself like these?

I was doing this to me.

* * *

I went into a slough of depression, an enclosed world I'd never before entered. I wouldn't have chosen this – I had nothing to do with it. Without my volition, I was appropriated. Slow to realise what was happening, I became apathetic to everyone and everything. Depression is without emotion: sterile – leaving nothing palpitating. There's no before, there's no after. And the platitude 'Remember, there are others less fortunate' is a form of misplaced sophistry. But why had it taken so long? This was a year after Cordelia's death. What mysterious toxin had been at work while all the time I thought I was performing all right with Michael, Tamsin, friends and teaching?

Nothing since has been as eclipsing as grief – not even physical pain. It was the most apocalyptic experience in my life: an incubus that lay like a beast in wait whenever I went down behind my eyes.

Although time doesn't heal, the momentum of living can give one a shove.

Dylan Thomas's 'force that through the green fuse drives the flower' was the force that finally drove the revival of my spirit. It had happened after my mother had died when a new life had grown within me, and although she never lived long enough to hold her granddaughter, the birth of Tamsin gave me that impetus through regeneration. When years later Michael died, Tamsin was pregnant with our first grandchild.

When Cordelia died, something germinated without deliberation but from a place beyond my rationale.

The seeds of resurgence are not always the obvious ones.

Within two years of my sister's death we became caught up in the complexities of adopting a child.

With my grandsons in mind – Sureen's two boys, Benjamin and Laurence – it's imperative that I write in detail about how their mother's life moved from Asia to Europe when she was a child. What a momentous result when by chance we deviated off the Bangkok–Lopburi road on our way home. Some day the boys may be curious about their ancestral country. The story of their origins, the beautiful monarchy of Siam, the place Sureen left at the age of seven – Sureen who, if asked, has only fugitive memories of those early years. Fortunately, apart from the letters I've been sorting, Michael left us photographs of all our travels.

At present the collection may be of little interest to my grandsons, but one day I hope the boys will open the albums, and if I'm no longer around, both Michael and I owe them their history.

In the sixties Thailand was full of unwanted children; abandoned, orphaned, disabled, unacceptable, they filled institutions with their smell and extended bellies and hands that surreptitiously curled round the fingers of every visitor who crossed the threshold. Anyone who thought that taking an abandoned baby, and giving it a home, would be simple had no idea that every question they asked in the world of bureaucracy floated like dandelion seed into the air and landed nowhere.

Walking through homes full of disowned children led us into worlds full of anguish and nebulous answers, through a twilight zone of equivocation and heartbreak. No boundaries, no recognisable logic, no prescribed system, and always, built into the situation, were smiles and questions without answers. As with many endeavours that start with a plan and an assumed outcome, had we known from the beginning would we, like Robert Frost, have taken the other road instead of the 'one less traveled by'? The one, in fact, that 'has made all the difference'?

Why were we doing this? There is no rational answer. Rather it was a motley collection of influences. The country? The times babies had been offered to us for sale in the more remote provinces where we travelled? Our neighbour's child – plucked from an orphanage – who often came to play 'cooking' and 'shops' with Tamsin in a corner of our compound? How do you rationalise something that has gestated from goodness knows where while living at the forefront of life?

Sometimes it's better not to ask the question when the only response is a dusty one.

We visited places where babies were for sale, where two toddlers shared one cot; homes for prostitutes' babies; nurseries housing babies left on clinic benches; institutions for older children abandoned in a fallow waste for ever waiting to be claimed. The mandrake shriek of a baby – a torn root drawn the length of the ward – the sound of a child ceaselessly banging its head against the wall – the deformity of malnutrition – pleading fingers reaching through the bars . . . The search became a recurring ordeal; we were groping and everything felt warm. Hard answers were impossible to find.

'You want baby?' – smiling – 'No problem! Which one you want?' The question, direct, simple, was too raw to answer. Despondent, we geared ourselves up each time to face the ordeal of walking among children with indifference that belied our inner turmoil.

The system appeared straightforward. It worked like this. Thais who sought a child to bring up as a kind of servant and handy helper about the place could take a child without any formalities. The method was not as heartless as it sounds. We saw this at first hand. A family living next door to us that had a young girl from an orphanage used her for carrying the shopping and to run errands; she went to school, came to our house to play with Tamsin and – most crucially – had a place she called 'home'. Conditioned by our way of looking at things, we may think this cavalier, of dubious morality, but in fact it was a workable alternative to leaving a child to moulder away in limbo.

That was the way it worked for the Thais. For foreigners it was something else altogether. We needed pieces of paper, official permission, a passport and a legal adoption that would allow us to take the child out of the country.

One day – God knows how long after visiting countless institutions and receiving the usual equivocal responses – we were told of two possible babies for adoption, except, as usual, details were elusive. No one knew if the parents could be traced, were in prison or in an asylum, or had promised to return. A young girl showing us round, twittering helpfully by our side, explained that the 'high person' was not there that day, but 'You come back. You take. Mother not want baby.'

Amidst the sour smell of urine, rubber sheeting, damp bedding and humid concrete I wrote the names of two children on the inside of my diary. In one almighty stroke, by a random gesture, by a hair's breadth, we were about to change a child's life and our own.

The next time we could get to Bangkok we would try again. But it was weeks before we could return. We had no telephone, there was no way of making an appointment – anyway that sort of thing was moonshine; appointments were bunkum. The only way was to drive the slow road to Bangkok, taking the chance that we might find the 'high person' on the premises. We visited again, but she wasn't there.

We stayed overnight with Malcolm (my saviour when I'd been bitten by the sea snake) and, because the orphanage was on the north side of the city, we tried again. We were lucky; the principal was there that day. Serene, smiling, without an inkling of how portentous the occasion was, nor how casually we'd decided to deviate from the main road on our way home, the matron led us into her office. We showed her the two Thai names in my diary. One had already gone, she told us, but that one, pointing to the name on the page, was still available. She led us into the nursery. Here were the children whose days were spent in boredom and lassitude, deprived of identity, language or love, yet once an adult moved towards them, paused to speak or held out a hand, their response was immediate. Their desire for attention was pitiable. Sureen was no different. Propped up in a corner of a playpen with three others, her smile was instantaneous.

'You can have this one if you like,' the matron said, picking her up and holding her out. (But I wasn't going to put my arms round her until I need never put her down again.) The look on the child's face as the matron replaced her on the floor was catastrophic as she remarked, 'No one will want her because her father is a prince. It would be a loss of face for a royal baby to be discovered in an orphanage.'

In the past, royal progeny were so numerous that titles spread like veins throughout the dynasties, making it necessary in the following five generations for each prince or princess to lose a grade. This meant that great-great-grandchildren born to the monarch finished up as Mister or Miss. The father of the child on offer to us – as a descendant of King Chulalongkorn – had the title of *Mom Rajawongse*, the Honourable (whose own father was *Mom Chao*, Serene Highness) and his daughter, being one notch down, had the lowest title, *Mom Luang*. This made it undesirable for any Thai family to take a child with such majestic lineage to bring up as a servant. Any children the daughter had would inherit the royal title *Na Ayudhaya*. Inevitably, nowadays, as monarchs no longer have several consorts, the system is on the decline. (There's a satisfactory sequel to this. Many years later, in 1979, Sureen's first job after leaving the London School of Contemporary Dance was to take the part of one of her ancestors at the London Palladium. She danced as a 'minor wife' in *The King and I* with Yul Brynner and Virginia McKenna.)

Back in the office, sitting on chairs with overstuffed embroidered cushions covered with plastic that stuck to our backs, we faced the principal. Behind her stood a glass-fronted cabinet with an unopened tin of Johnson's Baby Powder and a collection of toys (given by kindly charity ladies) that were never distributed.

'You see, the staff would take the toys home unless we kept the cupboard locked,' she said, giggling behind her hand, and then added disarmingly, 'You can take the child now, today.'

Stunned, deflected from our assumption that certain formalities should be observed before actually taking a child, Michael said, 'Give us time to think. This isn't how we planned it . . . Goodness! We haven't even a bed for her.' I said, 'Of course we'll take her.'

How naively innocent of us, enticed by the gentle charm and good humour of the Thai faced by the unsubtle onslaught of the Westerner's idea of doing business! There is oriental amorphism – or there are shopping lists. Solutions evolve, they are not tabulated. No notes, no registration, no birth certificate or health records. No one even asked for our names and address.

Sureen was handed to us naked. The garment she was wearing was needed for another child. (How strange she felt, like a peeled stick. What was I doing with this small creature lying across my shoulder whose contours, weight and smell felt alien?) With bones deformed by malnutrition, a runny nose, a black front tooth and a scarred forehead (from a fall or abuse?), she was still unable to speak. Smiling, the matron assured us as we left that if we changed our minds we could always bring her back.

We were incredulous: 'Are we talking about a human being or a commodity?' She was ours for keeps. There was no question.

How many times since then – long after that day – have I looked at Sureen with a sense of perturbation at the fortuitous moment when, almost casually, we carried her back with us? But I haven't forgotten all the shadowy children – the ones we didn't take home.

Unsure of her age, her health, or whether she was deaf or dumb, we bought Sureen some clothes and then went straight to a missionary hospital in Bangkok to consult an American paediatrician. Sometimes missionaries with their zeal and dedication are infallible oracles when it comes to scientific answers. This kindly doctor took on the screaming child, going over her from top to toe, and handed her back with wise advice: 'I'd say she's more than two years old but less than three. Look, she still has her Mongolian mark.' And she pointed to what appeared as a bruise at the base of Sureen's spine. 'Asian babies have it for their first year or two. The black birthmark is a relic of the capacity of the skin to produce red blood cells in the womb. Post-partum this capacity fades, but in newborn Asiatic children the evidence remains.' Her smile was reassuring. 'She's neither deaf nor dumb, her squint will cure itself, the scars will heal, and, with care and nourishment, her bones will straighten. Worm her immediately – she's sure to have a tapeworm, they all do – and if you intend taking her from the country you'll have to get a birth certificate for her. Good luck and God bless you.'

Thus Sureen entered our family. When I think of the arbitrary way we found her, I can only believe in some strange sense that we had been moving towards each other long before she was put into our arms. Pathetic, unloved, communicating by tears not words – for no one in the home had time to talk to her – she responded with immediate enthusiasm to everything on offer. Food of course. But bathing, childish rhymes, lullabies, toys of her own and, above all, love. She accepted it all as though she had never known any other life. But bedtime was a contest. Tamsin, delighted to share her bed with her new sister, was most upset when it didn't work. Sureen had never slept in a bed, just lain on a mat among other bodies. For weeks the only way I could get her settled was to lie on the floor beside her, my arms enfolding her as a cat lies with her kittens until she fell asleep. In a tropical climate the floor is the coolest place to lie, but without supporting children surrounding her Sureen rolled during the night until by morning I had to extricate her from under the chest of drawers.

In our small town it was soon spread about that the *ferang*s (the people with 'rice water eyes') had brought back a child from Bangkok.

'Why such a black one?' asked the governor's wife, a woman who was always asking me to order face cream from England to whiten her skin, with disarming frankness. The colonel's wife remarked gloomily, 'She won't be able to eat your kind of food of course.' Little did she know that our 'kind of food' was Thai, and every course which appeared at the table was greeted by arms outstretched and wails of desperation from Sureen, fearful that unless she was quick she'd miss out on what was on offer. It took weeks before she felt secure that there would be more food tomorrow.

Sureen learned to speak Thai and English simultaneously. How enviably easy it is to learn a language at that age, and if at times her words slid about overlapping one with the other, it was an engaging confusion. Tamsin and Sureen became bilingual companions, intermeshed so closely that I doubt if they thought about their dissimilar origins. And what endless giggles they had together when 'cow pat' was on the menu. *Khao phat* was the mainstay as we travelled by train around the country or stopped to buy a dish of rice from a street vendor.

In spite of her insecure origins, Sureen has grown up to be the most generous person I have ever known. Irrepressible, any excuse and she arrives loaded with presents. She finds it impossible to meet her nieces without bringing them a collection of pretty clothes. Lasting psychological damage may occur in the first year of a child's life, and there was certainly deprivation in hers, yet despite her agitation at meal times in the beginning, it's Sureen whose arms are now outstretched in the act of giving.

Of course I had moments of panic. How could I not? Questions kept me awake night after night. David, being much older, already had his own identity, but what about Tamsin, now a four-year-old who suddenly had a ready-made sister? I was aware that for her, a younger sibling coming into the family as a baby growing in her mother's body was very different from a two-year-old deliberately brought in from 'outside'. Tamsin might well feel usurped, particularly as Sureen from the start was an extrovert child with none of the tranquillity assumed to be inherent in orientals. She might have been my mother's natural grandchild, their temperaments were so similar. Whenever Sureen erupted, her demands rang through the household with a resonance that pulverised us all. Tamsin, a quiet child, found offers of hugs and teddies repudiated. While the tantrum lasted Sureen was impossible to placate; nothing could deflect her outburst until she decided for herself that it was time to stop. The following calm was a form of benediction.

I was also aware that we would be taking a child away from a place where her appearance was unremarkable. We were cutting her link with centuries of hereditary proprieties, louche tendencies and the profundity of Buddhism, replacing it with coarsened gestures, imposing our history, language and education. Yet watching her asleep I was appeased, knowing that, long before labels or nationality, she was just a child. Why anticipate complications?

Quite fortuitously, Sureen's bonding with the family was in a motor car. It was the rainy season of August 1961. David was with us for the holidays, and long before we'd known about Sureen we'd promised him a journey north, to Chiang Mai and the mountainous wilderness beyond.

As we drove through teak forests David amused the children by playing the fool whenever it seemed their spirits were wilting, keeping them happily curled up on the back seat, reluctant even to be winkled out when we stopped.

(Years later, when both Tamsin and Sureen were grown up, David – now production manager at Times Books in London – became their most reliable saviour in moments of crisis. On several occasions Michael and I called on him to drop everything and salvage some problem that required good-humoured and brotherly retrieval. He never failed us.)

Before the main highway had been constructed, journeys north during the monsoon meant taking spades and a towrope.

Progress was slow. Parts of the road consisted of corrugations of mud. Long before we were anywhere near Chiang Mai, we had to stop for the night. A village 'brotel', as it was called amongst foreigners, was basic but welcoming. The proprietor even insisted on moving the tables and chairs in the bar to allow us to drive our car indoors overnight. He didn't want anything to be stolen while we were his guests.

Sureen in every way except legally was now ours. But there lay the quandary: we were due to go to England on leave in April 1962; but as there was no formula at that time for foreigners to adopt a child, we waded into a morass of red tape. The majority of children in the orphanages were not actually available for legal adoption. Parents could not be traced, refused permission, were temporarily ill or promised to return but never did. And if the parents were married, the father's permission was needed to sign the adoption papers, yet half the time there was no record of the parents' marital status.

As soon as we thought we'd found the right office, clerk, piece of paper, signature, we were sent in another direction. We learned the Siamese art of getting nowhere while sipping coloured water in numerous public welfare departments with overhead fans and strategically placed spittoons. Finally in one – the women's hospital – we triumphantly acquired Sureen's birth certificate.

'That is the easy part,' said Prawanee, the lawyer whom we employed to negotiate the adoption. 'But nothing can be done unless by hook or by crook you have the father's signature on the forms.' The father! Good God. Who and how? And where was he? For all we knew the man we were seeking might be surfing on Bondi Beach.

'Of course . . . you understand . . . there are easier methods. You know . . . hanky-panky . . . a little monkey business.' Prawanee looked at us across her desk, inscrutable, dead earnest. 'It's a piece of cake if you can pay someone to sign in his place.' She saw our reaction.

'Oh yes, it is often done. You must hold out a carrot to certain people in offices and so forth and so on.'

But we wanted everything to be legal. We were dealing with a child, not authenticating a shady deal, and we lived in dread of failing and having to return Sureen to institutional no-man's-land. Without officialdom's stamp on every piece of paper it would be futile to go to the British Embassy in Bangkok to apply for a passport for her.

Anyone who has tried to penetrate bureaucratic entanglements abroad will understand how happiness depends on martinets. The worst kind, the ones who pick their teeth while talking to you, who wear dark glasses and flashy watches, and keep a row of miniature bottles of Cointreau, Grand Marnier and Scotch whisky among Dunlop-tyre ashtrays and Carlsberg beer mats on their desks. Passed from corridor to department, anteroom to office, person to person, we found the process to be fiendish. We felt as though we were being held up, not so much by red tape, but by the aimless leads we pursued towards oblivion. Unable to think of anything else, I felt witless, out of control; suspended in a buffer state, I woke every morning distraught.

To live long in Asia is to know increasing bewilderment, but at last the hint of achievement presented itself. Through a random encounter, we were given a blurred newspaper photograph of Sureen's father and the name of the town where he was living. Lawyer Prawanee was cool. Unfazed, she reminded us, 'He is an important man – what you call "a bigwig". We must now use someone suitable in the town to find out his address. He must be approached with kid gloves.'

The cuckoo clock hanging on the wall behind Prawanee's head struck ten alpine notes, instantly crystallising our impatience into Swiss pragmatism.

'I will look for someone up-to-the-mark who will discover if the father is willing to sign the necessary papers.'

I couldn't speak. The love of clichés sprinkled through the language of those who had learned English through old-fashioned phrase books usually delighted us, but not now, with Sureen's future 'hanging on a thread'. Nothing would ever be funny while apprehension, perplexity and frustration bordering on despair had taken over.

'I shall make inquiries. I can pull the wires, you will see. No problem! Meanwhile you must get a certificate to prove that the child's parents were legally married.' It seemed that otherwise we'd have only needed the mother's signature, but why hadn't she told us before? So much time wasted.

We got up to go. As we made the *wai* gesture – palms together, head inclined – to each other, Prawanee smiled. 'Leave it in my hands; I shall leave no stone unturned.'

Michael and I were despondent, chafing at the invisible obstacles forever delaying our progress as once more we drove back over the potholed road to our town.

Yet miraculously – weeks later – our lawyer 'gave us the nod' to board an overnight train for the distant town where Sureen's father was living.

At that time Thai trains were magnificent things: polished bottle-green or black with brass fittings; punctual, fired by wood, they panted patiently at every station while a man continuously swept the floor from one end of the train to the other. (Footprints on a lavatory seat were puzzling until we realised that squatting was the natural position for defecation.) None of the carriages were air-conditioned, so at every station we leaned out of open windows to buy food from children running the length of the platforms. Grinning, they scrambled and shoved, offering us coffee in evaporated-milk tins hanging on shreds of raffia; pieces of cooked chicken coated with curry paste; chunks of pineapple threaded on twine; coconuts with drinking straws implanted through the shells. Woven trays, loaded with whatever fruit was in season, were thrust towards us by smiling, pleading faces, impossible to ignore. This was one of the great pleasures of train travel. A pleasure that has been lost since air-conditioned carriages were installed and passengers sealed from contact with children, passing smells and sounds from forest or village. Buying cooked food from itinerant vendors was always safe compared to other Asian countries.

To the soporific clacking and rocking of an express train going at thirty miles per hour, we travelled through agricultural landscape scattered with thatched houses on stilts. By dawn we were among uninhabited hills and deeply forested gullies; we passed a man cleaning his teeth beside a stream; a girl sitting outside a shop at work on a treadle machine with a cloth modestly covering her legs. *Samlor*s filled with four or five blue-and-white-uniformed children on their way to school waited at a crossing, and vendors carrying food on poles across their shoulders walked along dykes bordering the paddy fields.

This was to be the final journey. It had to be. We were slowly being destroyed by legal uncertainties. All the hours spent in municipal offices facing closed doors must lead us to this final denouement when we would confront Sureen's father with the fate of his child. Oblivious of what was closing in on him, we

were apprehensive of his reaction. To have foreigners corner-
ing him over a bit of his past would be embarrassing. How
would he react? Not that he had reasons to object, Prawanee
had assured us – 'No problem.' Although we had reached the
point of no return, she reminded us that he must be handled
with delicacy.

'Face' was everything, and his had to be preserved.

At the friend's house where we were staying, and through a
convoluted sequence of contacts, a message was relayed to us
that Sureen's father went to the barber at the same time every
day. At eight o'clock the following morning we were parked
in a tree-lined street, out of sight of the barber's, waiting to
confront the man. If that failed we were prepared to kidnap
him.

As he emerged we recognised him instantly from the newspaper cutting. He was good-looking and taller than most Thais.
We didn't hesitate. We walked up to him, introduced ourselves,
explained what we wanted and as deferentially as possible
press-ganged him into our car. Touching a stranger would have
been disrespectful, but I do remember how we stood either side
of him. We didn't frog-march him exactly, we kind of hustled a
bit without causing him embarrassment in the street. Anyway,
once in the car, we depended on him to direct us.

It was done. With unaffected grace and fatalism the man
was ours. Two hours in the district office was all that was
needed to fix what had been eluding us for months.

During those two hours our quarry made no attempt to
escape, or plead other appointments, or take evasive action.
Instead it was he who courteously explained to the official
what we had come about. Authoritative stamps on duplicated
forms were needed; carbon paper between pages; signatures
galore; the conversion of our parents' dates of birth to Siamese

years, all written in elegant script across pages in a book the size of a paving stone.

I thought of the child, the unloved infant ignorant of this momentous meeting, and I could have wept. While clerks padded barefoot to and fro bringing us glasses of pink water, the conversation between our hostage and us covered every subject but the one in hand. We'd already learned that the custom of never coming to the point for what seemed like hours of polite trivia had to be maintained. We spoke of the revered Queen Sirikit, discussed Thai silk, the temples of Bangkok, teak forests, elephants, orchids, the climate and whether, being foreigners, we could eat Thai food. Never once did the man refer to his child, ask where she was, show any interest in us, her future or why we were living in the country. His manners were impeccable, his reticence diplomatic.

Somewhere, in a small provincial town, there's an official book where this most consummating event was recorded authenticating our legal contract.

Before we left for leave in England we decided to get Sureen a Thai passport. The bureaucratic palaver for this was nothing compared to what had gone before, and although we could have put her on one of our passports it seemed imperative that we give her the option to reclaim her nationality in later years should she want to.

In London on 23 June 1962 we went through the British adoption procedure. The distinguished chairman of the Juvenile Courts, Baroness Wootton of Abinger, reputed to be outrageous and fierce at times, was intrigued to preside over a trans-racial adoption, which at that time was fairly unusual. She was charming and encouraging, and the sight of a three-year-old Siamese child blundering among two languages endeared Sureen to everyone in the court. She now had dual nationality. Some day in the future the choice could be hers.

Those critics who protested that we were removing Sureen from her culture can never have entered those infernal regions stacked with unloved children. If they had, they might have stopped to ask themselves, 'What culture?' Festering for years in an institution until puberty sends children one way or another is hardly likely to implant in them a deep feeling for their civilisation, which is why the current neurosis over trans-racial adoption misses the point. And to the question of how it is possible to feel the same for an adopted child as for one's own, anyone with more than one child knows each is different, that responses, shared pleasures, problems and empathy with one or other is special. My mother loved both her daughters. I knew she regarded Cordelia as her 'blessed first-born', which was something I could never be, but then I shared with her other things that were not my sister's territory. Did this make my mother love one of us more than the other?

I remember some years later, when we were living in Greece, the gauche question a German woman asked: 'But can you love an adopted child in the same way?' Then, looking at seven-year-old Sureen, she added, 'And anyway, who will marry her?'

The business of the umbilical cord is a red herring. Even so, with Michael's family, we had to tread carefully. Like so many with in-built frontiers, 'not one of us' was an assumed credo that applied to background, class or children. We decided to wait until we returned with Tamsin and Sureen to England before telling Michael's mother and sister that Tamsin had an Asian sister. This wasn't a problem for me, and, had they lived, I knew that both Phyllis and Cordelia would have approved. A child was a child. Free from moral, political, religious attitudes, 'not one of us' wasn't part of their vocabulary. Only the pragmatist classifies adoption as second best.

Sureen now has two sons. One was born with the Mongolian mark at the base of his spine authenticating his origins just as *Brighton* does through a stick of rock. Sureen's skin, hair, eyes label her, yes, but those are superficial traits. In every other way she is Anglo-Saxon. She was a child lifted out of a no-man's-land when, had the light fallen differently, she would have landed elsewhere.

Conversely, her sister feels un-rooted. Although Tamsin's fragmented education in Greece, Italy and Austria finished with her getting a first at an English university (where her Classics tutor told her she'd written a 'sizzling unseen') followed by a doctorate, growing up in different countries has left her in a strange way uncommitted. But not Sureen. Her identification with England was total, exemplified in London once when I happened to comment on the number of foreigners who stopped to ask me the way somewhere.

'How odd, Mummy, no one ever asks me.'

'Look in the mirror, Sureen, to see why they don't.'

She'd forgotten – a long, long time ago she had forgotten.

The Rain Tree (*samanea saman*)

In 1962 we moved north to Chiang Mai, once the capital of an independent kingdom. The invasion of American soldiers with handfuls of dollars on R & R from Vietnam had not yet started, nor had the country become polluted by tourists and entrepreneurs.

There was still innocence.

There was still the old Railway Hotel: a place redolent of Graham Greene with its wide carved-teak balconies, ceiling fans rhythmically creaking through sultry air, and coils of mosquito repellent, green and acrid, burning in saucers beside bamboo basket chairs. Nightly, beating a gong, the watchman walked along the lanes. On days when the royal family were in their northern palace, foreign kings and queens, presidents or diplomats were greeted at the airport with music and by dancing girls wearing spectacular headdresses and curved brass fingernails. Flanks of eager schoolchildren waving the relevant national flags jostled and giggled as royalty proceeded along the main street. For several weeks we lived in the Railway Hotel while we looked for a house and a school for the children. (The hotel has long since been pulled down, the population has grown, and hostelries of every sort have proliferated. The town is now a place on every tourist itinerary.)

We were exhilarated by our new venue: a change of pace; an absence of traffic; the hiss of *samlor* tyres on wet nights; the banshee voice of a girl wavering through the dark at a distant cremation – we felt excited by the northern-ness after the monotony of the south. Chiang Mai – famous for its silversmiths, weavers, wood carvers and lacquer ware craftsmen – had temples less glittery and opulent than those in Bangkok. Carved figures and birds of gold were barely visible through the umbrageous surroundings of frangipani trees, trees with the same symbiosis with temples as yew trees have with churches in Britain.

The house we moved into – within the secrecy of a seventy-foot rain tree – was wooden, built on stilts to withstand annual flooding during the monsoon of the river Mae Ping. The tree, also known as monkey pod or cow tamarind, and reckoned to be one of the most symmetrical trees in the world (the French have a more poetic name for it: *arbre à pluie*), dominated our lives. Early travellers believed that during the night its closed leaves allowed rain to trickle through as a gentle shower.

Among the branches were parasites: the orchids. They clung to their host with the sinuous tentacles of an octopus searching for its prey. Others with aerial roots reached into space for something to clasp like Gollum, the groping, lisping monster in *The Lord of the Rings*.

In contrast to our Lopburi house, this one beside the river had no embellishments. A vernacular building made of teak – the hardest and most durable wood – it had walls made from woven cane with floor-to-ceiling windows on three sides protected by shutters and mosquito netting. The teak floor, with gaps between the planks to allow for seasonal movement, meant that in the monsoon when the roof leaked we put pot plants beneath to catch the rain. In the dry season our bedroom appeared to be breathing from the sunlight and stippled shadows reflected off the river; we woke to the placid sound of the gardener watering below the window, to the whistling phrases of the common magpie robin, and to the bubbling song of red-whiskered bulbuls ransacking the *lamyai* trees, whose laden branches were supported by wooden frames. All day the birds gorged on fruit.

Opening the shutters at dawn to the watery pallor at the onset of the monsoon was a benison. Getting soaked in a country where rain is as warm as tears was inconsequential. Under sliding volumes of cumulus and the fluency of showers, we walked through a garden of rain-blotched leaves and predatory creepers throttling our trees. At other times rain falling in corded skeins flung pots of ferns from pedestals; cisterns overflowed; screens banged; unsecured shutters crashed against the house causing the woven walls to quiver. Driving the car at night, our headlights pierced shrouds of spray among the trunks of trees whose heads roared and swayed in a cataclysmic upheaval.

*　　*　　*

While we'd been living in Lopburi and Michael had been teaching adults at the teacher training college, I had volunteered to teach English in a primary school. The children, who had never been taught English before, were instantly responsive to the 'direct method' which meant a good deal of movement, gestures and, best of all, singing. They loved learning English through song. Their language, being tonal, seemed to give them a special aptitude for picking up tunes.

In Chiang Mai education was very different. There were missionaries. In remote places they worked among the tribes; in town were their two schools – Presbyterian and Catholic. When I was asked by the Mother Superior to teach at the Catholic school even after I'd admitted I wasn't one of them, I accepted. How could they not take me on – an agnostic, a fertile soul who had not yet found God? I was a challenge. The challenge was theirs, and all through the years I taught at Regina Coeli their prayers for my salvation never faltered.

Compared to the po-faced American Presbyterian school, mine – with nuns from France, Yugoslavia, Australia, Holland and Spain – was far more dynamic. So too were the Jesuits who taught at the university. (There was one, Father Goman, who when in mufti wore a T-shirt on which was written 'Go-Man Go!')

Few conversions were made among the students: it was more a matter of pragmatism. The nuns offered them the best education in the town – anything else came by the way.

I loved the nuns. One in particular, an elderly Irish sister, told me of her youthful days playing tennis before she took holy orders and went to Thailand in 1929. She was a constant and beloved friend who, ever optimistic, lent me books on the visionary French Jesuit Teilhard de Chardin and on converts such as Graham Greene and Evelyn Waugh, as well as biographies of both St Theresas – of Lisieux and Avila – hoping for my conversion.

Another nun told me in confidence that it wasn't necessary to be a virgin to be a nun. Was she offering me a chance, I wonder? And the first time I heard one of the nuns describing in Thai a pupil as 'mean', *khi neo*, I was surprised that, literally translated, she was saying 'sticky shit'.

Then there was my great friend, a young nun who taught me yoga.

'Come into the music room and I'll show you,' she said. In this tiny space, mostly taken up by a piano, she instructed me: 'Keep an eye out for Mother Superior.' An intimidating but charming French woman with the grace and courtesy of a socialite, she went on: 'Watch this. I'll show you the Candle.'

Of course I was watching. I couldn't take my eyes off her. Lying on the floor, raising her legs high, like a ship's sail unfurling her white robes revealed woolly white stockings and black buckled shoes. A shower of rosaries and crucifixes fell from her garments, and from under her stiff white collar, fallen across her face, she trumpeted, 'Now look' – as though I wasn't – 'this is the Plough.'

Over her head went her legs, knees round her ears, as, with a display of white bloomers, she proclaimed this position ideal for constipation.

During the years I was teaching at Regina Coeli, the instruction came from Rome that the nuns' uniform should be modified. No longer were their faces enclosed entirely with white wimples with not a hair showing; instead they wore a veil fixed at the back. Having never been exposed to the tropical sun, their skin was revealed as tender as a baby's. Laundering may have been simplified, but with the change of habit went a certain imposing magnificence.

After I returned to England I kept in touch with some of the nuns. My Irish sister, who enclosed decorated prayer cards in her letters, still prayed for my conversion. Among her letters is a scrap of paper on which, in a neat script, she'd written: 'There was needed nothing less than the labour, terrifying and anonymous of primitive man, and the long beauty of Egypt, and the anxious waiting of Israel, and the slowly distilled perfume of the oriental mysteries, and the wisdom one hundredfold refined of the Greeks, that, upon the stem of Jesse and of Humanity, the Flower could open.

'When Christ appeared in the arms of Mary, he lifted the world.'

No one has prayed for me since.

After the Lopburi market with its alleys awash with slop alongside the continual slurp and suck of the river, Chiang Mai was all about feet, their splayed precision, their practical adherence to the ground; each toe, separately jointed and allowing accumulated debris to ooze between the digits, was as elemental as the trays of produce we stepped between. Had I been an artist I'd have lain on my tummy to paint market life at ground level, where a single line would connect the earth to the produce as well as to the feet.

Through outsize umbrellas oiled against rain, suffused sunlight cast a glow as rubescent as old cabbage roses over the samples of halved fruit. A papaya with shiny black seeds exposed its coral flesh oozing drops of juice; segments of a mangosteen, with papery skin dark as 'Queen of Night' tulips, lay piled next to finely veined watermelons and 'prickly' rambutans reminiscent of sea anemones. Jackfruit, with knobbly skins, were heaped beside pomolo, custard apples, pineapples, varieties of bananas and sapodilla – a small brown fruit tasting of burnt sugar. Tamarind, bamboo shoots, chillies, jelly mush-rooms, soya beans and water chestnuts were massed alongside corrugated cucumbers and green aubergines the size of golf balls. Coconuts eased from their shells provided refreshing drinks through straws stuck in their flesh.

Caraway, turmeric, cinnamon and saffron filled the air with pungency: other odours less tempting included wet dog, washed-up wrack, rancid bone meal or mouldy leather. Most overpowering was the mordant tang of *kapi*. Roasted and wrapped in a banana leaf, *kapi* is the basis of a sauce made of dried shrimps, garlic, chillies, lime juice, tamarind, palm sugar and fish water that leaves piquancy on the tongue after eating it with raw or pickled vegetables.

In the north, glutinous rice, soaked in water before being steamed in a basket, was kneaded into a ball, then dipped with fingers into one of several savoury dishes; most delicious was sticky black rice when blended with cane sugar and covered with coconut milk.

Trays of *khanom* – sweet confections glistening in syrup – were morsels of gluttony. Folded in banana leaves with the dexterity of turned hems, these melliferous comfits made from fruit, sago, tapioca, lotus seeds, coconut and rice flour were steeped in jasmine or rose water. Our favourites were *foi tong*, golden strands made from pandanus (screw pine) leaves, sugar, eggs, perfumed water and jasmine-flower decoration. We would return home with shreds and blobs no bigger than a cotton reel, embellished with gold leaf. Any leftovers Tongdee would pass over our fence to novice monks from the neighbouring temple who came to chat her up when the abbot wasn't looking.

The Thai for eating is 'eat rice', for hunger 'hungry rice'. The simplicity of the grammar – no declensions, no conjuga-tions – is eclipsed by the hellish subtleties of tones: five of them

– middle, low, falling, high and rising. The joke on foreigners was to try them out on 'New wood doesn't burn, does it?' which requires the one word *mai* to be said in the five different tones. With a Sanskrit-type script of forty-four consonants and about thirty-two vowels or vowel combinations, the language is a linguistic trap.

For a long time, using the wrong tone, I called a child next door 'Pubic Hair'. Too polite to correct me, the girl always responded to her inappropriate name. And the gardener, when I asked him to put a pot of flowers in the sun, didn't flinch when I told him to put them in the genitals of a woman.

And *khi nok*, which means 'bird shit', called out by a little boy to a passing foreigner always prompted an appreciative but misconstrued smiling response.

During the four years we lived in Chiang Mai we became familiar with the seasonal ritual of rice-growing in the valley. Ploughing with water buffalo at the start of the rainy season was followed in early August by stooped figures – reflected upside-down in the flooded paddy – transplanting seedlings from the rice bed to the field. Slow and painstaking, the process had none of the fluid agility of reaping. In November the women cut bunches of rice with a curious sweep of their sickles, before the sheaves, heavy with grain, were carried on poles to the threshing ground by men taking small rapid steps. In late December the sheaves of ripe grain were either beaten on the threshing floor or else shaken loose by two buffalo walking round and round like a pair of black somnambulists. Most graceful of all was the sight of the women winnowing the grain. Tossing it into the air from shallow woven trays, they let the rice fall in a heap on the ground, leaving the chaff to float away in dusty drifts.

Every phase of the harvest was without urgency, ending with a procession of oxen, ponderous and clumsy, carrying the rice in high-wheeled carts to the granaries. Standing on tall legs to keep the grain out of reach of rats, these buildings were as handsome and as valuable to the villagers as their houses.

At first we'd had plans to explore the unmapped terrain beyond the encircling rice fields, venturing into mountains lapped in cloud and treetops where woodpeckers screamed among the foliage. But there were no roads, only tracks for pedlars and elephants, so we exchanged our car for a Land Rover. Most accessible was the umbrella village outside Chiang Mai. Here women and girls working under the raised houses, painting with rapid dexterity blowzy blooms of some unnamed genus. Finished, the umbrellas were laid in overlapping layers of glowing colours in the sunlight. Tamsin and Sureen took plain ones back with them to decorate at home.

Unlike the watery arteries that penetrated the landmass of Thailand, the Mae Ping – rising just across the border in Burma – carried no navigation: none of the life on barges, river buses and floating markets of Bangkok. Occasionally instead we'd see a leisurely column of elephants lumbering along on the opposite bank, more like a herd of cows returning to the meadow than a cavalcade of baggy creatures on their way to the jungle. When the river was low, a line of fishermen would wade forward in unison, tossing their nets in floating arcs sparkling with drops of water. Fat-bellied baskets with narrow necks hung from their waists for the catch. Only the smallest fish escaped.

And every morning at sunrise the daily ritual – hardly changed over two millennia – took place along the lanes where pots of water with coconut-shell ladles stood on shelves for the benison of passers-by. A procession of saffron-robed, shaven-headed monks with begging bowls would pause to receive offerings of food to be consumed before midday from the women emerging from their houses. Buddhist monks are forbidden to own anything; they depend on the necessities being given to them – their robes, soap, towel, food, tobacco and betel nut (for those addicted there's a book with the riveting title *Betel Chewing Equipment of East New Guinea*) – augmented on holy days by a bamboo 'money tree' sprouting leaves of one-baht notes. On the *katin*s, or feast days (and there were many throughout the year), the monks would receive lavish amounts of food. As well as bunches of purple lotus flowers they would return to the temple with copious helpings of curry, vegetables, rice and leaf-wrapped packets of *khanom*.

Michael and I used to go next door to the temple and join our neighbours sitting on the floor before a dais on which the monks sat cross-legged intoning prayers, cooling themselves with fans decorated with rabbits (odd, because we never saw a rabbit in Thailand). Among clusters of candles, the soporific scent of incense and the muted gold of Buddha figures, we temporarily entered their world. Incomprehensible and hypnotic, the rise and fall of their modulation removed any thoughts of a temporal existence. Their religion was benevolent, non-confrontational. No questions were asked; rather, it brought immediate harmony.

The cycle turned. Three clearly defined seasons displaced weather, changing the light and the mood, and for us, living beside the river, the volatility of days altered the tempo of our lives.

In the gummy heat of April, when the moon is full and lethargy returns like a malady, *songkran*, the Buddhist New Year, is celebrated. A few nights before the festival, the undertones of adults and children collecting sand from the river would reach us from beyond our garden. By spreading sand over the temple ground they gained merit, the same motive behind the sale of small caged birds which would be bought and then released. But freedom was short-lived. Easily re-caught, they would be sold by boys back to the original vendors, who perpetuated the transactions by bringing merit to everyone except the birds.

Within the temple a less materialistic method was gained from women sprinkling sacred water on the figure of the Buddha. *Songkran* – once a decorous festival when families came to pay homage to their elders, who blessed them with water in silver bowls – had become a light-hearted and good-humoured celebration. Like the rest of the town, we waded into the shallow river, where everyone splashed each other till we became soaked. In the streets people threw buckets of water – often from trucks – to drench passers-by. Everyone was easy prey. Hapless tourists, travelling in open *samlor*s and regarded as fair game, were not always amused. The rest of us behaved with childish abandon and later, with adult stoicism, put up with a cacophony of drums, gongs and chanting from our temple throughout the night.

Courteous and gentle, the monks often invited us to their rituals, including their most sacred, the Birth, the Enlightenment and the Death of the Buddha. *Visakha Buja* took place in May, when chanting and praying went on continuously, culminating in a candlelit procession round the temple. The monks, their begging bowls full to overflowing – ask for nothing, refuse nothing – shared the superfluity with us. A group of figures followed by child-attendants carrying a surplus of edible offerings processed down our path bringing a *khan tohk* table, a low, lacquered tray on a pedestal bearing many of the choicest perquisites. Given the dignity of their progress and their robes the colour of the canna lilies flanking the path, the bizarre occasion was emotive and surreal.

The memory remains preserved for ever like a bug in amber.

The season changed, the tranquillity of the solstice came with the first full moon bringing the three-day festival of *loi krathong*. In contrast to the hilarity of chucking water over each other at *songkran*, the Festival of Lights was quiescent. Secretive and supplicatory. In miniature boats made from pieces of furled banana leaves, galaxies of candles floated down the river, each one carrying tokens of belief in the beneficence of kindly spirits: incense, a coin, a flower and a candle whose light while it lasted bore the prayers of those who launched it. Throughout the town – on gate posts and window sills flanking paths or carried by hand – were hundreds of candles. Shadows enlarged and diminished in air cleansed by rain.

One year Karen and Thanin Kraivixien (Thanin became prime minister in 1976 but was deposed by the military in 1977) and their five children were with us. Karen was Danish: the mixture of their ancestry produced startlingly beautiful children. Sitting beside the river with them, our children and Tongdee – having cast our boats down river – we watched hundreds of lights pass by the bank before disappearing round the bend accompanied by sighs of regret when one foundered. Ribbons of candlelight diminished in the brilliance of a full moon.

As the last light within the foliage of our rain tree turned the orchids along the branches luminous, I waited for dusk to deepen. Slumped in lassitude from the humidity, I gazed up at flowers – like butterflies poised for flight – dependent for life on their predatory roots. The temperature dropped; the humidity eased. Skin separated from skin.

From the crook of a tree a chameleon – five inches of prehistory – clung by its prehensile tail as it changed from madder to opaque mud. Immobile, it watched as I walked among the bougainvillea. The scent from the unclenched buds of the frangipani, funereal and heavy, overwhelmed a jasmine suffusing the evening with perfume so impenetrable that I pushed out my hands to move the scent aside. A voyeur, I put my eye to the interior of a canna lily as translucent as a boiled sweet, to watch a green insect violating the pistil of the flower. A kingfisher, a streak of brilliant turquoise, skimmed across the surface of the river. Red-whiskered bulbuls, shuffling among the *lamyai* trees, and the clack of armoured beetles hurling themselves against a lamp were the only sounds.

As I walked towards the house, the tang of chillies, onion and garlic roasting over charcoal engulfed the soporific fragrance of the garden. Thailand is a country of smells – ambrosial or nauseous – nothing smells middling. The hot northern sauce, *nam prik deng*, was being prepared in the kitchen to accompany glutinous rice: a classic dish of Chiang Mai.

Sorrel was coming to dinner.

We had met her at a party the night before. How enigmatical is the chemistry of friendship. For most of my life this aspect of instinctive warmth to one person but not to the other has been something out of my control. From the moment we met Sorrel we instantly recognised some indefinable fusion that made her stand out amongst the others in the room. As she lived at the other end of town we brought her home with us.

Next morning, lying spread-eagled across a divan, her limbs flung about like discarded appendages, her face pale from a hangover, any vestige of human stamina was absent. Distant songs on a radio, sung in strangulated androgynous voices, interspersed our conversation.

'I'm spinning out of the frame,' she mumbled, gazing myopically at Michael.

As an overseas volunteer Sorrel worked at the municipal asylum, a grim place: a Hogarthian madhouse set down in the tropics where the ostentatious entrance and fountain balancing ping-pong balls on waterspouts were bait for government functionaries convincing Western mandarins to grant cash to the asylum.

But go where Sorrel goes.

Go beyond the colourful façade to a world where centuries drop away to medieval bedlam. Inmates wearing loose cotton garments shuffle due to a mind-numbing lack of stimulation. The smell of soiled people was her home for two years: a wooden shack, a small bedroom, a lavatory/washroom and a porch with a table and bamboo chair.

The governor, hoping for a quiet life, expected a *ferang* to add prestige to the asylum and bring in Western aid, not someone like Sorrel, a termagant with radical ideas. She understood the inmates' blank stares out of eyes like pebbles, their lack of curiosity; drugged, their passivity was assured. Discovering some patients permanently locked up, she went berserk. For the first time in years she gave them access to move freely in the compound. The more docile ones she took on outings, saying, 'The airport's their favourite place.'

Sorrel and her troupe of shuffling figures became a familiar sight, gathering crowds of jeering children as she made her Pied Piper amble up the road to the airport. The sight of a foreigner accompanying a line of 'lunatics' was too good to miss.

'Idiots, idiots!' the children yelled. In the eyes of adults she was demeaning herself. She was losing face.

Sometimes Sorrel sang to them. The repetitive verses of 'Where Have All the Flowers Gone?' held them fascinated, nodding with pleasure, shuffling closer, nudging, drooling, staring beyond the realms of sanity, spellbound. Nothing like this had happened before in their damaged lives as she encouraged them to dance and sing – anything to bring back dormant responses. Her spectacular 'miracle' was the day it 'rained' cigarettes. From an upstairs window Sorrel tossed out handfuls, to their joy and bewilderment.

How could we not fall for Sorrel, not offer her a refuge from her institution, not include her in family outings into the wilderness of distant mountains?

I look at the photograph of her sprawled across our divan and remember a certain evening when Michael and I were on the veranda waiting for Sorrel.

It was dusk. Silvery moths appeared and disappeared in the assembling shadows; bee-eaters had ceased pursuing insects on the wing; flowerpeckers and sunbirds had deserted the garden; the crickets and the rusty croaking of frogs started their discordant undertow as a single rasp set others off one by one. And from far off we heard the large-tailed nightjar, the tok-tok bird whose monotonous note was background to the scene by the river.

Presently the monks in the temple beyond our garden began chanting a legend of the Buddha in Pali with the same continuous intoning as a drone on a bagpipe. The hour was magic, heat was dispelled, and for a brief while human beings were nicer than at midday.

Into the circle of light Sorrel walked through the garden wearing a cotton blouse and a *pasin* (a piece of ankle-length material folded into a pleat held in place by a silver belt), carrying a gift of sliced green mango, sprinkled with powdered ginger and coarse sugar, wrapped in a leaf. Tonight, rather than Thai whisky (based on glutinous rice, yeast, molasses and mould, and described by one old inhabitant as 'the best drink of its kind east of Suez'), it was martinis. Michael's were lethal. The alcohol steamed as he poured it into freezing glasses with rims wiped with lime: 'A good martini should cling to the glass like tears.'

After one sip the temporal bones in the skull ached. Much later we floated indoors to eat chicken cooked in coconut milk flavoured with lemon grass; slices of the strange root *kha* (galangal); a *som tom* salad of green pawpaw and raw beans dressed with lime juice.

Drinking coffee on the balcony, mellow, relaxed in the balmy darkness, the monosyllabic 'ook, ook' of a Scops owl audible from across the river, Sorrel, temporarily freed from the asylum, spoke of her life and loves in the crazy world where she lived at the other end of town: 'I must tell you. I've met a man in the most unromantic circumstances imaginable and we've fallen in love. It happened like this.'

Sorrel was to escort an asylum inmate back to a Yao village north-east of Chiang Mai. Into a sparsely inhabited mountainous region beyond the cultivated plain where, across the invisible frontiers of Laos, Burma, China and Thailand, live the hill tribes: the Lao, Karen, Meo, Lahu, Lisu and Yao, who live by growing maize, rice and opium poppies. Their diet was mainly maize and pork; their income came from opium harvested when the poppy petals had fallen and the pods were slit for resin that oozed, hardened and sometimes was smoked in its raw state before being refined into morphine and heroin. Speaking diverse languages, wearing embroidered costumes, silver jewellery and outlandish headdresses, the tribes were popular with American graduates chasing PhDs in anthropology.

The journey by bus and ox wagon would be arduous. For Sorrel it was an adventure that resulted in a Jewish anthropologist from St Louis coming to the rescue of a girl with cholera.

Before she left Chiang Mai, a cyclone in China resulted in unprecedented rainfall. Far to the north precipitation had turned streams and rivers into torrents, creating a deluge that, once it reached the Mae Ping, was cataclysmic. The whole of the lower town of Chiang Mai was flooded.

Stealthily at first the water rose beside our house. Wooden markers we stuck in the ground under the 'Bead Tree', so-called for its yellow berries, were submerged in minutes as the Mae Ping, grown turbid with sediment, flowed past like a mobile arboretum caught in spate. Water swirled round the posts holding up our house. Inundating the garden, it gushed out of the gate, into the temple and on down the road where, surging through the school to the delight of the children, it swept among houses until it merged with other water, consolidating into one uncontrollable force. The town was afloat. Overnight Chiang Mai metamorphosed just as European cities are transformed by snowfall.

When the flood receded, leaving drinking water polluted by sewage, cholera spread with catastrophic speed. Too late every child was inoculated; no one could enter the market without a jab; each passenger arriving by car, bus, plane or train was accosted by a girl with a hypodermic. The hospital filled until, like effluence, patients overflowed into the grounds, creating a macabre scene for a painting by Hieronymus Bosch. The sick lay outside on beds with holes cut in their bases, with a bucket underneath for those too weak to reach the pole spanning a pit. (Rising clouds of flies indicated when the pole was in use.) Other patients squatted beside their beds: the result was a rapid outbreak of cholera throughout the town.

Cholera is an undignified and charmless disease. Diarrhoea, vomiting and violent cramps need instant medical attention. Dehydration, the imbalance of body fluids, can result in death within twenty-four hours. When it struck Sorrel – miles from a tarmac road – her only chance of survival, having neither drugs nor the replacement of salt, glucose and potassium chloride, was for someone to continuously pour water through her body.

Into this unromantic situation Piers – an American anthropologist studying the Yao tribe – appeared as a guardian angel. No trumpets, no wings, but with a conscience and a love of humanity. The limp figure of Sorrel lying in the dark corner of a wooden shack roofed with overlapping teak leaves – weak, soiled, her hair matted – had been left alone by villagers fearful of touching the body of a stranger, not so much through superstition but through custom.

Piers, recognising that Sorrel would die if neglected any longer, took charge. He had to replace the liquid that was running out of her by forcing water down as fast as she could swallow. As she was too weak to protest, he cleaned her up and changed her clothes, then organised a bullock cart to get her to the nearest track. Water and time were vital. If either failed – without medication – there was no way of saving her life. He guessed it would be a five-hour journey to the nearest logging camp where teak trees were felled and floated down the river and where, most crucially, he would find a jeep.

Piers's life in St Louis had not been happy. His parents kept strictly kosher; Hanukkah, Passover, Purim, Rosh Hashanah, Yom Kippur were all observed; quantities of sour cream, cheese curds and eight days of eating latkes were the norm; a curmudgeonly father and terrifying mother ran the household. As a child Piers had watched his mother stabbing a needle through cloth or hoovering up spiders with intense spitefulness. Animosity billowed round the house while he cringed in terror until old enough to escape. He fled to the freedom of academia.

At university he did well. He achieved his doctorate and had a promising future until he contracted polio, leaving him with an imperceptible limp and maimed self-confidence. To prove he was not a cripple, he took up skiing. He became a fearless cross-country skier, pushing himself to the extreme whether under a blue sky among cones of drifted snow, flutings, funnels and spindrift or among fractured ice, crevasses and blizzards. His physical shortcomings fell away, but it was not enough – he needed something more.

Meeting Piers for the first time, with his taciturn expression, people found him prickly, defensive. Treading warily, he moved with caution, waiting until he knew a person well enough to feel at ease. Later they would discover a compassionate heart that belied his gritty exterior.

'I remember nothing of our departure. I suppose I was unconscious,' said Sorrel. 'Later I was aware of an arm holding me up, forcing water down me, lifting me down to squat beside the cart. What an obscenity. But what did it matter? There are times when dignity is irrelevant. I felt so ill . . . with such cramps that at times I raged at Piers "I'm dying, dying!" but all he said was "It's still no reason for being bad-tempered."

'That was the moment I fell in love.'

The journey down the mountain in a wheeled bullock cart with curved shafts of silvery-textured wood, normally used for carrying rice from the winnowing ground to the granary, was not ideal for the invalid. Juddering over every rut, Sorrel's ankles, hips and arms rattled like a puppet's when the strings are loosened. Piers walked alongside murmuring of nights hearing the desolate wail of a train crossing the continent of America, the fog horn in San Francisco, the first time he had heard the liquid trill of a curlew and the call of a muezzin, although he knew she wasn't listening.

Once they left the mountains, a dense tree canopy closed over their heads as they made their way through the vernal grandeur of the forests that still existed then in northern Thailand. Teak leaves the colour of burnt almonds lay in their path like deceiving stones; overhead racket-tailed drongos flew among shelf upon shelf of foliage. The metallic bluish-green birds have two twelve-inch tails narrow as ribbons, with feathers at their tips that appear like a pair of bumblebees flying in the birds' wake.

Hours later, when they reached the logging outpost, one glance at the collapsed malodorous figure in the back of the wagon brought offers of transport, more water and cloths in which to wrap Sorrel, who by now was insensible. And when finally they arrived at Chiang Mai Hospital, Piers was relieved but wary of leaving her: he'd been long enough in the country to know patients were dependent on their families to do the nursing. It was not unusual to find a grandfather reposing in a bed while the ousted patient lay underneath it among his relatives who'd come along for the novelty. A doctor, back from medical training abroad, told Piers that it was impossible to teach his staff mouth-to-mouth resuscitation: 'Lips were considered unclean. A few nurses tried but only through gauze. In the end I gave up.'

Cholera is an acute infection, but for those who survive it leaves no lasting effect. Sorrel, when she was recuperating, wanted to know why: 'Why did you do it, Piers? The journey, I mean.'

'Well . . . what would you have done? You don't stand by while someone is dying. Action was imperative and no one else was doing a thing.' He shrugged, teasing her gently. 'Anyway I needed a change from anthropology – it was a fortuitous break.'

Michael got up to bring us more drinks. A river snake slid into the water with the sound of an exhaled breath. Sorrel continued: 'When we met I was a washed-up stranger and he . . .' – Sorrel made vague gestures in the air – 'he appeared like a heaven-sent apparition with strong arms, brown eyes, a smile that lit up his saturnine features, and he spoke my language. He rents a small house in Chiang Mai where he writes up his notes. In his village he hasn't any privacy. Even the place to wash and defecate is a kind of sentry box with a raised bamboo floor surrounded by a loosely woven screen. The kids love to stare through the gaps. They can't believe anyone can be so hairy.'

'Where are you now, in your relationship?'

'Out of my mind – he fills my horizon. I fell for his oddly farouche manner.'

Sorrel walked to the edge of the veranda.

'We hyperventilated in each other's company. Making love we became ossified one to the other . . . at other times he cooked. He liked making paste with crabs from the paddy fields, and steaming rice in those baskets with black-and-white patterns you find in the market. As I can't cook – I've no room in my shack – I sang songs instead.'

And into the darkness full of nocturnal latency she sang, ' "For the leaves they will wither and the roots they will decay,

And the beauty of a fair young maid will soon fade away, Oh
. . . will soon fade away," until we fell into each other's arms.
God, it was fantastic.'

The affair engulfed them. Communication was impossible:
Sorrel was in Chiang Mai, Piers in the mountains. No phone,
no post. They endured their periodic separations with impatience and a total lack of stoicism.

'Unlike the missionaries, who do their best to convert,'
Sorrel told us as we returned one day from the market, 'Piers
has no intention to "save" the hill tribe he's working with. He
wants their confidence. He speaks their dialect, though once,
when he was offered dog's penis served with root ginger, he
did baulk. "Sorry but I don't like ginger!" But the missionaries fail, they're too earnest . . . apparently a Presbyterian had
told him of a colleague sent to a remote tribe they were trying
to convert in South America, who had, after several airlifts
of food to soften them up, been dropped in by parachute. He
was never heard of again. It was assumed he'd been taken as
another edible contribution!'

Another day with Sorrel, when the call of a brainfever bird – a
parasitic cuckoo repeating a series of descending notes alternat-
ing with a plaintive ascending scale and known in Malaysia as
the 'dead child bird' – could be heard across the river, she told
us that Piers had taken her to his village: 'The people were so
friendly. I wanted to live forever among them and be his Rima, I
told him as we went for a walk, like in Hudson's *Green Mansions*
. . . and when our daughters were marriageable they could . . .
as the village girls do . . . tie a pair of gourds to their sashes as
symbolic testicles that'd clatter provocatively at the young men
and get them rich husbands with droves of black pigs.'

In a pool of clear water they cleansed the dust from their
bodies and Sorrel, floating, with hair swaying like weed round

her head, stared up through layers of green cavities perforated by shafts of sunlight until Piers pulled her under, gazing at her eyes as lustrous as those of a seal.

'He told me I looked like an oriental naiad escaped from the waters of the Acheron.' She turned to us. 'You see, Piers had me spiralling until I spaced out . . . but the man had faulty wiring.'

'We unfastened slowly. We didn't admit the kissing had to stop, but I'd sensed his restlessness after he returned from a visit to the *wat* . . . hospitable places to pilgrims from whatever provenance. Piers took me once . . . oh yes, it was all seduction. Among fruit trees he followed a procession of monks to the temple where he joined the chanting, their hypnotic droning: *Namo tasso* . . . among candles, lotus buds and incense. Feet folded beneath him, head lower than his mentor's, he wrestled with disciplines of the Noble Way of Buddhism, the Teaching of the All-Enlightened One, the Eightfold Path and Self-Enlightenment.

'What chance had I? The intermeshing of Hinayana Buddhism, Brahmanism and animism confused me and when he explained that Buddhism teaches that "of all the lusts and desires, there is none so powerful as sexual inclination" . . . I knew I'd had it. His karma, erasing the past, relieving him of ethnic roots, of guilt, gloom . . . the whole bit . . . an upbringing bound by the rigidity of the Talmud . . . hell, I was nowhere. He was off . . . Transcendental Wisdom and Selfless Compassion . . . places I couldn't follow into his mystic withdrawal and Ultimate Truth. "You cannot see the wind, only that the grass is bending."

'Anyway if I did pray who'd be there to listen? And worshippers murmuring prayers at the foot of the shrine – how could their abbot, their spiritual shepherd as a Buddhist cognisant in the aspects of doctrine, allow them to waste time when he knew *no one* was listening?

' "Tell me, need there be a listener to make prayers effective?" was his reply. I had no answer.'

Back in Chiang Mai, Sorrel wrote Piers a letter she left in his house: 'I shall return to England in a few months. Desire, with its separate volition, goes on in the same way beards grow on the dead after death . . . I remain a becalmed kite with no one on the end of the string. The girl you once knew, my beloved incubus, cannot live in your slipstream.'

After Sorrel left Thailand, the sight of her malnourished figure walking down the path at noon was irreplaceably lost. Among the itinerant foreigners who wandered in and out of our lives – the backpackers, anthropologists, linguists, botanists, refugees, the unwashed, hungry, idlers or freeloaders – none had the singularity of Sorrel with her complexity of strength and of frailty.

The children missed her, missed their wild games together. When the Mae Ping was sluggish they used to swing over the river on a rope suspended from the rain tree before dropping into the water, their cotton *parsin*s trapping the air, allowing them to float like coloured balloons before landing on the bank further downstream.

Letters from Sorrel hurled into the house from time to time: 'Life seemed big when I was with you. My insecurity is total . . . feel like the neurotic woman who, imagining she might not survive till morning, ate her breakfast the night before.'

When we heard she had married, was pregnant, we assumed that with her husband Damien she was facing another way, at peace, so we were dismayed to receive her next letter:

'Gossamer was born to The Rolling Stones and black coffee and Damien huffing and puffing beside me and a midwife called Falstaff who'd been captain of hockey and kept shouting, "Hold your legs apart and PUSH." And when suddenly Gossamer burst out I thought all my insides were going, forgot what it was about and shouted SAVE ME. And then there she was crumpled and new and marvellous. But later it wasn't good. I threw things at people and walked in my nightdress through the streets in a sort of desperation to hang on to some bit of me I recognized.

'I went home after a week and went really mad. I was taken off to the loony bin where I stayed two months. There's no lock on the lavatory but I was allowed to throw water and cornflakes everywhere and Gossamer came with me and when I disowned her they looked after her. I believed I'd hit upon the cure for cancer and the Vietnamese were only having a snowball match so it was all right. When I came to it wasn't. What's really real is our world of love and shit. So they sent me home and here I am washing nappies and cleaning the house and wondering why we do it all.'

She swung through phases of psychotic quicksand rejecting her baby, rejecting Damien: 'I ought to be happy after nine broody months creating another being but I'm waterlogged. I still dream of Piers. He's lying against my back, arms encircling me, holding my breasts as we draw warmth from one another before dawn in his mountain village among the rag-tag-and-bobtail of young and old bodies shuffling, snoring, farting, gurgling, whimpering. In half-recollected dreams I whimper too.'

For a time after Sorrel left Thailand, Piers used to come to see us. His saturnine features appeared more serene now that he was studying sacred Pali scripts, meditation and detachment.

Looking up at the chiselled orchids along the branches of our rain tree, he spoke in little bursts, running along corridors of thought: 'The abbot is teaching me, or trying to, that words and possessions are not necessary. Abstractions are the reality, not those parasites up there collected by Western predators to sell in New York flower shops.'

Turning towards us he added quietly, 'You see, that's what it was. Sorrel was out there searching for the tangible while I was pursuing my own nirvana without ever looking back. She once told me, "My bones create discord. Can I do without breathing? Press my eyes like over-ripe figs to issue their seeds and see things differently the way you do." She tried to convince me that happiness lies in the fulfilment of the spirit through the *body*. "My body possesses me, don't you understand, Piers? Where else can I live? Know I am alive – unless through my flesh?"

'I teased her: "Your body? Oh Sorrel, not that again?"

'She replied . . . "No, Piers not again . . . *but still*!" '

That was the last time we saw Piers.

Tamsin and Sureen were no longer at the Thai school but at an international school attended by the children of the many foreigners who lived and worked in the locality. Most were Americans – missionaries or working in the university or the consulate. Tamsin returned from her first day asking us why they keep talking about the 'Guard'.

On the girls' birthdays, which occurred within two days of each other in January, we gathered up some of their friends and took them in our Land Rover into the forest for a picnic. Having been used to birthday tea with ready-mixed Betty Crocker chocolate cake with candles on a table, the children ran about like released birds, and when two mahouts brought their elephants to bathe in the stream almost at our feet, the day was perfected.

By now the girls had become experienced travellers. Exploring nearby or distantly, both children were agreeable companions with their instant responses and endurance on lumbering bus journeys; hanging around frontiers; crossing rivers in an unstable boat; sleeping in bamboo cabins; being stared at and eating unfamiliar food. Our journeys added to their innate curiosity and to their ability to curl up anywhere.

On the days when we looked for ways through the nearby forests stretching for leagues into the wilderness, we'd drive along narrow tracks among trees with roots like buttresses and branches hung with cordons of creepers. Lurching over boulders through the vegetal gloom, we found a waterfall where we lay in the water clinging to a branch listening to the susurration of bamboos with leaves like folded grasshopper wings and the noisy but invisible tailor birds. Rare, yet once heard never forgotten, was the whistling song of a black-napped oriole: a flamboyantly yellow bird with a black band circling its head. And caught momentarily in funnels of sunlight were flights of butterflies – vermilion, sable, topaz, cobalt.

We patrolled the boundaries of our country, curious to look across forbidden frontiers. Once at Mae Hong Son, on the border of Burma, Sureen – with a similar appearance to everyone else – walked across the bridge inaccessible to us, merging naturally with an endless stream of people passing to and fro bringing back packets of small jewels to sell in Thailand.

On the northern frontier one cold season, we warmed ourselves at nightfall with glasses of Ovaltine made from condensed milk while from our car we watched an outdoor movie being shown to a group of villagers, of James Mason in a kilt. His, and all the other voices, were dubbed by one man speaking Thai from inside a giant Ovaltine tin.

And once, in Laos in the hot season, we were led into the jungle by a fanatical botanising Jesuit who risked tearing his black habit as he scrambled up a tree to drop back to earth with orchids loosely bound in his cummerbund.

In the far south we drove to the final sliver of country where the border merges into Cambodia. In the Gulf of Thailand we stayed in a small wooden 'hotel' with two rooms, carved shutters and balcony, and a *klong* jar containing water for washing. Old Siam was slipping away under our feet.

The urge to travel kept us exploring countries close to Thailand. As we set out once more when the schools were closed for a long break during the hot season, we knew there was no fresh geography left in the world and that our sort of travel was superficial, skimming countries with antennae extended but never landing. Without preconceptions we looked, tasted, swam, cycled, rode and walked with a sharpened awareness that only comes from first encounters.

In our imaginations anything that magnified distance produced a sense of latitude where, if we kept walking in a northerly direction, we would wander into the wastes of Mongolia, to tundra, and find buried mammoths. Or should we retrace our steps towards the west we would reach the unattainable: my childhood Shangri-La, a land with the bewitching name 'The Empty Quarter'.

There would be a time for stability in the grave.

When we flew to Nepal in a small aircraft, our first sight of the Himalayas appeared as pearly vapour floating at such an improbable height, we expected Blake's Creator to lean towards the universe with outspread compasses. With three-year-old Tamsin we camped under Annapurna, which rose majestically to 26,504 feet.

In Java we witnessed the political suppression of President Sukarno. At nine each morning – as an example of the efficacy of a dictator – everybody had to get out of their cars and sweep bits of the surrounding road. A far less low-key event was being escorted across the airfield by soldiers with fixed bayonets to catch a plane to Bali. Once aboard we were given anti-shark powder to sprinkle round ourselves and around Tamsin should we come down in the sea. The island of Bali – in those days bereft of tourists – was fecund: shimmering with costumed people holding festivals along the shore or deep in jungles where we gazed through lianas as though through a theatrical scrim.

A journey to Luang Prabang, the royal capital of Laos at the confluence of the Mekong and the Nam Khan rivers, revealed a small monarchy caught in a time warp. All was fabulous and latent before political turmoil changed the place irredeemably.

Malaysia was different. Unrest may have lain like an undertow beneath plantations of rubber and spices, yet at that time (more than forty years ago) there was an affable ease afforded to the traveller passing through. Islam thrived in the peninsula with non-confrontational amiability.

Michael loved these peregrinations. He'd been nourished on travel: 'Every winter we used to go to Switzerland. The rapture of my first train journey at the age of nine, hurtling through the night with banks of snow piled up beside the track kept me spellbound. Cocooned in the compartment I was unable to pull down the blind and turn back to my berth I was so excited.'

Michael's father had taken him rock-climbing and skiing, teaching him the names of the Alps till he knew every one.

When we lived in Greece and were often travelling across Europe, Michael would recite a litany of those peaks, recapturing his childhood memories of alpine huts and the smell of ski wax. Now he found our aimless straying into the forest compensated for his war years in India, Burma and China, when the menacing circumstances and the arboreal density of Asia had been a threat. Six years lost. When he returned the world had shifted, but he forever regretted his youthful conformity to military drinking and laddish behaviour in the Air Force rather than meeting the people of the countries in which he was billeted: 'I hated the maleness of service living. We were stupid and insular! We never discovered the fascination of those eastern countries. What a waste.'

How different were my memories of Switzerland compared to his boyhood holidays in the country to which I'd been banished after having mastoid. The photograph in my hand of myself at the age of ten standing beside my mother – each of us wearing the heavy dark blue skiing gear of that era – brings the whole miserable desolation back with a vividness I'd rather not recall.

There I learnt the invasiveness of homesickness – an emotion with no way out. The first time my mother left me, the Swiss International School had decamped during the winter holidays from Lake Geneva to a ski resort at Grindelwald. It was there for the first time that I saw the ancient Chinese practice of cupping being used on the children. A common practice, it seemed. I watched horrified as the hot glass cups were placed on the back of a child, causing a painful vacuum.

I should have loved the alpine life, been excited learning to ski and to skate, but instead, walking through the snow, tears running down my cheeks, I kept saying to myself, 'Yesterday Mummy was here, she passed this chalet, this fir tree, she saw that mountain.'

Among the letters I've exhumed is one my mother kept. One that, in light of more perceptive attitudes to bringing up children, should never have been written home by a child miles away in a foreign country. Inconsolable, bereft of hope, I'd written, 'Darling Mummy, I would MUCH, MUCH, MUCH rather have Masstoyed than stay here and if I have to I will put snow in my ear. Fetch me home.'

The cruel, middle-class legitimacy – even on the part of my mother, an enlightened woman – that condones sending a child away at such a young age is accountable for years of misery endured by children at prep school or, as in my case, 'for the sake of her well-being'.

I wonder who assessed that childhood chimera 'well-being'.

Homesickness is self-torture, and it overwhelmed me. I carried it as a penance throughout my childhood: an ordeal beyond the capability of a child to shelve, whether at boarding school or in holidays staying with relatives or a school friend. It was always with me.

And yet, and yet, somewhere deep in my unconscious, a love for that snowy, sculptured Swiss landscape has remained with me just as it did for Michael. We shared the thrill of waking to the first snow of winter.

In autumn 1966 we left Thailand. Siamese being their childhood language, Tamsin and Sureen spoke together sharing rhymes, prayers, puns (which the Thais loved) so that, as in the days of the Raj when the colonists annexed Indian words, certain Thai adjectives entered our family vocabulary. Very conveniently the Thais have a word for hot food and a different one for 'heat', a definition we often use, as well as their flat-sounding word *mun* for something tasteless. Among other Thai words we've appropriated, by far the most onomatopoeic, for something unclean, is the ridiculous sounding 'sok-a-plok'.

With our furniture, books and possessions – from textiles to carved musicians – that we'd accumulated over seven years packed in crates bound for Greece by sea, and our dog Becket left with friends in Chiang Mai to be flown to us once we had a home, we boarded a plane to Athens.

A week later we took a boat from Piraeus to Venice.

We disembarked at the Maritime Docks on an October evening in a state of enchantment. On our first visit – never to be experienced again in quite the same way – we walked onto the Zattere following a porter wheeling our luggage. The quintessential beauty of the city, after years of living among the architecture of the Far East, was hallucinatory. In the translucent reflections of the Giudecca canal, the constant passing of boats, the streets of Athens full of traffic and fumes fell from our memories. Tamsin and Sureen ran ahead with the freedom of colts, and next morning we woke to the surreal sight of a liner slowly passing La Giudecca.

We had the whole of Venice to explore, a whole week before us.

Some memories are kept for ever in pristine safekeeping.

Years later, long after Michael had died, I took all my family for four days to Venice. It was winter, when the city belongs to the Venetians. Tourist boats were silent, the melancholy siren of a passing ship sounded distantly through the mist, and as we walked along narrow *calle*s the shufflings of pigeons' wings rising before us were the very fabric of Venice just as opening shutters belong to early-morning awakening in Paris.

I hope that their first visit to Venice is for ever seared on the memories of my eleven- and fifteen-year-old granddaughters:

that they will never forget their excitement on waking their first morning to discover water flowing along the passage where they'd walked the night before.

How fortunate we are to be living while *La Serenissima* still survives above the encroaching tide.

Before leaving Chiang Mai we had ordered a French car to be delivered to us in Venice from Paris. Wishful thinking, stupidity or sheer naivety? Sometimes, though, improbable things do work. A Citroën – the colour of absinthe and with a slight trace of Gauloise cigarette inside – was waiting for us at the garage on the outskirts of Venice. We made a leisurely journey north, relishing the freedom to move among countries in a way that had not been possible in the East.

As we drove across Italy, Austria, Switzerland and France for England, the children marvelled at everything. They were still young enough to be excited by the new and the curious: getting out of the car to run and touch snow; the tactile responses from staff in hotels so different from the reticence of the Thais; bathing in hot water after years of scooping cold from a jar; wearing Austrian dirndls and aprons we bought them; eating spaghetti, salami, snails and French bread. (Children are the best companions, responsive and at times maddening, but I've always loved travelling with them, as I do now with my grandchildren.)

Trees, the lungs of the landscape with their mass, shade and deportment, outlast any floral exuberance in the flower beds. Their vertical architecture and bulky presence in summer contrasts with twigs outlined in rime in our northern seasons. They make me thankful for their visible definition in contrast to the tropics or around the Mediterranean where the Flame-of-the-Forest in Thailand, the catalpa in Greece in the desiccated beige, tawny or tobacco-coloured landscape – dead and dry for months – is followed annually in the East by canals of lotus buds and the miraculous eruption of sternbergia among the stones of the Pindus mountains.

Tamsin needed to know the name of every tree, unfamiliar after the majestic teaks, coral trees with claw-like blossoms and feathery casuarinas of southern Thailand. Her love of trees may have originated from that journey at the age of nine. Though she was never to see the most English of trees, the elms, whose leguminous outlines hollowed out the skies of my child-hood, her enthusiasm was certainly endorsed when we moved to Greece, to the olive trees on Corfu with contorted trunks looking as ancient as Palaeolithic fossils, which surrounded our house and under whose shade she and Sureen played together before the midday heat drove them indoors.

6

Who Will Pay the Ferryman?

'A strong wind blew and a wrack of long silver-rimmed cloud hung in the sky above the sea and the ghostly shape of Corfu.'

Patrick Leigh Fermor

On my eightieth birthday, with my children and grandchildren (though alas not with David's daughter Joanna, who was away at the Purcell School singing and playing the violin), we celebrated with a Thai meal.

Both my daughters are experienced Thai cooks, and Sureen has a friend – a Thai chef in London who receives ingredients by air from Bangkok every Friday – who provided, among many fresh ingredients, a durian (which I had to put in the cellar to avoid being overcome by the pervading smell) and one of my favourite dishes, *hor mok mo*. Either with pork or with fish the small parcels are superb but a terrible fiddle to make. Authentically the ingredients are wrapped in banana leaves secured with a sliver of bamboo, and because the finely pounded mixture, with all its elaborate additions and paste (requiring at least nine ingredients), is steamed, the result is subtle and unctuous and different from many fiercer-tasting dishes.

When we are all together like this, we occasionally set up an outmoded screen and projector to show slides of our travels, ones that Michael had taken long before the convenience of photographs via mobile phones or digital cameras. They show pictures of our lives well out of the frame of my grandchildren's experience – for the rest of us they resurrect the past.

'I'm Jocasta, your neighbour,' she said from under the brim of a straw hat decorated with poppies. She spoke with a Middle European accent: her smile was unconditional. Within her sunlit arms the child swaddled in spite of the heat was androgynous.

We were standing beside the gates of a villa on high land overlooking the Ionian Sea that Michael and I had rented on the island of Corfu as a place to live and grow olives and where the children could have a European life after our years in the East. The house overslept. No water, no electricity, telephone or kitchen – we had moved in with inept mistiming. A few days later, on 21 April 1967, there was a military coup. The prime minister, Panagiotis Kanellopoulos, was arrested and replaced by the extreme right-wing officer Stylianos Pattakos. Amidst violence in the streets of Athens, the king and politicians were arrested, tanks rumbled through the streets, and every province in the country was affected. The junta lasted until 1974. Far away on Corfu the rumours and counter-rumours only reached us gradually as we found the banks were closed, shipping had ceased, planes, letters and newspapers had been suspended, and our baggage forwarded from Thailand was stuck at Piraeus. A curfew threw a pall over the island, and the nightly fishing boats remained in harbour.

'Things will return to normal in a few days,' Jocasta reassured us, 'but if you need anything we live down the lane.'

I hate islands. I want the freedom of landmass. Having been born in this country where going abroad needs organising, I crave impulsive escapes. Yet here we were surrounded by sea and swaths of asphodels, a greyish-pink smoke among the olive trees. Distantly, between the mainland and the island, a chain of dolphins caught the sunlight as they rose and fell heading for the open Adriatic.

Tamsin and Sureen adapted to their new continent like chameleons on a frangipani tree. They accepted everything; went to school; replaced the Thai language and alphabet with the Greek language and alphabet. They made friends, thought coarse bread dipped in olive oil the best thing they'd ever eaten, became fascinated by mythology and the stories of Odysseus, and at school learnt by rote how to denounce the Turks and glorify the Greeks.

Tamsin, looking like a mermaid with her long hair, swam among the rocks and learnt the language by osmosis, and Sureen, collecting old tales and superstitions from the neighbourhood children, scattered affection wherever she went. Tamsin learnt *katharevousa* – the formal language the junta had imposed on schools. Sureen stuck to demotic Greek. And David – having moved on from his first job – was learning the compositor's language of 'Butted Slugs', 'Scumming', 'Cockling', 'Battered Type', 'Blind Blocking' and 'Bleeding Ink' at the London College of Printing. He arrived with a friend from England in a car perilously low-sprung for our stony lane. Michael, coping with our eighty ancient olive trees, regularly banned hunters from our land, exterminators who shot golden orioles for sport and hung them like trophies from their belts. Outraged and with a mixture of Greek and dramatic gestures, he confronted them, only to be met by the most agreeable acquiescence, which somewhat disarmed him.

The children went to Gastouri village school, not by *samlor* but on foot through an Arcadian landscape bounded by cistus, broom and Stars of Bethlehem. In their mid-morning break they bought two drachma's worth of bread to eat with olives from either Achilles or Hector, the two village bakers.

It was curious – Sureen at that time being the only Greek-speaking Thai in Greece, I imagine – that none of the villagers seemed to notice she was oriental, not Caucasian. Only when Athenians flooded the island at Easter did they stare and comment with uninhibited curiosity, quizzing her as to who her parents were. When she pointed to us, undaunted they would ask, '*Ochi, ochi*, no! Your real parents?'

More than the others I was reluctant to exchange the Orient for Europe. I remained stranded. Each morning as I closed the shutters against the rising sun my thoughts migrated beyond the Ionian Sea, Turkey, Persia, through the sleep of India and Burma, to a country for which I was homesick. And I thought of a friend – an Englishman – who'd made his home in northern Thailand, reminiscing about the war when he had been parachuted into Crete: 'There was sabotage, danger, hunger and fearless comrades galore, but what I most remember is making love to girls with wine-dark nipples. "Oh, where are you going my silver one? Where are you going my fresh sprig of basil?" ' He sighed from the memory as we filled his glass with *Mekong* whisky. And that's about all he told us of the country we were moving to.

Under the onslaught of swallows in spring the island was encompassed by vertigo; the earth tilted towards their geometric flight; their song strung on diagonals of light vibrated the air, and almost overnight, out of distorted black sticks, the green leaves of vines changed the skyline.

Summer began with fireflies. They appeared as a constellation of minute lights, moving in unison like a Mexican wave from the top of the grove flowing down across our lane. Summer also meant wholesale massacres. Moths, drawn by candlelight, circled the flame's cremating vortex: each morning I cleared away bodies frailer than a breath, with wings the colour of eucalyptus bark.

When the land was parched to neutral, in the third week of June, the schools closed. On breathless moonlit nights we'd walk among one-dimensional cypresses and olive trees with leaves turned to metal from the silvery light. By July torpor had overwhelmed the island. From noon till five inhabitants retreated. Animals, static as statues, dozed through the hours while we, in shuttered rooms, lay supine. The fledgling swallows – perched in the small, scented white rose *R. banksiae* (blessed Joseph Banks, the indefatigable naturalist who brought it from China) that scrambled through the olive tree outside our window – had ceased their chattering. And the screaming drill of cicadas shut out the age-old cry across the Ionian Sea: 'The great god Pan is dead.'

It was the hour of annihilation, of pagan spirits and the suffocating inertia that laid all creatures low.

Before light we'd hear the mournful call of the fish seller, '*Psa-a-a-ri-i*', followed later by the pony pulling the milkman's cart ambling listlessly by, and past the house where, before the war, the Durrells had lived – described by Gerald in *My Family and Other Animals*.

Among other itinerant pedlars who came along our lane was the haberdasher, carrying on his head a basket of buttons, beads, thread, elastic and safety pins. He would rest at noon crushing the wild thyme in the shade of a cypress tree. Another familiar figure was the tinker, whose donkey was laden with pots, pans, graters and tin icons as well as knives, brushes, plastic flowers and enamel mugs.

The draper came by van. He would arrive in the evening sliding back the door to reveal a kaleidoscope of cloth: plush, muslin, cambric, flowery cotton that ran at the first washing, and hard-wearing blue material for school uniforms. Our sheets, made from his seersucker cotton, became softer after every wash. And from the wide cotton bands of blue or pink swaddling cloth – still used at that time for newborn babies – I made a skirt for Tamsin. He also stocked dark-patterned tablecloths with fringing, silky tapestries of nymphs beside a fountain for parlour walls; and woollen vests, petticoats and long johns smelling of sheep, which encased the wearer in a lanolin skin and sucked up moisture like blotting paper. When we gave a lift to olive pickers in winter, the frowsty odour from damp clothes filled the car.

Life without electricity meant the daily chore of filling oil lamps; ironing with a heavy contraption full of hot charcoal; a fridge run on paraffin; a gramophone run on batteries; and once-a-week hot water made by burning olive logs in a copper cylinder standing at the end of a hip-bath.

Water was a perpetual problem: for our neighbours it meant waiting with their buckets at the standpipe in the lane for the supply to be turned on for an hour. As we had a car, each afternoon we drove down the winding road to the coast, where we filled our containers from a spring in the hillside and collected our mail. One afternoon, returning up the hill, we overtook a woman with a bundle on her head walking behind her husband riding his donkey. Michael stopped to offer her a lift. Her husband instantly jumped down and was affronted when Michael insisted on his wife getting into the car, not him.

Renting rather than owning our house meant that we lived suspended: unable to move on, to make the place habitable, to put in electricity or plumbing or paint a wall – we were stymied. The courtyard with its mandarin trees, a pepper tree, wisteria and slabs of blue iris in spring or honeysuckle in summer had high stone walls that would be perfect for festoons of roses, for clematis and for making a shadowy bower where we could dine.

For a year we remained thwarted. But then miraculously, or more likely pragmatically, the owners decided to sell us the house, the eighty olive trees as well as the separate olive press. At the same time our residents' permits in the Alien Department in Bangkok ran out. We could only return as tourists (except for Sureen, who had dual nationality).

Light. Four young electricians entered our house like a covey of warblers singing from room to room as they massacred the walls. Pecking, picking, tapping and hacking, with lambent eyes and luxurious hair covered with dust, they danced through our lives as we blew plaster from food and talked against the discord of splintering wood. In addition to Costa, Theodoros, Andreas and Nikos, three Spiros arrived to build drains, a cesspit and a bathroom. Weeks later cries of '*Founello! Founello!*' rang through the groves as explosions shattered the limestone rock for the electricity pole, and earth and pebbles fell among the irises and tiny orchids with their dragon faces and grinning mouths.

And we had light.

We also had visitors. Fortnight after fortnight our house was full. Extended meals – whether at a long table indoors or out under the vine – delightful as they were, meant that when Michael and I wanted a private conversation we had to meet at a particular olive tree on our land, our habitual trysting place some distance from the house. But the pleasure of summer visitors also meant that, just as when washed, colours in Indian cotton run, the same fault occurred with friends of friends. A form of leaching that wasn't always welcome. Letters would arrive about visitors staying for two weeks at hotels or a campsite:

'Dear friends of ours, we know you'd like them, and they'd adore meeting you! They're staying in a hotel in your part of the island . . . they haven't a car but are longing to see your house. If you have a moment we'd be so grateful . . .'

'. . . backpacker . . . appreciate a bath . . .'

'. . . has a gammy leg . . . not much good on his pins . . .'

'. . . with her first boyfriend . . . keep an eye . . .'

'. . . recuperating from a serious op . . .'

'. . . sure they'll get on with your children . . .'

'. . . bringing photos to show you of our grandson/garden/ holiday . . . just a drink . . .'

And so it continued until the last planes from England ceased and the days of sunbathing on beaches were no longer guaranteed.

In 1911 an Englishwoman, Sophie Atkinson, had lived in our house as a guest. She stayed a year painting, writing, walking and cycling round the island. In her book *An Artist in Corfu* she describes how the house '. . . is surrounded to its walls with olives, flowering trees and vineyards . . .'

Although the vineyards had long since gone, the almond tree below the terrace still produced galaxies of white blossom against the black limbs, and the four olive trees outside the courtyard walls where Sophie had hung her hammock were there. We'd sit in the shade of 'Sophie's trees' surrounded by the nutty scent of oleanders and drink to her memory. Of the olive harvest she wrote, 'the women and girls stoop and crouch day-long under the olives . . . The Corfiots consider that the trees are harmed by beating, so until the final gathering the fruit is just left to drop which it does steadily for months.'

Nothing had changed sixty years later. After school Tamsin and Sureen would join the women, swiftly collecting with both hands the sloe-like fruit lying among grass and between the roots. A continuum of chatter coiled around the trees or was projected to other pickers across the grove. In Sophie's day the landowner had increased payment from one drachma an hour to one drachma twenty if they kept quiet.

The olive press was now ours. Unused – our olives were pressed at a mill a few miles away – it had not altered since Sophie had written, 'small windows throw Rembrandt-like light over the uneven floor, clumsy machinery and moving figures set in a most etchable mystery of shadows.'

The huge supporting beam, the wooden screw, the millstone and the horizontal pole to which the pony had been harnessed were all there. Cobwebs, mould and the powdery olive flowers which percolated through the tiles on windy days softened outlines on machinery and stone vats.

When had been the last pressing filling the air with the pungency of crushed olives and topaz oil, the last time, according to Sophie, that 'the women bringing in the olives wring out their dripping skirts and gather round the wood fire'? The grandson of Tsipis – the overseer in Sophie's time – was our neighbour.

Another neighbour was Aretusa, known by the children as the 'fig woman' after their first encounter when she gave them a basket of figs. Sweet, smiling and gentle, she'd call to her hens each morning or to her cat, which came cantering towards her with its tail stuck up in the air. She lived with her brother Aristeides and his wife Maro. Aristeides, meeting the children on their way to school, would exhort them to maintain Greek proprieties and to work hard. Not far away lived Olga. Before she came into sight her stentorian voice shouting orders to her daughter-in-law Elvira resounded through the trees. Large and bosomy, Olga exchanged her working costume for dazzling finery on feast days, appearing like a fully rigged brigantine in a blue silk skirt and magenta apron. Festooned with gold she sailed up to the village booming '*Kalimera*' as she passed our gate.

Water shortage meant that most of the villagers had a *livadhi*, a fertile plot of land they cultivated in a valley two miles away irrigated by a network of canals and dykes. In the autumn we'd be taken there by Olga or others from the village, to be presented with a cornucopia of peppers, tomatoes, sweet-corn, aubergines and grapes – the delicious muscats. When our baskets overflowed Olga would fill her apron with walnuts and our arms with zinnias picked from among the vegetables.

Some Sunday evenings a film would be shown in the village, on others there would be dancing in the small *plateia*. Tamsin and Sureen with neighbouring friends would walk up the lane carrying their best shoes until, nearing the village, they would change, hiding their shabby ones in the bushes.

How lucky we were to be around when one of the dying breed of shadow-puppet masters came from the mainland to Corfu. There were still about eighty like him, he said, but not for much longer: cinema was taking over. Lean, with half an ear missing, he seemed such a used-up man, yet when he went behind the sheet he moved the puppets with agility, performing all the parts in the *Karaghiozi* epic (of Byzantine and Ottoman origin) with a voice that passionately declaimed anger or jubilation. In Thailand the shadow puppets were made from buffalo hide – nightmare creatures, titanic monsters that had the children screaming with terrified excitement.

On Christmas Day we walked to the village to give presents to our friends. This wasn't their tradition, but they knew it was ours. Angelica and her son Spiro – a school friend of the children's – welcomed us with kumquat liqueur and white cakes. Next door we were invited in by the mother of Tamsin's best school friend Katina (who, like my mother's school contemporaries, has remained her friend ever since). After more liqueur and cakes we met others: more white cakes, nuts and *sikopita* – a spicy, peppery fig cake laced with ouzo, as rich and moist as Christmas pudding – wrapped in walnut leaves. At Maria's house we had Greek coffee and left with four eggs tied up in a handkerchief. Her hens had just come into lay. Olga gave us a bucket of washed new potatoes tasting of clean earth and a flagon of rough red wine pressed that autumn.

Laden, we returned home to find the Gastouri band, arrayed in red and grey uniforms, blasting away on a miscellany of instruments at our gates. They all crowded into the house for refreshment and a lot of clinking of glasses and good-year wishes.

There were times too when we welcomed quite other people to our house, not for any sort of celebration but because we'd become a haven for Greek friends in a state of rebellion against the junta. Since the colonels' takeover, informers were everywhere. Political gossip in the *kafeneion* was silenced – any subversive talk could be betrayed by the man at the next table. With our doors closed, these protesters could gather round our kitchen table, where they freely expressed their frustration and repressed hostility until, overcome with a kind of inert nostalgia, they stopped to listen to our records of Mikis Theodorakis, the much-loved and exiled composer whose music was banned throughout Greece.

It was due to them, to their stories of torture and imprisonment, that I continued the letter-writing for Amnesty International which I'd started in Thailand as protest against the atrocities going on in neighbouring Cambodia. A solitary and boring occupation, it involved writing four letters in aid of the political prisoner I'd chosen from each month's Amnesty bulletin: to the head of state, whether monarch or dictator, to the Minister of Foreign Affairs, to the relevant ambassador in London and to the local press. Littering my letter, to some of the most despicable despots and tyrants all over the world, with 'Your Excellency' – sycophantic and courteous throughout – I became a toady on behalf of an unknown detainee to be allowed to see a relative, doctor or lawyer. Thankless, for there would never be a reply, yet the thought that somewhere, on every continent, there were others like me homing in on one particular prisoner of conscience justified what appeared an ineffectual task.

After we'd returned to England I kept up the letter-writing habit. Sometimes, on a summer's day, that month's Amnesty news would lie open on my kitchen table at the page of those to be taken up by other letter-writers around the world. His or her photograph would catch my eye as I moved about the kitchen. Outside the window a bee would be rummaging in a hollyhock; the scent of honeysuckle overcame that of cooking. I would stop: guilty, susceptible. Who are you? Where are you? In my kitchen or where they say you are? What days have you endured since I first folded back the page on which your photograph stares back at me? I hear the babbling of a dipper along the brook, but you? What sound, what air has filled your lungs? A ladybird gorges on greenfly, the scrolls of ferns uncoil.

Touching the edge of my life I pull the pan off the stove and sit down to write a letter. I am thinking of you, only *you*, as I extend my hand in its futile gesture of solace.

While we each in our own way were adapting to our new country, Michael and I had been conscious that we owed Sureen the chance to visit the country of her birth before its memory had been superimposed by life in rural Greece. Early in 1972 we took her to Thailand to refresh those years. We spent a few days in Bangkok and a day in Lopburi before going north.

Wherever we went, to a café or street bistro, we'd be surrounded by onlookers curious at the sight of Sureen. She looked like one of them, but her body language was perplexing, like a *ferang*'s, nor could she reply to their questions. It was Michael and I who explained that she was adopted and now lived in Europe.

We took the slow 'express' to Chiang Mai, visiting friends, familiar temples and remembered restaurants, and although there were more hotels and shops we only had to leave the town and travel into the villages and countryside to find Thailand as it had been on our arrival in 1959. With an old friend who'd made Chiang Mai his home we made a journey further north and east to the Yao village to which, years earlier, Piers had taken Sorrel in the midst of their dislocating relationship.

It was the Yao New Year, their most important festival.

About fifty thousand of the Yao hill tribe, who had originally come from south China as early as 2500 BC, were scattered throughout the highlands of northern Thailand still maintaining their traditional lifestyle, ancestor worship, artefacts and unique costumes. The women wore loose-legged black or indigo trousers decorated with cross-stitch embroidery in red, yellow, blue, dark green and white thread. The children wore embroidered caps from babyhood to adolescence 'to ensure if they die in childhood they have the right to play in a garden of flowers and butterflies in their next life'. At puberty girls exchanged the caps for turbans made from five yards of black cloth, tightly bound to hide every strand of hair. The folds of their headdresses were used as pockets and at night as pillows.

Wearing red plushy edging to their jackets, woolly pom-poms at waist and on shoulder bags, earrings, bracelets, rings, buckles, buttons and hoops of solid silver round their throats, and walking with rigid steps, feet turned out, added to their theatrical splendour. It appeared incongruous to see a woman stirring pig swill or milling grain under her top-heavy, outré turban and dressed in all that splendour while carrying it off with the stateliness of a courtier.

The spirit doctor greeted us on arrival, leading us past the Great Door – through which the dead are carried and the ancestral spirits return – to the other side of the house. Entering a huge room, opium, the rank smell of bamboo shoots and smouldering wood engulfed us as we were welcomed by members of the tribe. As in a daguerreotype, in the crepuscular gloom from smoke filtering through the roof I could just make out, hanging from the rafters, bird snares, tools, bunches of maize and baskets mellowed to burnt umber from years of usage. On the floor were baskets lacquered with sap from the 'varnish tree' (*Rhus verniciflua*) for gathering honey from wild bees.

'According to what Piers told us,' Michael said, 'these baskets are gradually being replaced by plastic buckets, and any day now they'll only be found in museums or, worse, in Pocatello, Idaho, as ethnic trophies. It's just another form of erosion like their "slash and burn" agriculture that's gradually ravaging the mountains, and I suppose each of us as tourists is just as much to blame as the road builders and the loggers.'

I peered into a basket. 'Nectar. It smells of mythology. How sad if they lose the art of weaving honey baskets in exchange for plastic.'

That evening we shared the family supper of pumpkins, root ginger, bamboo shoots and coarse rice. The meal was sparse in preparation for the next day's feasting, but the rice whisky flowed from a fat-bellied jar with notched patterns, shiny from frequent handling. Now and then a cup was taken over to a young man crouched in the corner printing 'spirit money' on paper made from bark using a wooden block made thirty years ago by Yunnanese. Unconcerned by our presence, the lad inked, thumped down and put aside the pieces of printed paper in a state of repetitive monotony as though already well away on drugs or drink.

'What's it for?' Michael asked.

'It's an imprint of a horse. Tomorrow it'll carry the money to the land of spirits in preparation for life after death.'

Sureen, throughout the day – experiencing strange customs, language and food, and bombarded with a whole lot of impressions unlike anything she'd adjusted to in Greece – remained unfazed. Thirteen years old and as adaptable to her changing background as a chameleon, she helped carry food to the pigs rootling about outside.

During the night to the thump of the money printer, to the guttural dragging voices of the Yao, Michael, Sureen and I slept fitfully among other bodies woken now and then by the dozy grunting of pigs penned outside, uneasy, perhaps, with premonitions of their fate. Beyond the slumbering people lay silence across mountains covered by folds of uninhabited rainforest where spirits lurked – the malevolent phantoms that tormented life among the Yao – possessing and preoccupying the significance of humdrum chores. Even among household objects there were evil spirits.

We woke to demonic screams of pigs. Slaughter day. Outside the fence a child – a baby bound to her back – was chopping up a banana tree for the fire; two others sliced pieces for pig fodder. The sound of trotters being dragged across the ground for ritual massacre made us retreat. We weren't going to witness preparations for the coming celebration. Instead we escaped.

'Let's get out, leave the killing fields for a nearby Akha village,' said Michael. 'We'll return when the blood and butchery are over.'

We walked across the hill, past their ingenious cobweb of forked sticks carrying bamboo troughs criss-crossing the falling land. Water trickled through holes to irrigate the young maize, and at each T-junction a leaf could be placed to deflect water into another aqueduct.

The Tibeto-Burman Akha people – whose villages are sometimes as high as three and a half to four thousand feet – grow opium. Animists, they believe that spirits pervade everything – the hills, trees, streams, stones or cooking pots – and need placating. And because they dread water spirits in particular, the Akha people appeared grubby compared to the Yao.

Their village, made of flimsy houses thatched with reeds, was guarded by sacred gates to ward off evil spirits and phallic figures with outsize genitals to ensure fertility. The bizarre headdresses of the Akha women rise in tiers decorated with tassels, dyed feathers, silver coins and strings of beads: height denotes the status of the wearer. Bare-footed, bare-breasted – only unmarried girls keep covered up – their heavily pleated skirts reaching to just above the knee are worn low on the hips, the most sexual part of the body. In contrast to their headgear the colours of the woven gaiters swathing their legs were indistinguishable from an accumulation of wood ash clinging like pollen does to stamen. Among a press of children and old women – the virgins had gone to the fields – we were invited into a low-roofed hut. A woman was standing with her foot on the treadle of a loom, so narrow that the woven cloth was only eight inches wide. Hospitable and chattering, the villagers' merriment increased as maize whisky (70 per cent proof) was passed around. Although our form of stumbling Thai and their mumbled dialect through a mouthful of betel nut made conversation somewhat stilted, their friendliness was unmistakeable. But we had to leave.

Back at the Yao village a feast was being prepared.

The savoury scent of barbecued meat after that morning's porcine pogrom reached us long before the village came into sight. Dressed in newly woven garments, members of the tribe, plus many others who had converged from distant settlements, greeted us. Already happy from rice whisky, plus the rarity of eating meat between one celebration and another, their enthusiasm remained uncurbed by the variations of pork dishes for the next few hours. Using chopsticks or fingers, they ate pigs' livers; pickled pork; chunks of pork with vegetables; and pork and chillies, as well as highly spiced raw chopped pork. When everyone was replete and Sureen and the other children had fallen asleep, a satisfied calm descended on the elders smoking their cheroots.

The prone figure of an emaciated man smoking a hookah lay in the corner of the room. Holding kneaded opium over a flame and inhaling deeply, he fell into a state of beatitude, drifting beyond the four walls, beyond the forest, beyond space and time to sublime forgetfulness, repeating the operation whenever he surfaced from the mist of oblivion.

Happy man. Lethe was attainable from poppies growing just beyond the frontiers of his village.

* * *

We returned to Corfu and to Tamsin. She had been staying with friends in London who had loved her since she'd been born, and she now was old enough to enjoy a world different from rural Corfu. Theatres and museums, concerts and galleries, plus the unknown world of department stores before we all returned to the embraces of our neighbours, intrigued by the curious souvenirs we'd brought them from Chiang Mai.

What remained in Sureen's memory of that brief return to her country is questionable, but it had given her a reminder of Thailand that in later years she'd be able to pass on to any children she might have. (Years later, when as an adult she went on holiday to Thailand, I asked her if she wanted to make contact with her father as it wouldn't be difficult to trace him. She looked at me with amazement. The thought had never crossed her mind.)

That same year, Tamsin, needing a wider education than what was on offer on Corfu, went to live with an Italian family in Florence while going to an international school run by Americans, which meant that several times a year we were driving between Corfu and Florence with the children. To while away the hours and with no car radios or cassette players, we'd pass the time singing. Michael sang old music-hall ballads, I sang songs from Fred Astaire and Ginger Rogers films of my youth, and Tamsin and Sureen sang Greek pop songs learnt from the radio. Later, when they were both studying in Austria and we were making even longer journeys up and down Italy via different routes, the habit continued and our repertoire expanded.

But all has changed. Now on long car journeys my grandchildren remain isolated, in a world provided by gadgets clamped to their ears where any form of interrelating is impossible.

*   *   *

Some friends had made Corfu their permanent home. They were people who had been living on the island for years. Apart from them, few visited us in winter from abroad, except for those passing through on their way home from Thailand with grisly accounts of the massacre at My Lai: the turning point in the Vietnam War.

The others, seeking sun and a sybaritic holiday, fell from our lives like leaves in autumn until Easter. They missed months when the island closed in on itself. No shuttered rooms at noon, no motor-scooter accidents on coastal bends, no disco music from bars along the coast.

Dusk darkened the inner curve of the island as Aunt Jobiska's 'lavender water tinged with pink' was reflected in the sea from snow on the mainland, just as Edward Lear would have seen it when he painted his watercolours on the island. We hibernated. We had evenings of uneventful tranquillity, reading aloud to the children as we sat round the fire of our upstairs sitting room facing east towards the Ionian Sea. Like fireflies spread across the water, the fishing boats left harbour at nightfall, only returning at dawn, towed back by the throaty throb of a diesel engine.

In late afternoon, while the children went to dancing classes in town, Michael and I shopped along the lamplit colonnades and flagstone lanes or visited the church of St Spiridion, warm and glittering with icons, candles and hanging silver lamps. During the day the narrow lanes were festooned with laundry between the five-storey houses from whose upper windows a small dog would be lowered by basket to perform in the street, or a shopkeeper would place goods in a basket that could be hauled up several floors. The Greek method of mute communication intrigued us as someone on the pavement with fingers bunched upwards and with a quick flick of the wrist could ask 'What?' to a friend leaning out of a window. An upward motion of the chin and a downward slant of eyelids with eyebrows raised meant total rejection. And biting of knuckles on a clenched fist signified 'Keep quiet. Don't tell!'

Other gestures were equally explicit. Scolding a child, when not within reach for ear-twisting, could be indicated with an outstretched hand slicing the air. Pain was registered by an indrawn breath with top teeth clenched over the lower lip, accompanied by the floppy shaking of a hand. A circling flat hand was a silent 'Po! Po! Po!' or 'Crikey!' but most disconcerting the first time we heard it was a low 'Pssst' meaning 'Hey you!'

And once we watched a man on the telephone gesturing with his hand until, needing more emphasis, he tucked the phone under his chin to be more expressive by using both.

On winter nights, rain clattered against our windows from an easterly wind making the old house creak, ripping olives from the trees and causing the pliant cypresses to curtsey to the ground. We knew then that we'd wake to crystalline air, to a different perspective – metamorphosis – the mainland had moved nearer in the night. Hills, roads and shoreline were defined with such clarity that we'd take off for the north, for the summit of Mt Pantokrator, for views of the Othonian Islands, of the Albanian lake Butrinto, and south to the island of Paxos. After months in summer when the distance had been hidden and the sky had been white from humidity, a day like an aquatint was not to be forfeited. A stormy night also meant the olives had been shaken from boughs too high to reach. The women would be out for the first of the season's harvesting, and woodcarvers, eager to spend their winter evenings using the hard olive wood to make satin-smooth objects with beautiful grain, gathered any fallen branches.

One exception to this winter desertion by our friends was the author Kevin Andrews, who, regardless of the season, would come for a fleeting visit bringing with him an almost tangible effervescence for life. American, born in China in 1924, married to the poet e. e. cummings's daughter with whom he had two children, he arrived from the mainland with a fistful of narrative poems and dynamic anti-junta articles. By the time we met he was separated from his wife, had become a Greek citizen and was living a nomadic life. His knowledge of travelling through the Peloponnese had inspired his youthful book *Flight from Icarus*. Reprinted many times, it has become a classic much admired by Hellenic enthusiasts.

On hot evenings in midsummer we took food and wine, drove north to a secluded cove and swam naked among the rocks. In winter, sitting beside the fire, Kevin recounted grim stories of intellectuals being imprisoned by the colonels and of his own police harassment, of being beaten up for writing seditious articles for the American press.

I have just reread the letter he wrote to me in the spring of 1989: 'News of Michael's death sent me to my diary of October 1968 – packed with anecdotes and remarks by him and you, descriptions of Corfu and your house, Tamsin and Sureen, accounts of how we read aloud to each other by the fire, talked, chortled. Apparently I did have the wit to tell you, on leaving, that my visit with you had been one of the happiest weeks of my life.

'What I don't understand is how, after such a radiant time, I could have let 21 years go by without an attempt to find you again.'

Oh Kevin, Kevin, beloved friend, you died too soon. He suffered from epilepsy. In the middle of a conversation he'd go silent; his eyes would go blank as a seizure – petit mal

– overwhelmed him. In later years the malady became worse. In the autumn of 1989 – the same year as Michael – a rare and life-enhancing friend was lost to all of us who knew him.

Among all the foreigners who came to live on the island were two who changed the bias of our life radically. Elizabeth and Christopher Glenconner. They arrived the same year as we did. At the port, where we'd gone to claim our crates of possessions shipped from Thailand, were theirs. Relieved to see they lived on the other side of island – we weren't going to find ourselves among a ghetto of foreigners with all the social commitments that involved – we found as usual our pre-judices were unfounded. Although they lived at Paleokastritsa and neither of us had phones, we began leaving notes at the grocer in town to arrange our next outing together: on picnics, at tavernas as well as sharing our visitors from one side of the island to the other. Frequently Elizabeth and Christopher took us and the children on their caique to the islands north of Corfu, or we would drive them to the mainland on moun-tain explorations, staying in village houses in the Epirus or travelling further south to classic sites in the Peloponnesus or crossing by ferry to Italy, to visit towns and cities and once to London.

A tangible legacy of that friendship remains. Elizabeth, appalled I'd arrived in Greece with clothes suitable for the Far East – gave me a length of such superb Scottish tweed to make myself a warm skirt, I still shake it out of mothballs every winter.

Now and then I remind her of this generous gesture made thirty-odd years ago.

Coincidence can be diverting or disastrous, or sometimes appear as implausible. Quite by chance in 2005 I discovered, through having contributed a chapter in the same book on adoption as Robert Dessaix, that he'd written a novel in 2001 called *Corfu*. Intrigued, I bought the book. On the jacket it said, 'One Easter a young actor [an Australian] far from home, rents a house in Corfu from a little-known writer called Kester Berwick.' The house, cluttered with Kester's papers, pictures, photographs, books and clothes, left his ghostly personality – the inspiration for Dessaix's novel.

The coincidence happened because many years before, soon after we'd arrived in Corfu from Thailand, Kester had become a close friend. Reading Dessaix's book was strange: we were seeing Kester through the imagination of the author, slightly skewed but vivid enough to bring into focus a man whom we'd known well.

Kester had arrived in Gastouri in 1968 from Lesbos and, further coincidentally, like both Robert Dessaix and Stella Bowen, he had been born in Adelaide. By chance Michael and Kester discovered they had both been to the same drama school before the war. A gentle recluse, grateful for a meal and the use of our bath, Kester had given Tamsin guitar lessons, and we had given a party for him and all his friends when his book, *Head of Orpheus Singing*, had been published. 'Doing a Kester' entered our family vocabulary because, to the children's amusement, after we'd finished a meal and moved away to sit by the fire, he'd become so absorbed relating in great detail the story of a film or a book that he'd remain at table talking to the wall.

Kester lived on a meagre pension in a shabby house in the middle of the village. Here, with great ingenuity, he contrived gadgetry from bits of detritus to make his life easier. With no bathroom, his shower was a cold trickle through holes punched in the bottom of a plastic bleach bottle – attached to a hose from the sink – which he'd suspended on a clothes-hanger from the ceiling of his stone-flagged kitchen. His barometer was one of Tamsin's long hairs fastened to a feather that moved across his chart, as it lengthened or shrank, according to the moisture in the air. His home-made harpsichord, made from a packing case, played barely audible, whispery music as long as the cicadas outside weren't too loud.

We visited him often, either sitting outside on rickety chairs surrounded by condensed-milk tins filled with tomato or bean seedlings, geranium cuttings and marrow pips, or else indoors among his books mouldering from the damp. He was always welcoming and warm and the villagers loved him.

Robert Dessaix's book revivified – years after Kester's death – one more of our friends who had come in and out of our lives like the fabled smile on the Cheshire cat.

In the sixties and seventies, there was an influx of foreigners buying and restoring houses once owned by the Corfiot aristocracy. Built under the influence of four hundred years of Venetian rule, many had been abandoned by families whose offspring moved into the town. Deserted and crumbling among the arbutus, with swallows nesting in every room, the villas on large estates with the dimensions of the Golden Section, were highly sought after, as were village houses where discarded cans, painted blue or white and stuffed to overflowing with geraniums, were placed with unaffected artlessness on steps and window sills. On the thresholds stood a tin of basil, not for any culinary use, but as an aromatic sprig for a departing friend. With outside stairways and stone arches over double doors with locks to take ten-inch keys, they were bought up by energetic enthusiasts who rescued discarded transoms, corbels and roof finials; hinges, bolts and shutter fastenings; tie-bars, fragments of majolica or rusted pergola supports.

From abroad came writers, artists, actors, publishers; those who had retired and entrepreneurs who renovated houses as holiday lets. Sophisticated and gregarious, they added greatly to our life on the island. Usually they came to their restored villas or newly built houses – open-plan living rooms, wide terraces and swimming pools – only for a few weeks in summer. Among the fair-weather, decorative butterflies or the hard-drinking escapees, they lived in clusters within the proximity of others speaking their language.

Not far from us on our hill, but along the coast, was a coterie of like-minded people. Among them were the playwright and actor Emlyn Williams and his wife Molly. (Before the war Michael had taken over Emlyn's part in *The Corn Is Green* when it had gone on tour.) Endlessly hospitable and entertaining, Emlyn repeatedly responded to nine-year-old Sureen's request for his funny story about a parrot, and her curious habit of emptying her pockets of accumulated detritus in their waste-paper basket before we left for home never seemed to faze these amiable people.

Their neighbours were Roger and Ines Furse, whom Emlyn described as 'the only ex-Etonian married to an ex-Estonian'. (Ines disarmed us when Roger was dying by asking us, 'Oh darlins, Roger promised his eyes to the hospital. Vat should I do and ven?') Roger, art director and costume designer, was a delightful and amusing raconteur, laid back and an excellent cook; his two Oscars propped up his large collection of books. I have a pencil sketch he did of Sureen helping him at the kitchen table as they made Thai curry together. The drawing hangs in my hall as a reminder of two engaging friends who added another complexion to our life on Corfu. When Roger was diagnosed with lung cancer, we drove them back to London for him to see a consultant. Roger was the most ideal travelling companion. Somehow he had a nose, an instinct, for the right restaurant where the most delicious but inexpensive meals were to be had and then chose the right wine to go with each course, even in the most unlikely place, Chamonix, where we stayed the night.

Near to the Furses, the publisher Jamie (Hamish) Hamilton and his wife Yvonne had built their villa. Great party-givers, they entertained lavishly; drink flowed amongst an assortment of authors, film stars and Italian aristocrats. Jamie disconcerted me the first time we met. Instead of putting his arms round me he put his hands on my breasts, a far from appealing trait and one I took care to avoid on subsequent meetings. Yvonne too could be disconcerting but in a different way. The first time they came to us for dinner she remarked, 'You do have a lot to do on the house, don't you?'

Taken aback, we thought it already perfection with its patina of age lying over everything. But Yvonne was eyeing the faded shutters, the large iron hinges on the front door, the creaky wooden floors, the swallows' nests in the children's bedroom and the ancient trough at the end of our kitchen where once the wine had been bottled.

These, our nearest 'foreign' neighbours, came and went seasonally, bringing with them heady days of a metropolitan and recherché milieu and a blast of worldly living.

One of our indigenous friends was Marie Aspioti, who had worked for the British Council until – in protest over the British position on Cyprus – she had resigned. Her account of childhood picnics when, in carriages loaded with family, servants and food, they crossed to the west coast of the island to spend a day at Paleokastritsa sounded idyllic. How different from those halcyon days were her lurid tales of village betrayals and clandestine love affairs.

Inadvertently Marie was responsible for my most clumsy clanger concerning our royalty. One day she brought a princess to visit us, one of Prince Philip's sisters – humorous, charming and interested in our old property. Many months later Michael and I were asked to have tea with her. Sitting in her drawing room surrounded by old family photographs, there was one of her with her three sisters as children standing in a row wearing white dresses next to a smaller boy. I asked where each sister now lived (they all married German princes), and pointing to the little boy, forgetting her lineage, added absent-mindedly, 'And where does your brother live?'

With complete composure and without doing a double-take, she replied, 'Buckingham Palace.'

Is there a certain sense of ethics, of probity, to friendship? Peripatetic friends can be real and interactive. My mother was unshakeable regarding her friends who bypassed the wreckage strewn throughout her love life. In Thailand our friendship towards some of those we met had all to do with context. Once we left the country, only a few remained, but those that did have stayed in our lives for more than forty years. The others – ignited with genuine intensity – lasted only as long as we shared physical proximity.

On Corfu two couples in particular became friends, for their generosity, empathy, wit and idiosyncrasies. Rapport was instant.

We were fortunate. Had we taken a house on the other side of the island we would never have met Jocasta and Lucien. Warm-hearted and erudite, they helped us cope with exchanging the reticence of the orient for the full-frontal approach of the Mediterranean. Hospitality – *xenos* – was customary.

Everything hung out. Give a lift to a Greek woman on a road far distant from anywhere, and in no time we were sharing disaster, disease, ruin and tears. In Thailand there had been nothing like that. The Thais' oblique approach was innate.

Fluent in European languages, informative on the ancient world, Jocasta and Lucien beguiled us with directions on how to find inaccessible monasteries in the Peloponnese, where to fill up our wine flasks, dates of the village *paniyiris* (festivals), the significance of name days and ritual behaviour at funerals.

Through their friendship we entered Greece by a side door.

Lucien, with an ebbing hairline, had the appearance of comfy clothes – nothing fitted. Good-looking in a soggy way, he was enfolded by a troposphere of indolence, affable as a passer-by in County Cork, feckless as someone who lets the end of Sellotape stick back on the reel, and – like a cat – assumed he was always wanted.

Jocasta's world was ethnic. Sometimes she joined the village women (the older ones still wore medieval-looking costumes: full black skirts, full-sleeved white blouses under black waist-coats and headdresses that varied from village to village) sitting together on the *pezouli*, a ledge running the length of a house. Other times she sat with the young women as they worked at their dowries. Towels, pillowcases and sheets embroidered and trimmed with crocheted cotton lace were stored in the traditional *preeka* chests decorated with leaves and flowers that were to be found in most village houses (years later they were to be found in antique shops).

One evening, drinking wine and eating *mezedes* on our terrace, Jocasta told us of her childhood in France: 'The Dauphiné . . . really primitive, anyone beyond fifteen miles was an *étranger* . . . my grandparents spoke the ancient language of Occitan . . . a goose girl guarded the geese and each commune had its blacksmith, wheelwright, carpenter and saddler. The best bread ever – better even than Greek – my mother baked in a wood-fired oven . . . we kept the loaves on a hanging shelf safe from vermin. Every autumn I helped my grandfather to bring our sheep down from high pastures . . . from a distance their movement expanded and retracted like fieldfares do rising like a cloud from stubble . . . and how I wish you could taste the local cheese. I love *fetta* but it doesn't compare with Saint-Marcellin or Beaufort from the cows browsing in the Haute Savoie.'

When marginal farming was no longer a way of life, Jocasta's brothers moved away. One left for the Beaujolais vineyards: 'One February I visited him . . . fantastic . . . the pruners' long garments dragged in the snow as they burned the pruned twigs in mobile incinerators made from metal drums mounted on wheels. Blue smoke rose all day into the wintry sky, it was beautiful.

'I was happy!'

Her ebullience was catching: her buoyant spirit was a great source of enjoyment in the long dark days when the island was shrouded in rain for weeks on end and when meeting in cafés or the market was the highlight of our social life. It was a time when there was only seasonal food in the shops; none of the produce whirling round the world today was then available. In their allotted time came artichokes, mandarins, lemons, dried figs – still moist from summer – and the sweetest walnuts. Oranges were the fruit of winter, and at Christmas we'd eat small honey cakes, *finika*, sprinkled with almonds and dusted with cinnamon. At Easter salted cod with *skorthali* was followed by all the fruits in sequence. Apart from the delicate *fraises des bois* which the children sold on the roadside, holding them out in baskets lined with leaves, larger strawberries only appeared along with all the other imported fruit after we'd left the island.

We were in a village *kafeneion* at a table covered in plastic saying *Kalimera* on it and with the usual toothpicks and damp salt, drinking retsina, picking at the olives, *mizithra* (an unsalted ewe's-milk cheese) and freshly fried *kalamarakia*, when we first met Celia and Stavros. With her broad, frank face and large milky-blue eyes that protruded slightly, their lids always visible as in portraits of Medici princes, Celia had a look of naivety.

'I used to faint at the sight of mannequins in shop windows until I came here where there aren't any.' Loquacity flowed out in a breathless stream. 'Now I merely shock the locals . . . who keep their woolly vests on till July, Stavros told me . . . by sunbathing topless with my feet uphill to tan the underside of my breasts.' (Topless bathing has become ubiquitous since then, but at first village women protested. A friend of ours used to walk along the beach covering them with their towels.)

Stavros, an optimistic lecher (reminding us of a friend who arrived in Thailand with a case full of nothing but condoms), used to communicate with the pilot by short-wave radio when the Athens plane was approaching. If any pretty tourists were on board he'd be at the airport (in the sixties a small informal place) in time to welcome wide-eyed girls game for anything. Celia had been one of them. She was easy prey for Stavros, but when they were married and living in the family house her mother-in-law sucked the life out of her.

After a couple of years she fled – into the arms of Meredith: 'With the curly hair of a cherub he wrapped me in charm and benign radiation. Too late I discovered he was a compulsive nomad. For a time he'd lived in a squat in Haight-Ashbury among all the counterculture ... Bob Dylan, Joan Baez, Jack Kerouac, Ginsberg ... when we met he'd been follow-ing Pausanias, his classical Baedeker, through Lakonia and Arkadia until he and his dog, with a pelt like loose underlay, washed up here to write his novel *Shell-less Ego*.'

Yet Meredith chafed. To write he needed stimuli, the ebb and flow of human interactions whether in the Abruzzi or Catalonia. It was time to move on. Celia, as she came to say goodbye, said rather plaintively, 'I used to try soothing him by playing music, but he had the same ear for harmony as Beethoven, or as Tiresias had eyes for art.'

Crossing to the mainland, they wandered among the people of northern Greece, the Vlachs and Karagounis; they traced mythological underworld rivers: the Acheron, the Acheloös, the Peneios and the Styx rising in Mt Chelmos. The last we heard of them they had come to rest among the wild flowers of Messini.

Celia and Meredith, Jocasta and Lucien had been among those rootless friends who came in and out of our lives during the years on Corfu, but once they left, our close involvement – nour-ished on spasmodic meetings – evaporated. Keeping friendships intact is double-edged. Some shrivel through neglect; others thrive however great the distance, however long the pauses. Then meeting again, amity rises like leavened bread.

So it was with Sorrel.

Turning on the spit of a hot afternoon, Michael and I are sitting under Sophie's trees surrounded by oleanders reading a letter from Sorrel. Although long pauses spread between our correspondence, she has a way of jumping events in her life or sending us squibs such as: 'my friend hank, fart he said but he didn't mean fart he meant these bananas have gone bad and this is the problem of communication.'

The letter we had today is longer: 'This year I'm thirty that really is grown up. I can't do handstands anymore. I've been in hospital in Bedford for the last nine weeks, having visions like John Bunyan in prison . . . though not being a sinful creature bound for Hell obliged to give up dancing and bell-ringing . . . I hang onto the word Bed Ford, crossing over – bedlam. The Hospital of St. Mary of Bethlehem – a place for lunatics in the sixteenth century – is my personal Nemesis, my Slough of Despond.

'I'm living in the background of my life. There is no fore-ground. But today my birthday I long to be with you, your family and Piers my first, my deepest love, lumbering across eastern Thailand as we once did to Vientiane. How can I bear it?'

She replied to our invitation to visit us on Corfu: 'Before I do I must first get home to Gossamer who, with the wisdom of a sibyl, has coped with her loony mum.'

But she didn't go home. She wrote from hospital, 'I carry Piers like a parasite, like orchids in your rain tree, he's my resident tapeworm. He once wrote: "Waking with naked skin, head on my shoulder at midnight – sweet woman, where are you now? If by closing your eyelids I could annihilate past and future and suspend you in the dark water of my love you could loosely lie, sprawled child, forgetting what and if." But the earth tilted the other way and all my ancient certitudes are lost.'

She used to say that the problem her patients had was that their interior living was at odds with the exterior: 'In the end it's a matter of which one wins.'

*　　*　　*

We left Greece in 1976. We sold the house and returned to England, to where the children's lives had taken them. Sureen to the London School of Contemporary Dance, Tamsin to university, David to Times Books, Michael and I to Shropshire.

Which is stronger: attachment to people or to houses? To people or to hereditary homes? For me it's people every time. I've always felt I could transplant myself into places in the world and take root if the right person or people were there. But for others, the wrench of leaving their familial base remains a consuming regret for the rest of their lives. For Vita Sackville-West, the loss of her ancestral home at Knole lasted her lifetime. Nearer home, Tamsin never forgave us for selling our house on Corfu, which she loved, yet at the same time regrets not having attended an English school and learnt about Bunsen burners. As for Michael, our return to the Midlands (which, according to Hilaire Belloc, 'are sodden and unkind'), was a definite form of homecoming to the landscape of his childhood and his schooldays.

Two years later we heard of Sorrel's suicide.

Mourning is built into old age, but the colour of grieving changes when a person dies young.

My husband and my mother had lived over threescore years.

Cordelia and Sorrel left with years unfulfilled.

Why did I feel an oblique responsibility for them both? For my sister, I was certain, at the time of her death, that I could bear being dead more easily than she could. With Sorrel, momentarily, and with an overweening sense of power, I thought I might have prevented her suicide.

Sighing has become a component of growing old – increasingly so. Some tweak of memory, a person or an occasion

– gone from my life for years – surfaces through a letter or a photograph.

In my hand is a photograph of Sorrel sitting on a bench at the Chiang Mai asylum between two of the inmates, shaven-headed, baggy white clothes, with their spread-toed feet bare. She's showing them a small object in her hand. I can't see what it is, but from the intensity of those slack-mouthed figures either side of her, something is absorbing them. No one is turned towards the photographer.

Nothing lessens thoughts of Sorrel that slew and yaw over the most forsaken act in the world. I am stuck with them.

Held between my fingers is a moment petrified. While I'm still alive the occasion will remain immortalised. Later someone will come across the photograph and wonder, 'Who is that young woman with hair folded like ravens' wings framing her face?'

And throw it away.

Suicide is a matter of outwitting. Arrangements have to be made. Dorothy Parker wrote:

> Razors pain you;
> Rivers are damp;
> Acids stain you;
> And drugs cause cramp.
> Guns aren't lawful;
> Nooses give;
> Gas smells awful;
> You might as well live.

People who choose an overdose play Russian roulette – there's a chance they will survive – but Sorrel didn't play games. Hers was no gesture – no cry for help, botched overdose, garage fumes or ineptly cut wrists, no stomach pump or open window clearing the kitchen of gas.

Friedrich Nietzsche wrote, 'The thought of suicide is a great source of comfort . . .' Maybe, but suicide is also the ultimate selfish act, leaving the living with minds unable to let go, as we found for ourselves when we heard that Sorrel had leapt off the southernmost point of the Peloponnese.

Had the Mani lain dormant in Sorrel since her hippie days when she'd explored the Taygetus Mountains and beyond? So it is that I see her poised among wild orchids and iris, stepping out of her sandals, hear her cry protesting the logic of gravity before contact with the merging surge of the Aegean and Ionian seas. I keep her there – thrumming in her ears, hair wrenched to filaments – on the way but never arriving. I don't want to hear her last cry united with the crowing of shearwaters tirelessly skimming the waves as she dispossesses herself of her heart's reproach for the day she walked away from Piers. As a petal turning in water, moved by the current, with waterlogging lungs, she floats through luminous blue darkening to ultramarine, her limbs trailing ribbons of phosphorescence until she lies rocking to the pulse of the ocean.

Her grave is among sea urchins, barnacles, molluscs and kelp. Her companions – the fastest of creatures, outpacing the whale, beloved of Poseidon – are the dolphins rising and turning, fluid flesh parting the water with centuries of ease.

7

Time with a Gift of Tears

Before the beginning of years
   There came to the making of man
Time, with a gift of tears;
   Grief, with a glass that ran . . .
Swinburne

I thought I'd prepared myself for the day when, calling his name as I entered the house, I'd get no response. I used to look at Michael asleep in an armchair, wearing his dressing gown, dying from a malignant brain tumour, and I'd think: this is the man with whom I've shared my life, our children, our love of poetry, good food and our garden. This is the man who has comforted me over countless sorrows, who has remained patient with my outlandish schemes. He is the companion with whom I've travelled, whose empathy I depend on and from whom I am bracing myself to be for ever deprived.

However prepared you think you are, the finality of death cannot be rehearsed.

*   *   *

Universal advice to the bereaved is: wait. Slow up. Do nothing precipitous. I didn't. But after living through the four seasons I knew that the garden Michael and I had made together no longer held any charm: the quintessential alchemy that had arisen between us as we walked about the land, planted bulbs, trees and old roses, no longer held any felicity. The contours of living had changed shape. Without Michael, homecoming was a non-event.

There is something profoundly satisfactory about an occupation with someone you love: the person you know so well that words become surplus. So it was with us, and so it was with friends of ours. Working together in their studio, Lesley Heale used to say to her husband Jonathan, 'Twenty-five years we've spent passing the paintbrush between us.' In other milieus, couples have co-operated writing books together, and famous acting couples throughout their professional lives have walked the same stage, yet for others that way of living is abhorrent: 'Impossible. We respect each other's work, but we keep that part of our marriage separate.'

For Michael and me the act of *shared gardening*, not the *garden*, was what had mattered. We may have disagreed, argued about steps, walls or wheelbarrows, Latin names and weed killers – in fact the basic grist of creation – but we were both suckers (not intended as a jokey pun) for roses. We never disagreed about them. Instinctively we moved in step, and when we wandered through a rose nursery in full spate, we found we'd listed the same ones without a word spoken between us.

The consultant who told us in April that Michael hadn't long to live was wrong. After the operation to remove as much as possible of the tumour, frail, aged by twenty years, stuffed with chemicals when headaches crippled him, Michael never surrendered. That summer Tamsin and I took him to France, where at a gentle pace he was able to enjoy the scenery, the food and the imaginative revival of past journeys in the warmth of the sun. By Christmas, with all the family, we took him to a quiet hotel in a village across the Channel, where Michael, determined, prolonged every enjoyment left to him.

Without support from one another I doubt if we could have endured an occasion we each knew was terminal.

Michael died in the spring. Yet it wasn't until the melancholy days of winter, when the stillness was immutable, my breath carved the air, and my footsteps crunched through frost, that within this caul of quietude I could release my grief. Looking had nothing to do with it. Rather, on a day of suspended activity some interior deliverance surfaced.

Anyone who has read Antoine de Saint-Exupéry's allegorical story *The Little Prince* will remember his reassuring aphorism: 'What is essential is invisible to the eye.' On my bedside table I keep a collection of non-confrontational books – pre-sleep stories such as the romantic tale of love and youth in Alain-Fournier's *Le Grand Meaulnes* or David Garnett's fantasy *Lady Into Fox,* and *Twenty Years A-Growing*, about Maurice O'Sullivan's idyllic childhood on the Blasket Islands off the south-west coast of Ireland.

Escapes, escapes, through literature, not drugs or sleeping pills.

Being an agnostic allows me the freedom to move across many latitudes, among spiritual places where I don't belong. When I hear the service of Compline I'm moved by an inexplicable perception as I listen to its pure simplicity at the end of the day.

For a time in my life I attended a Quaker school where the integrity and belief that God resides within one's self made me envious of their self-contained ethos.

Buddhism surrounded us in Thailand: 'From the moment of birth we are becoming shadows of our former selves.' Admiring its width of boundaries in contrast to more formal practices, Michael and I attended many Buddhist ceremonies, but though I struggled with meditation it constantly eluded me.

Belonging nowhere, the first time I heard the call of the muezzin with its mysterious portent from a minaret in Istanbul, I stopped, entranced by the sound of quarter-tones alien to my ear.

With a Greek friend we were introduced to the theatrical ceremony on Good Friday at one of the smaller churches in Corfu town. Following the bedecked bier we processed along the street to the dim interior of the church full of the scent of incense, glitter, icons, candles and the deep voices of Orthodox chanting.

But landing nowhere, having no framework, I'm aware that an instinctive response to things – whether the proportions of a building, a piece of music, a painting or a friend's benign biopsy – leaves me at a disadvantage. I have no one to thank, no one to whom I should make my supplications for a child in a Mexican earthquake up to her chest in water as rescuers try to extricate her legs from a fallen beam. For two days, across the world, we watched as adults shouted down encouragement to a small face smiling upwards to the cameraman, her dark eyes full of confidence that soon they'd rescue her. But the hours passed; her valiant spirit ebbed as the crane needed to lift the beam from across her legs trapped below water never appeared. The rescuers needed more time; the child had none.

Yet as long as I remembered her, surely that child wasn't dead? Not entirely.

There were others. Children I mourned nightly, keeping them alive in some sort of other dimension through intense recall. Having no religion I hadn't any extraterrestrial comfort, no panacea to placate black thoughts when remembering a child – the legacy of Ceauşescu's Romania – lying on her side, sucking on *two* hands for greater comfort. Nor have I forgotten the young fair-haired hostage caught in the crossfire of a terrorist attack on a bus in Germany. Who were they? A handful of nameless children thrown aside like detritus with such vandalism, in such violent circumstances that the pain of their deaths postponed sleep night after night. Perhaps it was after all a form of prayer? There must be a kind of healing as long as their deaths aren't allowed to sink into oblivion.

Nor did I have anyone to thank for having no intimation of the last twilight Michael and I would walk together among our roses, and for that I am profoundly and everlastingly grateful.

We were gone, and the garden with us. When I left I knew it was finished. The garden could not be perpetuated, nor should it. And I recall the Frenchwoman whose garden I once visited: 'When one disappears, that day the garden will be over.'

Chilling words, but the truth.

This last part is for my great-grandchildren – as yet unborn – to tell them how I came to be living in Ludlow, where I'd like to think one or other of them might live to spend May mornings looking into the branches of the magnolia tree as I have done for more than two decades.

A year after Michael died I moved to a town seven miles from where we used to live. I had never bought a house on my own. The moment I'd agreed with the agent I panicked.

Michael and I had done everything together. What was I doing plunging about in the deep end with no firm edge to hang on to? Dismayed, I rang our son David, asking him how I could get out of it.

'Everyone feels like that,' was his laconic reply. 'Go ahead.'

I did. Ludlow is an elegant town. A castle where Milton's *Comus* was first performed and where the 'little princes' were imprisoned before being murdered at the Tower of London, the magnificent St Laurence's parish church dating from the twelfth century, and the Buttercross, formerly a market. The streets of handsome houses, the narrow lanes and the two bridges across the river Teme were where Michael would have enjoyed living in his declining years.

My lamentations are not just for myself but for him.

With the enthusiasm and urging of the three children I moved into a terraced house with a long back garden and into a new phase of my life. Friends, concerned that I was living on my own, need not have been. Opening the door into an empty house was something I accepted, knowing with certainty that if Michael couldn't be on the other side, no one else would do. (A door in a doorframe would be my luxury if I were banished to a desert island: the gestures of turning the handle, opening and walking through and, conversely, closing a door behind are fundamental, each with their singular merits.)

Returning home – in a town small enough that when I forget my purse I can still do my shopping – and opening the door into an empty house has become a serene act.

My house is between the castle and the river. I remember, years ago, sitting with friends in their London garden, having the curious impression that, although we were overlooked by a terrace of high houses, the surrounding walls gave us a sense of seclusion.

Ever since then, the lure of back gardens had intrigued me. I brooded on them when in the country I paddled among our streamside primulas or sat among the lily-flowered tulips in the orchard. With our limitless space, perversely, I thought of courtyards, a place of paving and pots, where an outstretched hand touched a definitive boundary and where there was no chance of trespassing further. I imagined a minimalist sanctum of stone and shadows, of walls painted with trompe-l'oeil perspective, or maybe a garden of paradise inspired by the Moghuls of Rajasthan. And occasionally, when driving through urban streets, I'd be curious to walk through the front door of one of the houses to the back, to a secret, personal space created by a stranger. And then there was the enjoyment to be had by looking at back gardens from a train where individual use of space was visible, perhaps the charm of allotments with their small sheds and higgledy-piggledy layout, displaying someone's vegetable commitment.

But now, since moving to Ludlow, my focus has altered. From a first floor window looking beyond my thirty-by-seventy-foot back garden, I plunder gardens outside my boundaries appropriating everything in sight. Near or far is my estate. Through the changing seasons I regard with concern or jubilation the return of blossom in the gardens of neighbouring streets: with guiltless cupidity the domed mosque of a distant copper beech and a horse chestnut with its annual ranks of white spires are both mine. The pinkish young growth on my neighbour's eucalyptus flutters in the wind; a ceanothus drapes across a dividing wall where its ultramarine intensity lasts for weeks; a white wisteria, a buddleia with damson-coloured flowers and the conflagration of a creeper are all within my tenure. While on a patch of grass outside my front door I've laid claim to a sixty-year-old magnolia. A tree of such splendour I've stood each spring gazing into its branches, hoping I'll be doing the same again the following May.

Margaret Drabble once described a magnolia at Hidcote Manor: 'up there against the heavy skies of Gloucestershire bloomed weirdly, impossibly, the large white flowers of China. Great single blooms like vast butterflies, like resting birds ... Too beautiful to be plausible, yet petals the size of saucers floated down to lie on the hellebores, as pledges of its vegetable truth.'

Did she know, I wonder, that she was describing *my* tree? The one I have annexed since I moved here? And how her words, so descriptive, so perfect, are written in my Commonplace Book to be read again each May?

Other things too have been recorded there at incidental moments since I was in my teens. Poems or prose which resonated at the time, and some that, decades later, still does. Once, hearing the daily litany of a shipping forecaster warning sea captains that the weather south of Rockall was 'drifting and losing its identity', I wrote it down, adding – obviously in a black mood – 'Don't we all?'

I know I go on about gardens, but we all need something. There are those who go on about their finances, their golf handicap or their operations: weight, cats, how much to a gallon, their digestion. For me it used to be gardens when it wasn't friends, food or travel, but now I'm left with merely residual recollections of a long time ago. Thirty years I've confirmed from looking in my 'Idiot Book', the place I used to record everything we planted and how it fared, alongside small snapshots Michael had taken of things at the pinnacle of blooming. I also noted the number of cruciform signs in the margins, proof of how vicious winter frosts were killing rosemary and cistus, magnolia and dogwood.

After Michael died I took my bad habits with me. A back garden in a small town and I planted twenty-eight trees in a space seventy by thirty feet. I tortured them, cutting the tresses of a Kilmarnock willow; allowing rust to be a dominant colour; using the cheesecloth from Stilton cheeses to stick round plastic pots, giving them the appearance of antiquity. Feral violets washed up against a garden table, clematis bound up every vertical, smothering, strangling, and I used the wrong sort of paint: water-based colours on the summer house, benches and chairs to allow the grain of the wood to show through. Every two or three years it's easy to renew. And there's hardly one male visitor who doesn't warn me: 'I'd get that valerian out if I were you, before it pulls down the wall!'

But the intervening years have eroded my gardening vigour. With passive acceptance I now let the far end of the garden become more dishevelled year by year. I'm doing the same. We, the garden and I, lose control at the same pace. Only my courtyard still fizzes. The colourful flourishes, the declamatory embellishments where I've painted the chairs a muted orange to tie in with pots of tulips and pansies, which I know will soon curdle when cascades of pinkish roses take over, is a sight I relish. Even on overcast days the outlook glows. And temporarily it appeals to a wild duck who has been hatching her eggs – unseen by me – at the end of the garden. She now brings her brood of eight newly hatched ducklings to my back door for breadcrumbs.

How could I not rejoice that orderliness has been usurped by wildlife?

After my book *A Gentle Plea for Chaos* was published (the year Michael died and our daughter Tamsin was pregnant with his first grandchild), this led on to others, to talks to gardening clubs here and in America, and articles about important gardens where I'd drive to some superb location forgetting that there were campanulas growing out of the dirt in the back-door hinge of my car. Unlike Michael, who in his youth had cared about cars and owned a series of racy vehicles, mine was just a machine to take me from here to there. I hadn't cared that one winter morning my five-year-old granddaughter Cassandra had irreparably inscribed her name through the frost across the bonnet of the car.

The idea for another book came about entirely from the chance remark of a librarian telling me of elderly people who, on wet afternoons, browsed the gardening shelves looking for answers. Left to cope alone, these marooned widows and widowers were stuck in the past.

'My husband loved his lilies – spent hours cherishing them. What am I to do now? I haven't the know-how to deal with them, but whenever I see them wilting I feel so guilty.'

Their guilt was my catalyst.

A Breath from Elsewhere was an attempt to strengthen their resolve – bereft and coping alone for the first time – to move in another direction, face another way, release themselves from self-censure, and to remind them that what was *then* no longer applied. Burdened by misplaced consciences, their self-imposed culpability had become intolerable.

Yet I know gardens are a lifeline; they form a small calm eye in a world gone mad. But when these guilty people are overwhelmed by summer amplitude, they shouldn't feel persecuted by siren voices outside the window.

Don't be bullied by greenfly on the bud.

What was *then* applies to me too when I'm asked if I mind returning to where Michael and I made our garden, and where now my daughter Tamsin and her family are living. Such places cannot be perpetuated. Once the creator has left, the quiddity – which made the garden what it was – has been lost for ever, to be replaced by something else.

If you are a gardener you grow light as well as flowers (illumination is what I mean, not weight), a component I hadn't been aware of until, seeing the sun shining through the petals of a group of meconopsis, I noticed how the blue profundity became as pale as the white of a baby's eyes. The same with clematis, where one petal overlaps another – the colour is dark, not blue at all but turbid purple. On an overcast day colours appear more radiant and white flowers more luminous at twilight. Really it is to Stella Bowen that I owe my dawning awareness of light, transference, refraction when I first watched her at work at her easel which, as a child, I carried up a hill somewhere for her to paint a green scene of pastoral England.

What a legacy. Years later, with a small lens, I peered into flowers, to a bee's-eye view, a form of voyeurism by looting the territory of insects where spines, filaments and seed heads are visible. Look! Look closer. Insects inhabit these places of gilded forests and dusky voluptuousness as they drown in honey sweetness. Deep in the interior of flowers pillage and rape are going on, insects – invisible to the naked eye – are foraging among stamens. Deeper still the shuddering stigma, the anther and the ovary, indicate that gang-bang chaos is taking place.

The libido of flowers is arcane. Gazing myopically into flowers, at the ecclesiastical plush of peonies, at the barbarous hooks on the seed head of vermilion-coloured clematis, I move slowly through the garden. The centre of a Japanese anemone is as homely as yellow jelly surrounded by custard, and the convolvulus has hair-line fractures running the length of its petals as fine as those on the face of an ageing oriental. The scarlet heart of a potentilla is far from innocent: within the flower there are black stamens glistening with lascivious spit.

Once having entered this realm of minute observation I can never again be unaware that what I see is all there is to see. A palimpsest is fixed for ever in my looking. How different when on a foggy day in November – without distance or shadows – the garden becomes a cipher. I walk with damp hair and moist eyelashes through coils of mist: I hear the river, the church bells and, far off, the lowing of a cow, yet see nothing. The garden I thought I knew has become opaque.

However, not everything is so illusionary and passive. There are mundane days when I stand on my doorstep looking for a man. In fact occasionally I put my card out in the hall saying: *Help! A Man.* No wonder wised-up male friends hesitate to cross my threshold; they know they will be hauled off to move a bench at the end of the garden, to bring indoors the Greek urns too fragile to withstand the frost, or to climb a ladder I'm too wimpish to climb on my own. King Richard III may have pleaded for a horse, but an aged commoner prays for a man.

How can something so simple be so *increasingly* unattainable?

A Breath from Elsewhere describes how I made this garden, but now, in a different phase of my life, I have put down my spade. I no longer write about gardens, visit them for an article, pore over plant catalogues or travel miles to nurseries with a list of names. My garden no longer fills my horizon.

And if gardening is a form of self-expression, there are days when I think I can do without that exposure.

Faced with physical dilapidation, I have accepted the inevitable: old age means I can no longer stoop, climb ladders or lift a stone slab. Nor can I keep the garden the way I made it when I first moved to Ludlow and groups of English or American gardeners came to see it. At that time Rosemary Verey – who had been a supportive garden guru to me ever since hers was the first garden I'd been asked to write about – brought the American artist and writer Robert Dash to stay the weekend. My lasting memory of their visit is of having to dash – no witticism intended – out for another bottle of whisky. I'd visited Robert's singular garden in the Hamptons on Long Island, returning to Manhattan on the charmingly named Hampton Jitney. And never to be forgotten was the night before, at a literary dinner, when I was delighted by my neighbour at table asking me to 'Shoot the mustard!'

But all that was years ago when my garden was worth the journey. Yet people still ask to see it, forgetting that both plants and people are transient: the place is a remnant of what once it was. They still expect – I no longer do.

A snowy Sunday and winter shakes my memory as I look into the black rigging of the magnolia outlined with white outside my window. Distantly, beyond the woods, I see black figures walking their dogs, and not for the first time I rejoice in living here.

Of course when I moved to Ludlow I brought a lot of impedimenta with me: emotional and physical. Despite half a century having passed since her death, two nights ago I dreamt of Cordelia – ill, not dead. The dream persisted throughout the day, but why, after so many years, should I encounter sorrow rising to the surface with undiminished force and with no apparent pretext? And why, after so many years, do I wake remembering our children when still in their fledgling state needing help getting dressed, easing knuckles like sightless moles nosing for the sleeve's end, toes like curling chrysalises into socks? How I wanted them to keep their fresh-seeing eyes, their ability to be confounded, but I let years slide by thinking and planning, looking forward to 'what next' instead of looking at 'now'.

I thought I had time, but childhood passes. Grown at a tangent, happening in my sleep, I found them older. If only I'd hung on to all that credulity before the frontiers closed, before their laughter became inaudible and childhood was replaced by the assumed 'age of reason', cynicism, rationalism or disenchantment.

As a zoom lens on a camera, edges of my life keep coming into perspective. Although the space between Michael and me is widening year by year, some habits remain amaranthine like the imaginary flower that never fades. Drawing back the curtains on snowy roofs, or waking to the gasping breath of a hot-air balloon frail as a butterfly, passing overhead, or watching a badger lolloping along the pavement up the hill, involuntarily I say, 'Look, Michael!'

Nonsense. But in-built responses are stuck, impossible to shed regardless of the intervening years. Being alone can be sad. Nothing profound, but a need to say 'Yes' out loud not always into an empty room. If that sounds mawkish, it is. Sharing enjoyment of small things is visceral.

So what about all that stuff on contentment and wisdom as we near the edge? The publication of my first book was not a life replacing a life, as had happened when my mother died and Tamsin was born, nor when my sister died and we adopted Sureen, but a creation of some sort, particularly as more than half the garden photographs had been taken by Michael, sadly published too late for him to see them. A photographer's eye is unique in the same way as an artist's. They are consummate sorcerers. When I look at a plant I also take in the blurred imagery on the periphery of my sight – but not the photographer. Constrained by the margin of a frame, their intent remains clear as they petrify a moment on the point of dissolving. Now those boxes of petrified moments lie neglected on shelves. Almost all our life together as we gardened or travelled abroad has remained transfixed by Michael on archaic slides that no one uses now or would have the time to sort through.

Other stuff – tangible and indispensable – also came with me to Ludlow. Love letters between Phyllis and Aylmer, diaries and photographs: one that reminds me how embarrassing she was when visiting me at school wearing chic, colourful clothes quite unlike any of the other mothers. They were all so dowdy: concerned with the intellect not the flesh. And I remember when she was married to Aylmer, when she dressed up for an evening in Soho at the Gargoyle Club – frequented by Dylan Thomas, Noël Coward, Augustus John et al. – she always added a long scented chiffon scarf that floated behind her – a '*Suivez-moi, jeune homme*' she called it. Oh yes, she certainly belonged to the world of the flesh as well as the heart.

Stella Bowen's paintings are here – they hang in rooms all over the house. Once they hung on the walls of my mother's house in London. I remember how, after I was married, whenever I arrived there she would welcome me with warmth and happiness, running me a bath with her traditional gesture of love. A friend commenting on Robert Frost's words 'Home is a place where, when you have to go there, they have to take you in . . .' wrote in a letter, 'I should have called it a place you somehow haven't to deserve.' A sentiment felt by Cordelia and me each time we went back.

And every week, winding the carriage clock Phyllis inherited from her mother, with its bevel-edged glass panels, solidity and weight, I see my grandmother in a dress hanging perpendicular from shoulder to ankles, black-buttoned shoes and a string of beads swinging to and fro across her bosom. Astonishingly, with insight and tolerance – considering the era into which she was born – she wrote to my father, admonishing him for forbidding my mother from seeing Cordelia and me when the turbulence with Aylmer was in full swing. I still have the letter. My grandmother had loved us with the kind of love that skips a generation, total and unqualified – an altogether different thing to parental love as I have discovered with my grandchildren – and the thread that links us remains unbroken from even further back in time.

How surprised my grandmother would be to know I sleep in the linen sheets (woven on such a narrow loom that there are flat seams down the centre) she inherited from her grandmother, who had been born in 1783.

Embroidered in minute cross-stitch is the date 1802.

And I brought Michael's scythe with me. Not for use, but because it was the cherished garden implement he used in the dog days of summer when even the dippers had stopped singing along the brook. In *A Gentle Plea for Chaos* is the photograph he'd taken of his scythe hanging in an apple tree. On an August morning, long after the lily-flowered tulips appeared under the wild cherry trees, through a mist of lengthening grasses, he'd take his scythe into the orchard. While I was making coffee I could hear, through the open window, the rhythmic swish of the blade with occasional pauses as he honed it with a whetstone. The essence of summer was in those sounds. Sounds that unravelled back through centuries of pastoral labouring until usurped by vast machines audible from fields away.

The blade, oiled, wrapped in sacking, the elegantly shaped wooden handle where his hands had worn to satin the two holding grips, Michael's scythe lies across a beam in my cellar: an heirloom for my grandchildren who never knew their grandfather. But I'm alive. And while I am, the link is not yet severed.

In years to come who, I wonder, will unwrap the scythe, wipe the blade and sharpen it with a whetstone?

Among all the memorabilia I've been sorting, cataloguing, ejecting or merely mulling over with indecision, I find an unexpected pleasure. Turning the pages of *Art, Love & War*, the 2002 Australian exhibition catalogue of Stella Bowen's work, I come upon a familiar picture which years ago faded from my memory.

In the curious way random connections happen, I heard of this exhibition – taking place on the other side of the world – purely by chance. The chance came through the late theatre designer Dr Julia Trevelyan Oman – a friend with a prodigious memory – who recalled having seen some of Stella's paintings in my house. When Marilyn Darling, in a letter to Sir Roy Strong (Julia's husband), mentioned the forthcoming exhibition of Stella's work in Canberra, Julia remembered, rang me up and put us in touch. In March 2002 the retrospective opened at the Australian War Memorial. The following February, while it was touring the country, I received a postcard from Julia saying how she and Roy had visited the show: 'It was beautiful and really rather touching . . . Stella's a great discovery of the Australians – by now a heroine.' (Oh Stella, if you could have read those words written on a picture postcard of your painting of flowers in a green pot!)

The paintings – traced, catalogued, measured and where possible dated – had been painstakingly assembled by Lola Wilkins, the curator (painstaking because Stella's work is scattered about the world), for a show of seventy-two canvases sponsored by the Gordon Darling Foundation. Thus through fortuitous connections one of Stella's self-portraits, which for years had been on the wall of my house in Shropshire, found its rightful home in the National Portrait Gallery, Australia. It was her *Embankment Gardens* (now in the Art Gallery of South Australia) that triggered my memory of her painting it pre-war from our top-floor flat off the Strand. It was after we'd moved from a large house in Belsize Grove, Hampstead, where the 'Stop Me and Buy One' ice-cream man, the muffin man carrying his wooden tray on his head, the coal merchant and the scrap man with his cart shouted out as they passed along our street.

Embankment Gardens was painted when Phyllis and Aylmer were living in the Adelphi and when Cordelia and I went to school every day by Underground from Charing Cross to Hampstead. How well I knew that picture. In the achromatic light of a winter afternoon, through an intricacy of twigs, is a view of Cleopatra's Needle (the obelisk from Egypt) and beyond, skeletal and shadowy, the arc of Waterloo Bridge. I can almost hear the subdued sound of traffic along the Embankment. In the foreground, surrounded by bare flower beds, is the bandstand: pretty, lightweight, with a filigree-edged cupola. In summer, as soon as Cordelia and I heard the sound of the bandsmen warming up (like cicadas at the start of a Mediterranean summer), we would rush down flights of stone stairs, through the iron gates and across the pathway to the musicians resplendent in scarlet and gold. Unlike the others, sitting in deckchairs, we never paid. The park keeper knew us.

One Christmas morning I looked down from our flat at two people walking past the bandstand as though it was a normal day. 'Don't they know it's Christmas Day?' I asked my mother, dumbfounded that anybody, on this of all days, could do something so ordinary.

Some of Stella's pictures I have are half-finished. Unfinished paintings have a poignant quality; there's an immediacy about them as though a moment ago the artist had put aside the brushes having been overtaken by twilight, a saucepan boiling over or a person from Porlock. Irretrievably something is lost. Can she have intended to abandon the picture only for it to show up decades later? Three portraits, one of herself as a young woman and two of her daughter Julie, are left in mid-sentence. Another, unframed, is of a pair of Ford Madox Ford's polished brown shoes on the seat of a chair over which hangs his jacket with a silky lining where the droop of the shoulders gives the appearance of it still being warm.

Au Nègre de Toulouse (even after their separation, Stella described how the painting was progressing in her letters to Ford) hangs over my fireplace. In the seventies, when Michael, the children and I were living on Corfu, Stella and Ford's grandson Julian – travelling through Europe from his home in Los Angeles – came to visit us. A charming young backpacker doing his European thing, and I remember how taken aback I was by his indifference to his grandmother's triptych *Au Nègre de Toulouse*.

As I opened the door into the room where the picture was hanging, I was moved that he should be seeing it, so remarkable and original, for the very first time. The painting hung between the two upstairs sitting-room windows of our Venetian house overlooking the Ionian Sea and distant mainland, where dolphins plunged through the waves and where the lights of the fishermen's boats could be seen at nightfall. Julian barely glanced at it; it meant nothing. He was concerned with the need to change money and with ferry times to the mainland. But he was young. And perhaps a portrait group of M. and Mme Lavigne – proprietors of a Paris restaurant in 1927 – was meaningless to a youth surveying the distant and unobtainable Albanian coastline with a hungry eye.

I value most *Au Nègre de Toulouse* – a testimony to the period between the wars when life was precious, impecunious and, more than anything, saturated by a vital flow of artistic creativity. The era was unique. The poorer quarters of Paris had reminded Marcel Proust of Venice in the morning 'with their tall, splayed chimneys to which the sun imparts the most vivid pinks, the brightest reds – like a garden flowering above the houses . . .'

Paris neighbourhoods of small, local shops were still extant. The kind where the florist was next door to the goldfish man; the *cordier* – dark, hanging with ropes and smelling of sisal – was a few doors down from the taxidermist from whose window a dusty barn owl looked out with glass eyes onto the congested pavement. The baker, the barber, the butcher with a red-and-white awning and the newsagent with postcards, books of nursery rhymes and scholastic *cahiers de devoirs* in the window provided the essentials in the locality. At the back of his shop the candle-maker worked among loops of cotton thread in an atmosphere pungent with paraffin wax and the acrid smell of tallow. Next to the art supplier's the dressmaker lived on the floor above the bookbinder. The *épicerie* and the horse butcher with his gold emblem over the shop were a few doors down. Goods were delivered: not just coal but milk and eggs and the daily unwrapped baguette propped against the door of the upstairs flat belonging to a night-shift worker. The second-hand clothes shop had a sign promising racks of *créations couture*; the picture framer handled gold leaf as delicately as though it were the wing of a dragonfly; the oyster man tempted his customers with promises of pearls.

Amongst all this merchandise, the courtyard Stella and Ford shared with the Ezra Pounds was '... a vision of summer greenery dropping down across the windows, dusty ivy on a tattered trellis, some ornamental shrubs, a stone bench, a few bulbs and the dark-stained façade of a shabby *pavillon*'.

Anyone who has once lived in Paris is forever homesick for, in Stella's words, 'the most hospitable quarter of the most hospitable city in the world'.

When the Pounds invited a crowd of people to their studio to meet them, Ford reminded Stella – the provincial colonial – that they were no longer in England where the arts were always in disgrace but in a country where to be an ignoramus in such matters was unpardonable. He proved it. When Proust died, Ford called the waiter over in a café, asking him where and when the funeral would take place. The waiter told him, naturally, Ford said, but had he asked an English waiter about the funeral, say, of Thomas Hardy, he'd have received a blank stare. And when they attended the funeral, it was impressively stage-managed in the Catholic tradition with 'groves of candles', festoons of black and silver, and Bach on the organ.

The central market, Les Halles – described brilliantly by Emile Zola in the nineteenth century – was still, in the twentieth, the nourishing source of life for the capital. Fed by innumerable arteries flowing into the city through the agricultural vastness of rural France, fresh produce was plentiful and cheap. The sound of horse-drawn wagons echoed through the streets at the same hour as late revellers returning home stopped to eat at one of the bistros for anything from woodcock to tripe. From the penetrating ozone smell of fish, the earthy pungency of mushrooms, to a fragrance of wood strawberries, a whole gamut of scents identified each locale. Raucous with the dialects of farmers from the Vosges to the Mayenne, the creaking of axles, the cooing of doves and the crowing of cockerels, the place heaved with activity. Before the sun had risen, in the lamplit hangars the farmers off-loaded their wares onto slabs of marble or trestle tables, leaving smaller produce in panniers and wickerwork hampers.

Stella described how the hotels, restaurants and shops sent their staff to bring back the freshest, the sweetest-smelling dew-covered produce whether from dairy farmers, stock breeders or fishermen. Tactile – squeezing, handling, smelling and discarding produce – the buyers were shrewd and sharp-witted, bargaining over every transaction, with the saleswomen dressed in heavy serge dresses and white bonnets, shouting their wares with guttural voices.

Was it from Les Halles (relocated in 1969 to Rungis, near Orly airport) that Françoise purchased the beef, calf's foot, pigs' trotters, onions, carrots, herbs, lemon and so on for the classic dish of *boeuf à la mode* at the home of Proust's aunt? Anyone searching for good bourgeois cooking – after a surfeit of the elaborate creations from starred chefs that proliferate in the second millennium – should turn back the clock to French time, to Proust and the many traditional dishes connecting that author to the sensual enjoyment of food, to the palate and to memory. And talking of sensual, the Goncourt brothers recorded that on Wednesday, 3 April 1878, at a house-warming dinner for Zola, 'He gave us a very choice, very tasty dinner, a real gourmet's dinner, including some grouse whose scented flesh Daudet compared to an old courtesan's flesh marinated in a bidet.'

On the table beside me is Ford's book *A Mirror to France*, with its dedication: 'To Phyllis in memory of Paris days, Ford Madox Ford 1st of May MCMXXVI'.

Had it been Stella and her tales of living in Paris that had unconsciously inspired my curiosity to find out what was left of their France when, decades later, I wrote a book on chefs, restaurants and bistros in my quest to find the legendary world Elizabeth David wrote about in *French Provincial Cooking*?

Changing from writing books about gardens to food, I needed a publisher. That meant, before anything was signed, a preliminary synopsis and a sample chapter had to be submitted. Having driven all over France with Michael for so many years, first from Shropshire, later from Corfu, and again when writing *The Secret Gardens of France*, I'd accumulated several notebooks of meals and travel trivia. Enough to make a book. The synopsis was not a problem and I had an outline of the chapters. '*Si on ne sait pas, on fait le coulis,*' one chef explained, throwing out his hands and grimacing. *Coulis* was on every menu: to such an extent that I wrote a chapter entitled 'Is There Life after *coulis*?'

But the sample chapter I submitted was something else: a scam.

The restaurant Chez Clotilde was an illusion, an imaginary restaurant based on an amalgam of so many small, out-of-the-way places we'd visited since our first journey across the Channel in 1951. I only had to draw on my pages of notes to resurrect a thousand details of kitchens, cooks, markets and menus.

I sited Chez Clotilde at the end of a road going nowhere. Michael and I had often travelled through the Chartreuse on our way to Italy and Greece – the *département* I chose for Clotilde's humble auberge. With care I noted the height of Mont Granier at the head of the valley where the Cozon stream flowed; I checked on whether it was chestnut or oak country; on the local produce, the local Apremont wine from the slopes of Chambéry and the game: the wild hare, boar and venison. Clotilde's relatives all had names I'd taken from a list of saints' days at the back of the red Michelin guide. Her husband Apollinaire who'd fallen on his gun, Aunt Solange who went to the bad, and cousin Crépin who was a bit simple. Names of such splendour: Tatiana, Gaspar, Angèle and Modeste were her family. In fact I really would have loved to have written the whole book like this, based on past and present notes of the people Michael and I had met. People who had been so inspirational it was easy to imagine what wild backgrounds, families and kitchen betrayals might have gone on. But I had a book to write – not imaginary but factual – about the chefs, markets, cheese makers, bakers and vineyards, and with the names and addresses of the restaurants listed at the back. *A Spoon with Every Course* was not my title – my editor insisted on using the heading of my chapter on Normandy where each diner is provided with a small shovel to scoop up the cream and Calvados sauce.

Pace Clotilde, whom I'd made elderly from the start. I knew she had to be dead by the time I finished the book. Sadly nothing remained where once Chez Clotilde had been in the valley of the Cozon, just an old menu still pinned onto the board after the last meal had been eaten. On summer evenings the sweet scent of clover filled the air instead of *queue de boeuf* or *pintade farcie*.

On one occasion when I was researching the book I was accompanied by David Wheeler (author and editor of the gardening journal *Hortus*) and the artist Simon Dorrell, who did the fine, meticulous illustrations. On other occasions Tamsin, plus her baby Meriel, came with me. Adept at coping with breastfeeding (something which astounded French women as primitive), we zigzagged across the country. Tamsin – an invaluable asset with her fluent and elegant French – took the numerous photographs from which Simon was able to make his drawings.

After the book was published, a well-known author, who'd written a series of informative books on the hotels and restaurants of France, wrote to tell me he was sure he had once visited Chez Clotilde.

Hallelujah.

I'm moving towards my decline willy-nilly. I'm getting so many brown age blotches on my hands – accelerating at such a rate – I'm hoping soon they'll join up and I'll be left with lovely brown hands so it will appear as though I never stop working in my garden. I've also become reconciled to the fact that by keeping books in the bidet my love life is over.

Among my indolent sighs there are days when I hanker for what I can no longer physically do. I know. It happens, never at an even pace but in lurches. I think I'm doing OK and then wham! My knees creak, I need a cataract operation, can't cut celeriac without using my pruning saw, open a new toothbrush, have forgotten your name and have almost reached the age when one book, one film do me because what I did yesterday is forgotten by today. But oh, there are still small intense pleasures to be had. On winter mornings I stand at my kitchen window and marvel at the fluttering feathers of nine long-tailed tits concealing my bird feeder before taking flight in 'irreproachable harmony'.

How tiresome it is that certain things remain in great detail when other, more pertinent and boring facts that would be useful to retain can never be recalled. At least that's what I'm learning to accept when a friend and I talk the sort of senseless gibberish beginning with, 'That book ... oh you know, with a title beginning with W about ... the girl who married ... what was his name?' And then my dear friend, often as equally gaga, helps me out with, '... Oh yes, you mean that one ... they lived at ... damn, where was it ... ?' and we giggle asininely, give up and open a bottle of wine.

Irretrievably, progressively and at moments obscenely, I progress towards my cul-de-sac. Of course at times I think about death and dying, but at other times, perversely, I start laughing. The physicality of laughter is a great relaxer even though it's into an empty room. The Prince of Wales may speak to his flowers; I speak to my organs. When a part of my body is giving me trouble I speak aloud, telling it to pull itself together, but I do wonder if I'm losing my marbles. After all I've been living on my own for over twenty years.

Yet how perverse. Inside, everything still pulsates. Thoughts like ripples in a pond keep expanding, activating and yearning. I do still dance in the house whenever something with a beat fills the space, whether it's wartime tunes I used to jive to or the old men singing at the Buena Vista Social Club. But I dance alone. The sight would appal my children and grandchildren.

And in spite of having lost the confidence of youth, when immortality seemed possible, I've reached the conclusion that I'm more adaptable over small setbacks than those who are younger. I'm not fazed, for instance, when we have a hosepipe ban, or when there's a panic over contaminated meat, snow falls, or there's an electricity cut. My grandchildren would freak out at the suggestion of having a once-a-week bath only six inches deep as we did in the war; at darning their socks; at turning sheets outside edge to in; at making clothes from parachute offcuts; at being rationed to one egg a week. And as for smearing our legs with beige dye and drawing a seam line with a black pencil all the way up the back of each leg before we went on a date, their comment would be, 'Yuk. Gruesome!'

The shortages in the war have remained with me. We had to manage without so much. The lack of choice was obviously something we didn't appreciate at the time, but which I now realise was an incentive. It's left me with an instinctive aversion to supermarkets, places I avoid when I can though I have used the one near the station when, leaving the train from London, I've been in need of a lavatory. What I don't need in these huge chain stores is choice on an intemperate scale: the racks of loaves, shelves of soap powder, aisles of biscuits, relishes and pet food, or the sly 'Buy One Get One Free'. Nor, like many others, am I tolerant of those friends who text messages below the restaurant table as we wait for the meal to arrive. Have we come together to meet each other, or is my friend so impatient, so insecure, she needs to be anywhere but here? OK, I've got the message . . . she came for the food not my company. Oh yes, the war has certainly left me with a miserly abhorrence to throwing away any leftovers that could be used up in a variety of ways, as my mother had to do.

I sound smug, but talk to people of my vintage and many will say the same.

Yet here my complacency ends. Coping for days with a mobile phone when my landline is out of order, or when my email blanks me, or gobbledegook terminology defeats me, I then know for sure I'm drowning not waving. I'm too old, too old. Technology has passed me by. It hurtles through the decades like an accelerating enigma.

Help. Where's Laurence, my nine-year-old grandson?

* * *

I may have rejected a felt shroud in favour of cardboard but not the thoughts that go with it.

Where to finish up? Not in a hospital ward if I can help it – a place I too often have to visit to see a bedridden friend surrounded by others waiting to drop off the edge. No one wants that. But pre-empting things can sometimes be taken to extremes, as happened when one of my mother's friends, afraid to be a burden to her children, put herself away in a home. Having mistimed her death, after ten years she took herself out again. In the end she died at home.

As far as I can see, the viable alternatives are to sell the house and spend the money on comfortable care but with no idea how long it will be needed, or to spend a dwindling amount paying for help at home while risking the money running out before I do.

How I admire Diana Athill (whose brilliant book *Instead of a Letter* I read many years ago) who has the courage to jetti-son her possessions and move into caring accommodation. Oh Diana, where do I find such courage?

I go down behind my eyes to the people, family and friends linked together by the universality of friendship, infidelities, loyalty, love and loss. Sadly – it is unavoidable and factual – the longer I live the more friends keep dying, and though the numbers mount up I can't bear to draw a line across their names in my address book. Some, like Jocasta and Lucien, were never transferred to my current one, and after leaving Greece we lost sight of Celia and Meredith. But some go back a long way. Helen, one of my mother's friends from school-days with whom in the twenties she used to go to the Turkish baths, had her hundredth birthday about twenty years ago. I went to her party among others who had also traversed many years of her life. Helen remembered me when I was born and now I was there celebrating her centenary. (She'd known my mother with plaits.) Her name remains in my address book.

Michael belonged to the lessening breed of gentle men – an increasingly rare quality that universally appeals to women. He preferred their company for their diverse responses to things other than continual competing maleness; those macho men who have to win every time are a bore, childish and predictable – attributes that don't always charm us. Among my male friends I'm lucky there are those like Michael whose underlying sensitivity is compatible with women. My mother always felt this rapport with him, appreciated his innate courtesy, and, as she'd known Michael since he was a little boy, their close friendship was constant. They remembered each other every birthday with books and little ditties which both of them were witty at composing. When she died he grieved for his personal loss in a way that isn't always the response to mothers-in-law.

Michael had always shied away from social commitments. Reluctant to go, gently complaining 'Do we have to?' yet when he went, he ended up by being difficult to extricate, having charmed others with his conversation and attentiveness, and always generous enough to admit how much he'd enjoyed himself after all as we drove home. That never prevented the next complaining overture for a subsequent event.

Forlorn as all this may sound, I don't feel hapless. It's a matter of paring down: the self-concerned anxieties of youth are gone, there's no longer time to spend on trivia, boring and time-consuming. Instead I have found an unexpected windfall: comradeship. New friends are an ongoing and blessed comfort. In spite of our disparate pasts, some sort of symbiosis or chemistry draws us together. When preconceptions and judgements on first encounters – which used to mislead me – are put aside, they no longer matter as amicability flourishes. Either we draw closer through instinctive empathy – where politics, partners, qualifications, income, jobs, appearance are immaterial – or nod in passing and move on. And what a compensation friendship is for all the dreary mechanical bits that cave in year after year. Conviviality, as we sit together round a table sharing a leisurely meal, makes for pleasure and for grace that never diminishes.

Women don't do jocular, but they do interrelate.

Those friends I have made in my old age are an unforeseen perk that is not to be relinquished. And it isn't always with those of my age. Friends young enough to be my children are an unexpected bonus.

One has been Katherine Swift, the brilliant writer whose innovative garden near Ludlow brings hundreds of visitors each year. She and I give talks together: a proper and an improper gardener. We never rehearse beforehand, but prefer to prod each other with provocative dictates as we praise, despair, agree or disagree over shrubs, designers or gardening fads. Kathy is an academic. For years she's been my amanuensis when I floundered among the Latin nomenclature of plants. Her book *The Morville Hours* is personal, touching and full of erudition, and she's been a blessed comrade since we were first introduced.

Another young friend, whom I first met in 1997, is the artist Jo Self. She arrived on my doorstep through a mutual contact like an exotic novelty: I'd never met anyone like her. From that moment we interacted through instinct not logic. As she lives in Brixton our relationship depends on correspondence, the old-fashioned sort – letters. Her inky, handwritten stream-of-consciousness epistles without punctuation or capitals have the immediacy of mainlining. The first time I visited her studio in Brixton she was on the floor painting an eighty-by-sixty-five-inch canvas black before transforming it into anemones. In *Modern Painters* Will Self – her ex-brother-in-law – had written, 'the black undercoat leaves the carefully described petals, stamens and leaves free-floating in the void, putatively divorced from earth and any possibility of regeneration.'

Utterly original, Jo had solved the problem of what to do underfoot in her back garden by covering it with thousands of surplus buttons collected from a nearby factory. There isn't a connection, but some years later she spent weeks in Dharamsala painting the Dalai Lama's garden, and just the other day she wrote that seeds she'd emptied from the box of paints she'd used have appeared, grown into 'a single pale magenta poenie [sic] . . . pure joy'.

Recently I've a new friend, years younger, who has led me through her passionate world of art and music yet doesn't know Browning's poem, 'Ah, did you once see Shelley plain . . .' and why should she? But it means that between us we have unknown regions to share. That can't be bad.

And something else. Theoretically I wonder if friendship is the paramount consideration as one grows decrepit, or would remaining at home – in spite of living in rural seclusion – be of overriding importance? What I'm asking is this: does familiarity, saturated with memories and surrounded by one's possessions, outweigh moving to a smaller, manageable place within touching distance of friends and professional help? The choice is isolation and the comfort of habitude versus convenience and human contact.

In old age, given the choice, which would you choose?

Eastern philosophy teaches that we only lose what we cling to. The abbot told his novices in our next-door temple in

Thailand the legend of two monks who encountered a woman too afraid to cross a ford. Regardless of the taboo that forbids monks to touch a woman, one of them carried her across, put her down and walked on. After some miles he turned to his outraged companion: 'That woman – I put her down at the ford. Are you still carrying her?'

Unfortunately I find there are still times when things rankle. Keep rankling. Apart from remorse for words unspoken, questions unasked or misjudging the appropriate time for pliancy not resistance, there are other regrets, things I can no longer do: never ride my horse again across the Shropshire hills, never skip down a hill holding a child by each hand. Or there are the things I've left too late to attempt: to have wind-surfed across the sea, eaten wild apricots in Tashkent or been to St Petersburg.

Although such aspirations have shrivelled, wanderlust – like malaria – reoccurs.

Meanwhile I have the boundless comfort of my daughter Tamsin and her family living only twenty minutes away in our old house. Forever willing to help when I need to fill in forms, when I press the wrong key on my computer or have an appointment with a specialist at the hospital thirty miles away, Tamsin had the wisdom to advise me not to replace my car when it was stolen but to relieve myself of the annual anxiety of the MOT, the expense – I used it so little – and take taxis instead. Being so near Tamsin bails me out on innumerable occasions. I don't take her for granted but mentally genuflect in gratitude for her good-natured willingness.

And what bliss. How I love the moment Tamsin arrives at my door on a day in summer as we set off with her children and with Sureen and hers for a holiday in a French *gîte*. I know these holidays are an endangered species. The children grow older and as they do their interests lie in other directions; they become individuals with their own agendas. Last year I believe I was the only one who had no reservations about going. I wanted the yearly events to continue, and each time we disembark at either Caen or Calais I remember other times, particularly with Michael, when we journeyed to and fro from Greece to England.

Anticipating a holiday with my family in a French *gîte* gets me excited to such an extent that I douse my eagerness in case, on the moment of departure, one of us is ill, a volcano erupts or we have a puncture. In my youth my mother's accounts of travelling through Europe with Aylmer, or Stella's life with Ford in Paris, had me hooked, however often I heard them. Surely the world atlas is the most divisive present to give newlyweds?

And how I admired the Frenchman's detachment at a garden I once visited when he said, shrugging, 'If the plant fails *tant pis. Alors*, I plant something else.'

It's easy to be objective over the pH of the soil. Not so easy with human frailties, so why do we wait for the person to be dead before saying the words they deserved to hear? Tender loving memories, expressions of gratitude or admiration . . .

Sentiments reiterated in commiserating letters that arrive when the person – the one who should be opening the envelope – is under the ground are mistimed. David – who had loved Michael in an undemonstrative way – had the sense to put his arms around him and tell him so before it was too late.

Inevitably I've had to confront unavoidable certainties – those impending possibilities that can't be dodged. Each lacks charm. It's this: either my brain goes soggy while my body remains intact, or else my wits remain but my body becomes infirm.

The best arrangement – to die at home and in one's sleep – rarely happens.

I look round at relatives, at friends, at other people's beloveds, and see evidence of these iniquitous alternatives. No one's health, in their declining years, works in harmony. I can't think of anyone in whom both diminished at an equal rate. Body and brain are not in sync. How cruel. What a fiendish arrangement that the physical and the mental are out of kilter.

Faced therefore with a destiny about which I can do nothing – were I given the option – I've come down on the side of remaining compos mentis, recognising my children and remaining lucid while acknowledging that my physical self, having caved in, means glaucoma puts an end to reading, arthritis keeps me living on the ground floor, and loss of appetite puts the sensual pleasure of gormandising off the menu.

Yes, I'd prefer that form of disintegration to being away with the fairies.

The fish in me turns to state the origins to my amorphous form as I walk the length of the garden breathing in the fragrance of a choisya, pushing aside branches of Winter's bark tangled with a rose drooping over the path, catching at my hair.

Each year, when the swifts return from their six-thousand-mile flight, I am reminded of Sorrel's question as we sat under our rain tree beside a river in northern Thailand listening to the song of the bulbuls. From under its branches supporting parasitic orchids she asked, 'Do you think swifts fly with their eyes open or shut?'

Now, hearing these magicians of navigation, the audacity of swifts diverts me, transfixing me with their piercing screams, and her question remains unanswered. Scooping up the air, mastering the sky, possessing the town for four months of summer before returning to Africa, the 'devil bird' is a piece of highly tuned engineering enclosed by feathers. Flying day and night, these birds spend their lives on the wing riding the thermals, drifting the down-draughts, scything the air with curved wings, sleeping in flight.

I'm waiting for my granddaughters Meriel and Cassandra to spend the day with me.

When I was writing this book – nearing the end – the eldest, unknown to me, downloaded several disparate drafts from my computer.

Why have I smiled since Cassandra told me?

I know what it is – it's her interest reminding me how I used to share with my mother a poem she'd just written. Cassandra is bombarded with a million options, doors closing while others are opening, yet the thought that bits of her grandmother's life should catch her curiosity – even if momentarily – moved me profoundly. In the midst of her university commitments she was making a gesture.

A small misdemeanour on her part. For me an outstretched hand.

Acknowledgements

Without my agent, Felicity Bryan, this book would never have got off the ground. Michael Fishwick, my editor at Bloomsbury, with his empathy, and Anna Simpson, with her infinite patience, are two people to whom I owe enormous gratitude; thanks also to Alexa von Hirschberg, Trâm-Anh Doan, Amanda Shipp, Laura Brooke and Penny Edwards at Bloomsbury. Thanks to Andrea Belloli for her copyediting, and Catherine Best for proofreading; to Janet Gough, David Reynolds, Valerie Thomas and Jocasta Hamilton for their critical input; and to James Roose Evans, Paul Binding, Peter Conradi, Katherine Swift, Erica Hunningher, Brenda and David Reid for their encouragement. I'm grateful too to Andrew Lawson for letting me use some of his photographs, to Frances Carlile for her illustration of the rain tree, and to *Granta* for permission to include the piece on adoption originally written for the magazine. And crucially thanks to my granddaughter Meriel who so painstakingly scanned the photographs for me, and above all to my daughter Tamsin, who helped me with the finished manuscript.

Index

A NOTE ON THE AUTHOR

Mirabel Osler is the critically acclaimed author of
A Breath from Elsewhere, A Spoon for Every Course,
In the Eye of the Garden, The Secret Gardens of France
and the classic *A Gentle Plea for Chaos.*
She lives in Shropshire.

A NOTE ON THE TYPE

The text of this book is set in Linotype Sabon, named after
the type founder, Jacques Sabon. It was designed by Jan
Tschichold and jointly developed by Linotype, Monotype
and Stempel, in response to a need for a typeface to be
available in identical form for mechanical hot metal
composition and hand composition using foundry type.

Tschichold based his design for Sabon roman on a font
engraved by Garamond, and Sabon italic on a font by
Granjon. It was first used in 1966 and has proved an
enduring modern classic.